Also by Bryan Greetham

HOW TO WRITE YOUR UNDERGRADUATE DISSERTATION

HOW TO WRITE BETTER ESSAYS

PHILOSOPHY

Thinking Skills for Professionals

Bryan Greetham

palgrave
macmillan

First published 2010 by
PALGRAVE MACMILLAN

Palgrave Macmillan in the UK is an imprint of Macmillan Publishers Limited, registered in England, company number 785998, of Houndmills, Basingstoke, Hampshire RG21 6XS.

Palgrave Macmillan in the US is a division of St Martin's Press LLC, 175 Fifth Avenue, New York, NY 10010.

Palgrave Macmillan is the global academic imprint of the above companies and has companies and representatives throughout the world.

Palgrave® and Macmillan® are registered trademarks in the United States, the United Kingdom, Europe and other countries.

ISBN 978–1–4039–1708–9   paperback

This book is printed on paper suitable for recycling and made from fully managed and sustained forest sources. Logging, pulping and manufacturing processes are expected to conform to the environmental regulations of the country of origin.

A catalogue record for this book is available from the British Library.

Library of Congress Cataloging-in-Publication Data

Greetham, Bryan, 1946–
  Thinking skills for professionals / Bryan Greetham.
    p. cm.
    ISBN 978–1–4039–1708–9 (pbk.)
  1. Thought and thinking. I. Title.
  BF441.G746 2010
  153.4'2—dc22

                                                              2010010499

10 9 8 7 6 5 4 3 2 1
19 18 17 16 15 14 13 12 11 10

Printed and bound in Great Britain by
CPI Antony Rowe, Chippenham and Eastbourne

*To Pat for so enriching my life and to two of the
finest professionals for saving it: Dr John Piper,
FRCS, and Dra. Maria de Lurdes Batarda*

Contents

Acknowledgements

As with any project of this kind, I have too many debts to acknowledge for these short acknowledgements. Friends, acquaintances, even complete strangers, have helped in one way or another. In particular my students have contributed to this, most without even knowing it. Thank you to you all for sharing your ideas with me and for allowing me to try mine out on you. I'm sorry that I can't mention you all by name.

As for the rest, first I would like to acknowledge the debt I owe to all those who have over the years taken seriously the task of teaching students and professionals how to think. Though few in number, educators, like Edward de Bono, John Wilson, Richard Paul and Tony Buzan, have set us the challenge of designing better ways of teaching thinking.

Equally important has been the work of all those teachers in schools, colleges and universities who have quietly accepted the challenge not to settle for just the easy task of teaching students *what* to think, but the far more difficult and much more important task of teaching them *how* to think. Their legacy in liberating their students from the thralls of authority to go beyond conventional wisdom and think for themselves is to be found not just in the diplomas on office walls, but in professionals who are capable of achieving significant breakthroughs in science and technology, and of generating innovative ideas to create businesses and jobs.

In the same context I would like to thank all my colleagues over the years, who have listened patiently to me extol the importance of developing our students' thinking skills and have given me their support, even when the institutional momentum moved irresistibly towards teaching students what to think at the expense of their skills. In particular, I would like to thank Professor Mel Gray for her support and encouragement, and for kindly allowing me to use the example of 'Suzanne and the Social Worker' to show how we can develop our moral thinking skills.

I also owe a considerable debt to all my editors over the years: to Suzannah Burywood, who began this project, to Terka Acton, who took it on, and to Pryanka Gibbons, ably supported by Melanie Blair, who saw it through to completion. Thank you all for your patience, professionalism and for your experienced judgement, when we had to decide which route to take. I would also like to thank Edna Rowe for her skilful detective work in tracking down the most obscure references.

Finally, there is my biggest debt of all to my lifelong partner, Pat Rowe, for being there when things got fraught and I needed someone to bring sanity and a sense of proportion to my work. I am also deeply grateful to my dear friend and constant companion, AH, for his inexhaustible sense of fun and adventure.

Introduction

In February 2009 Sir Tom McKillop and Sir Fred Goodwin, the former chairman and chief executive respectively of one of Britain's biggest banks, the Royal Bank of Scotland, both admitted to a select committee of the British House of Commons that buying parts of the Dutch bank ABN Amro was a 'bad mistake'. The £48bn deal not only wrecked RBS but threatened to bring down the whole of the British banking system. McKillop admitted that 'With retrospect, we bought ABN Amro at the top of the market. In fact, we are sorry we bought ABN Amro. The bulk of what we paid for ABN Amro will be written off as goodwill.'

Similar stories could be told about Lehman Brothers, Lloyds Bank and others. So what encouraged experienced professional bankers with long careers in the business world to go ahead with this and other deals at a time when the signs were that the credit crunch was already well underway? It wasn't as if this was an impetuous decision by the RBS board, which they regretted at leisure. They met to discuss it 18 times and still the directors were unanimous that the deal should go through.

Wider still, neither the Prime Minister, Gordon Brown, nor the opposition leader, David Cameron, had any doubts about the wisdom and financial acumen of the City and those who were making such deals. In his 2005 Mansion House speech Gordon Brown praised the City for its 'unique innovative skills, your courage and steadfastness'. And in 2007 he declared that, as a result of their ingenuity and creativity, 'A new world order has been created': we have the privilege of living in 'an era that history will record as the beginning of a new Golden Age'.

David Cameron was no less enthusiastic in September 2007, when there were clear signs that the banking system was in trouble. Thanks to the policies of previous Conservative governments, he confidently declared, a new world economy had been created. The Left's misguided belief in regulation had been thoroughly discredited and 'Liberalism' had prevailed. With the world economy now more stable than for a generation, 'our hugely sophisticated financial markets match funds with ideas better than ever before'.

And, of course, wider still, there were millions of ordinary individuals making decisions to take out mortgages, many over 100 per cent, on houses that were already overvalued by more than 30 per cent. Driven up by emotion and herd instinct to unsustainable price levels, many of these were bought for the long term as family homes, so losses and financial problems were bound to result when sanity returned to the market. Like the emperor's new clothes, such fantasy prices were sustainable only as long as we all believed in them.

Why did so many people make such poor decisions?

- the bankers
- the politicians
- the public

The explanation

1 Natural adaptation

At least part of the explanation for this collective poor judgement might lie in our evolutionary history. Over millions of years we have adapted to our environment to become routine, unreflective thinkers. For much of our existence our survival has depended on rules and patterns of behaviour well-tested by the thousands of generations before us. Learning to flee without thought in response to a certain pattern of colours and movement that signalled a predator was essential for survival. As a result, today we make decisions guided more by unchallenged rules and accepted patterns of behaviour than by rational analysis and reflection.

Despite appearances, we are inveterately conservative. Our minds are programmed for survival, not to seek out truth. Most of us are blindly credulous and confident of the working assumptions we all seem to accept. Even the rise of modern science, our most systematic attempt to challenge the authority of the past, is only a comparatively recent development. It was only in the seventeenth century that a small

> We are routine, unreflective thinkers guided by unchallenged rules and accepted patterns of behaviour.

number of 'natural philosophers' set out to reject traditional authority and invest their faith, instead, in the sovereignty of individual reason.

2 Social adaptation

But this is only one part of the story of human adaptation; the other takes place in each generation. Children are natural philosophers, blessed with untamed imaginations and deep fascination for speculative ideas. Over the years writers have drawn attention to the resemblance between the way children and the most creative poets and philosophers approach the world. At the birth of the Industrial Revolution, William Blake in his *Songs of Innocence* (1789) and *Songs of Experience* (1794) compared the spontaneous innocence and imagination of the child with the adult corrupted by the experience of a mechanistic, industrial world that diminished him to a mere machine minder.

Up until the age of nine or ten children seem able to resist the crushing pressure of conformity that forces them into 'normal' ways of thinking and behaving. In his book, *The Art of Thinking*, Ernest Dimnet says,

> They pretend to live with the rest of us, and the rest of us imagine that we influence them so that their life is only a reflection of our own. But ... they are as self-contained as cats and continuously attentive to the magical charm of what they see inwardly.[1]

Most children of that age have a mental life that is rich in ideas and insights, which they keep concealed from the adult world. Sunsets, patches of colour, water, waves, all generate wonder and curiosity. They might stare at a stone or a shell for what seems ages wondering what it is like to be this old. Concepts like eternity and infinity, space and time, capture their imagination and curiosity. Most children share the philosopher's doubts about the existence of the world, of God, the after-life, ghosts and spirits.

Harry Potter novels sell in their millions around the world with children clamouring for each new book on the day of publication. The capacity to step outside normal conventional ideas to imagine a world in which the powers of good and evil wage their eternal struggle, wielding all their magical powers, answers an insistent demand for speculative ideas that paint a world beyond our normal expectations.

A child's world is full of ...

- wonder
- curiosity

- imagination
- speculation

But then the spell is finally broken by forces working from outside. Parents and relatives clamour for a comfortable sense of conformity in their children. We learn from an early age to put aside childish thoughts and think according to the conventional norms of adulthood. We turn away from our childish imagination and speculative ideas. We begin to imitate adults and act 'normally', according to adult norms.

What child can resist behaviour that frees them from the fear that they might be regarded by adults as somehow 'odd'? Children begin to notice adults and think their thoughts. Education, too, plays a similar role by imposing other people's thoughts on them, rather than helping them get back to their own. We are more comfortable teaching students *what* to think than we are teaching them *how* to think.

And, of course, pressure from their peers elevates this need to conform to even greater heights. To survive in the environment of a large secondary school or high school means joining a clan, a group united by common ideas, behaviour and outward appearance. This is not the world of thought, but of survival and conformity – adapt or struggle! Satisfied with 'normality', children dismiss unconventional thoughts and questions. The interest that once filled their every waking hour recedes, giving way to the passion for 'having things', for comparing what they have with what others have. The child with flashes of ideas and inspiration is thought odd – a non-conformist. And once repressed it is harder for such inspiration to break through a second time.

> We are more comfortable teaching students *what* to think than we are teaching them *how* to think.

Of course, after we have left school and entered the world of work, the world closes in still further. Our concern is now to make money, to have things, to compare our lives with others. There is no question now of thinking seriously.

Life does the reverse of what we tend to think it does: we travel *away* from thought not *to* it. We feed our ego not realising that it is the shadow, not the substance, of life. Without the time to give expression to our inmost thoughts and ideas, year by year we become more anonymous, like everyone else. Most of us would be shocked to be told that we had more individuality at the age of, say, 21 than we do at 50.

The consequences

One of the consequences of this is that, like the many millions before us in our evolutionary history, we value action over thought, doers over thinkers. Business people are praised for their decisiveness, for being dynamic, even ruthless, while students go in search of the 'adrenalin rush' rather than ideas. One of the most successful sales pitches, celebrating the triumph of action over thought, insists that we 'Just do it'.

So, perhaps it's not surprising that we make such poor decisions, like the takeover of ABN Amro by RBS or HBOS by Lloyds. We routinely make decisions by applying yesterday's solutions to today's problems, when in fact we should be carefully analysing the situation and our objectives so we can discriminate more clearly between the alternatives from which we can choose.

Unfortunately, rational analysis of this kind plays a surprisingly small part in most decisions. More likely our decisions are driven by the same atavistic part of our natures that drove those of primitive man: our reaction patterns tell us to respond as others before us have responded. So whether or not we are bad decision-makers is not the point; we simply don't know how we do it. We follow established patterns of behaviour so automatically on the basis of incomplete analysis of the information that we simply don't know how we came to the decision.

In the banking sector in the 1990s and 2000s companies were successful through their acquisitions. Buy an under-performing company on the cheap, ruthlessly strip it of costs and you create value with a more successful company that produces the level of profits that shareholders are looking for.

When Sir Fred Goodwin committed the Royal Bank of Scotland to the £48bn takeover of ABN Amro, he was no doubt following the same pattern of expectations at a time when his concern should have been with the balance sheet and the liquidity of the bank and its target, rather than the cost-cutting potential. Not only did RBS go ahead with the deal, but it increased the risk to itself by offering a cash inducement. And, as we have seen, this is no isolated example. Others can be found who relied on their established patterns of expectations, failed to analyse the evidence and ignored the opportunities to take a different course.

The solution

The solution lies in developing the skills to think beyond the ruling patterns of behaviour. It's not enough just to possess the qualifications and experience in the technical aspects of our work. This alone will not make us good decision-makers and in times of change little in our past will have prepared us for the decisions we have to make. For this we need to be not only good critical thinkers, but good conceptual and creative thinkers, too. We need to be able to inhabit different worlds beyond our own and to think in different ways with new ideas and patterns of thought, out of which we can design solutions to cope with the challenges we face.

Thinking skills:
1. Critical.
2. Conceptual.
3. Creative.

This means developing the critical, conceptual and creative thinking skills to:

- analyse concepts and problems so that we can see more clearly the issues we have to tackle;
- generate our own ideas to solve them;
- synthesise ideas and evidence from different sources to see problems from different perspectives;
- use the different techniques to solve complex problems;
- present them consistently, coherently and persuasively.

In short, we must become genuine thinkers, better able to tackle the problems we confront.

This book

In this book you will learn simple methods and techniques you can incorporate within your professional and business lives to develop and use all of these thinking skills. They are the same methods and techniques that have been used by the most inventive minds of the past. They can be found at the heart of some of the most important breakthroughs in thought. As you learn them you will see your own insights peer through and inspiration take hold of your thoughts. It will lead you to wonder what brought a crop of platitudes where distinction and originality now spring naturally.

Part 1
Original Ideas

A radio producer in Washington DC, a few years ago, was awarded a promotion on the grounds that he was a 'good decision-maker'. Where most of us might have accepted it gratefully and said nothing, he wondered why, when so many of his decisions had not worked out well. The company, though, wasn't at all bothered by this. 'Being a good decision-maker means you're good at making decisions,' one executive told him reassuringly. 'It doesn't mean you make good decisions.'[1]

Recent evidence suggests that many organisations approach decision-making in the same way. It might explain why after 18 meetings the directors of RBS were still unanimous that the deal to buy parts of ABN Amro should go through. Given that the chairman and chief executive were prepared to make the decision, the directors were relieved of the burden of generating alternative ideas, analysing all their implications, and presenting and testing different solutions.

Most of us are not good at thinking in these ways, because we simply don't know how to. Given new, fresh ideas, we're presented with challenges we have no way of meeting; none of the skills, methods and techniques we would need. The more choice we have the more risk of making a mistake, so we get locked in a paralysis of indecision. Those who are more reckless, perhaps less mindful of the consequences, or who just come across as more certain about them, offer an easy way out.

And at this point, it's easy for the hierarchies of organisations to assume all the characteristics of a cult with those at the top deciding that any opinion which challenges theirs is a form of treason. Directors and employees learn to keep their silence and get on with their jobs. When Paul Moore, the head of risk at HBOS, warned Sir James Crosby of the risks the bank was taking, he was sacked, even though Halifax and the Bank of Scotland were heading for insolvency.

Decision-making would be so much simpler, if we knew how to generate ideas, analyse them and then create alternative solutions to problems with all the risks and benefits of each one spelt out clearly. In these circumstances decision-making would no longer be left to the most committed or the most reckless, who, like the Washington radio executive, are happy for decisions to be made regardless of the consequences.

In Part 1 we will learn how we can clamber out from beneath the suffocating weight of received opinion and the established routine patterns of response, so that we can generate ideas of our own. Then, in Parts 2 and 3, we will look at how we can analyse these ideas, reveal their structure and then work with this to create different solutions to the problem. In Part 4 we will learn how to test each of these, so that we can more clearly see the best solution.

In the process we will learn to be forward, not just backward, looking. Our aim in finding solutions to problems is not just to implement solutions of the past, the way things have always been done, but to see and adapt to the way things are likely to develop in the future.

Of course we still need to learn from the wisdom of the past, but we must find a way of being more than mere imitators. Presented with a difficult situation a good manager and professional can work with what they've got to find a solution, even though their training may say it cannot be done. They innovate and work with their ideas long after others have given up.

1

Reprogramming our Thinking

The way we understand a problem determines the range of thinking skills we use to solve it. So, to use a different range of skills, in this case the conceptual, creative and critical skills, we have to see problems differently.

Designing solutions, not finding them

Our standard pattern of assumptions tells us that solutions to our problems are found, rather than designed. They are already out there waiting to be discovered. All we have to do is to reveal them by chipping away those things that are obscuring them.

Over recent years one of the most welcome developments in university education around the world has been the acceptance that education must involve more than just conveying knowledge; it must teach thinking skills. Up until now, this has been limited to critical thinking skills, largely because these require no radical change to these assumptions. We assume that when knowledge and facts are unclear we can, through critical thinking, chip away the errors to reveal the truth hidden beneath layers of false reasoning. We don't have to design our own ideas and solutions, just make clear those we are given.

With the alternative pattern of assumptions, what we know is shaped by the act of knowing: solutions are not out there waiting to be found; they have to be designed. Largely ignored in education, over the years this has produced our most original thought and most of the important breakthroughs in our understanding of ourselves and the world around us. Even so, this is a more messy, creative process, involving trial and error, informed guesses, false trails and intuitions.

> What we know is shaped by the act of knowing.

Significantly, it is a model of thinking that feeds on error. In the standard model of thinking we use to deliver knowledge of facts and right answers, our aim is to avoid error. Students know that the way they pass exams is to exchange enough right answers for marks. But in the design model we're free to make mistakes as we fashion solutions to our problems. We're judged not by our failures, but by our successes. Indeed, failed ideas are important steps in the design of successful solutions.

Systems in which people are judged by their failures encourage them to play it safe, to avoid taking risk. In schools and universities students revert to regressive learning behaviour. Rather than think for themselves, they reproduce what they have read in authoritative texts, even though it may make no sense to them. To avoid risk we all imitate in the same way. We reproduce accepted wisdom and conventional ideas, rather than think for ourselves. But by doing this we're unlikely to fashion the new ideas and concepts that may be the answer to our problems.

Patterns and pattern recognition

Learning to think as a designer, rather than as a discoverer of hidden truths, involves reprogramming our thinking. However, some things are difficult to change. We all seek to minimise the levels of uncertainty in our lives. The millions of years of our existence have taught us routine ways of promoting our survival. A whole battery of unconscious controls influences our thoughts and behaviour, shaping the way we make sense of the world to relieve our uncertainty.

It works through pattern formation and recognition. The mind incessantly searches out and makes connections between ideas. It searches for patterns, creating them out of the isolated ideas that come its way. Our ability to understand our world and how it affects us depends upon our ability to recognise and respond to these patterns.

But as their influence on our thinking is largely unconscious, the mind creates patterns before we know that it has. These influence the way we process ideas without us being consciously aware of the restrictions they place on how we use our thinking skills. They will determine how we select facts, reconstruct events and develop arguments.

Example: Moral thinking. For much of the time this works perfectly well. In his book *Moral Thinking* the English philosopher Richard Hare describes the way we navigate the bewildering complexities of moral thinking. Rather than act as persistent calculators measuring the consequences of each possible decision every time we have to make one, we have certain 'prima-facie rules' or 'simple reaction-patterns' that we follow in the reasonable expectation that this will result in the best possible outcome. This he describes as 'intuitive moral thinking': he argues, 'it is highly desirable that we should all have these intuitions and that our consciences should give us a bad time if we go against them.'[1]

Problems arise when we only have partial information or, in times of change, when the information we have doesn't fit these routine patterns, making them irrelevant or ineffective.

Example: A chess master. A chess master will learn a vast number of patterns of play to navigate the immense number of possible moves open to him and his opponent. Rather than work through each possible move and all the likely counter-moves, the bewildering complexity of which grows geometrically with each move, he draws upon patterns of play he has stored from previous games, calculating which is likely to be the most successful in this sort of situation.

Herbert A. Simon and W. G. Chase demonstrated that the chess expert could look at any board with a game in progress and relate the moves that made up the entire game. But give him a board with pieces arranged in a random pattern, haphazardly, and he can make no meaningful sense of it.[2]

Problems:
1. When we only have partial information.
2. In times of change.

At times like these, when we have partial, unusual or just an avalanche of information to deal with, we are likely to make poor judgements. In times of stress and emotional confusion we're likely to recognise the wrong patterns and make poor decisions. We might find ourselves inexplicably rushing up and embracing a complete stranger in the street in the mistaken belief that he or she is a close friend.

In times of uncertainty, when there are fears of a recession, we might fail to judge accurately developments in the money markets or exaggerate the benefits that are likely to come from acquiring another company.

> *Example: RBS and the takeover of ABN Amro.* When the Royal Bank of Scotland took over ABN Amro the cost/income ratio (the proportion of a bank's income consumed by operating costs) was 47 per cent for RBS, but 96 per cent for ABN Amro. Sir Fred Goodwin's plan was to slash jobs, cut costs and generate profits, but it would have taken only a small fall in profits to turn it into a loss-making bank. As the banking crisis developed many observers thought this was more than likely to occur. But despite repeated warnings from inside RBS, Goodwin failed to see it. All he saw was the same pattern of factors that had justified similar acquisitions in the past.

Without a relevant pattern to interpret events and information we make mistakes. Members of the public, who witness the unusual events of a crime, struggle to produce an accurate and detailed report. Our minds reconstruct what we see to make sense of it, in the process drawing upon stereotypes of people and situations composed of preconceived ideas about race, age, sex and social group. Try it for yourself. Read the following familiar sayings in each triangle.

Most people don't see the extra word in each saying. So familiar are they that our minds selectively ignore and edit out the superfluous

words as if we haven't seen them. We see what our patterns of thought prepare us to see. Even though the evidence might be staring us in the face, we fail to see it.

Despite the astounding advances achieved by modern science over the last 350 years it too has struggled to relinquish well established theories or paradigms, even though there is a growing mountain of evidence for an alternative paradigm. From Semmelweis to Einstein, plate tectonics to quantum theory, the history of modern science is littered with stories of resistance, revolution and the struggle to overthrow theories.

In retrospect, as we look back on the poor decisions that leaders have made, it seems surprising that intelligent, experienced professionals and business people should overlook what is staring them in the face. But the mind does much of this unconsciously. It fills in the gaps in our thinking; otherwise, if we were to wait until all the information was in, we would never make a decision. It also reinterprets the pattern of information to bring it into line with established patterns. This, too, is a vital part of our mental processing. We see what we want to see: how we've always seen things and how we think things *should* be, not as they *are*. The mind reshapes and 'corrects' our experience.

Unconscious processing of ideas:
1. Fills in the gaps.
2. Reinterprets the pattern of information.

Read the following passage and see how well you understand it, even though the words in it appear to be largely unrecognisable:

Aoccdrnig to rseearch at an Elingsh uinervtisy, it deosn't mttaer in waht oredr the ltteers in a wrod are, the olny iprmoatnt tihng is taht the frist and lsat ltteers are in the rghit pclae. The rset can be a toatl mses and you can sitll raed it wouthit porbelm. Tihs is bcuseae we do not raed ervey lteter by itslef but the wrod as a wlohe.

In this case we get it right, but in many cases we don't. Our reinterpretation results in misinterpretation. Experiments have been conducted in which a person is strapped into a chair and the room is turned and tilted, while the chair and the subject remain stable. Usually the subject perceives the room to remain stable while the chair revolves. What is accurate in this report is the perception of the relative angular motion between the subject and the walls of the room. However, the interpretation given by the subject assumes that, because walls are normally fixed and upright, it must therefore be the chair which is revolving.

Making mistakes

So we shouldn't be so surprised that Sir Fred Goodwin and others make the sort of mistakes they do, misinterpreting situations, believing that new ones are just familiar ones repeated. Indeed, mistakes like this occur more than you might think. In their book, *Think Again*, Sydney Finkelstein, Jo Whitehead and Andrew Campbell catalogue a number of high profile decisions that went wrong because one pattern of information was misinterpreted as another more familiar one.[3] John F. Kennedy's presidency was marred by his infamous Bay of Pigs blunder and Mrs Thatcher's third term in office was cut short by her own party after her ill-fated support for the poll tax.

As for the blunders of business leaders, these have brought crippling damage to otherwise successful companies. Juergen Schrempp, CEO of Daimler-Benz, brought about the merger of Chrysler and Daimler-Benz, despite internal opposition. Nearly ten years later they were virtually forced to give Chrysler away. Lee Kun Hee, the CEO of Samsung, led his company into the production of cars, but, after mounting losses, was forced to sell the car division for a tenth of the billions the company had invested. And An Wang, the founder of the electronics company Wang, insisted that the company's personal computer should have its own operating system, even though it was clear that the IBM system was becoming the industry standard. The company no longer exists.

All their decisions seemed to have been driven by judgements based on their interpretation of the facts in the light of previous patterns of events and information.

Example: Quaker and Snapple.   In 1994, when William D. Smithburg, the CEO of Quaker, the very successful food company, decided to acquire Snapple, the leading company producing iced-tea and fruit juice drinks, it led to the downfall of Smithburg and Quaker.[4] Three years later Snapple was bought by Triarc Company for 1.4 billion dollars less than its purchase price, Smithburg retired and Quaker was acquired by PepsiCo in 2000.

The logic of the Snapple acquisition was that it would repeat the success of Quaker's acquisition in 1983 of Gatorade, the sports drink company. This was a company that produced a niche product, but was under exploited. The marketing expertise of Quaker was able to take the company to the next level and the same was expected of Snapple. But the similarities between the two patterns of information led experienced people like Smithburg and Don Uzzi, the beverage division president, to overlook the significant differences between the two.

Although our mistakes are probably not as catastrophic, we are all likely to reason in exactly the same way. As much of our processing is unconscious, we are not aware of the different ways we fill in the gaps and reinterpret what we see as we come to our decisions. For millions of years pattern recognition has ensured our survival. However, *strategic* thinking is rarely involved with questions of survival. To avoid mistakes in this type of thinking, we need to discuss and analyse the evidence over weeks, if not months, to identify and weed out the misleading assumptions we have unconsciously made.

> Strategic thinking rarely involves questions of survival and pattern recognition.

Unfortunately, once our minds have been imprinted with a particular pattern it can be difficult to dislodge, which probably explains how the RBS board could meet 18 times and still agree unanimously to the acquisition of ABN Amro, or how a chess master, whose mind is imprinted with so many patterns of play, fails to cope with one that is randomly organised.

Still, knowing how our minds can be easily misled, we are better able to recognise those situations in which they can get things wrong. We need, then, to learn simple techniques and strategies to analyse and criticise the assumptions we make.

First, though, we must reprogram our thinking and adopt habits of thought that will help us analyse and criticise our assumptions more effectively. Most of us would no doubt argue that our thinking is already guided by similar habits of thought. But as much of our mental processing is unconscious, to check it we need to take steps to make more of it conscious. We need to be more deliberate in our thinking, to play devil's advocate, particularly with assumptions that appear beyond question, and rigorously examine in detail the assumptions we make, so we can design better solutions as a result.

Four rules

These habits of thought take the form of four simple rules:

1. Tolerate uncertainty.
2. Suspend your judgement.
3. See things naïvely.
4. Make room for reflection.

1 Tolerate uncertainty

The British philosopher Bertrand Russell once said: 'To teach how to live without certainty and yet without being paralysed by hesitation is perhaps the chief thing that philosophy, in our age, can do for those who study it.'[5] This is not an easy lesson for those in business and the professions, when they are valued for their expertise and ability to make decisions and act on them. But action that lacks sufficient thought and analysis is almost always valueless.

Therefore, no matter how unsettling it may be, we need to learn to have the courage to hang a question over everything:

- we need to learn to question what we accept as certainties,
- empathise with others, vicariously experiencing their thoughts and feelings, and
- learn to present the other side of the argument as convincingly as we do the side to which we ourselves are committed.

2 Suspend your judgement

This means we must also suspend our judgement. In a later chapter we will see that good thinkers think about their thinking while they think. As they generate their ideas and develop their arguments they question the reliability of their own thinking: whether their arguments are consistent, whether they have seen all the implications involved in using a particular concept, whether their language drives their arguments in the direction they want to go, and whether there is enough evidence to support their conclusions. The willingness to question these things even when we are convinced of the reliability of our ideas lies at the heart of good thinking.

Good thinkers think about their thinking while they think.

The impressive achievements of modern science have come from just this disposition. No matter how perfectly a hypothesis seems to answer a problem, it is only after it has survived systematic attempts to falsify it that scientists accept it cautiously and provisionally. Among other things, it must have a good record over the long term of successfully passing all attempts to falsify it, if it is to be accepted by the scientific community.

Good thinkers ask ....
1. Are my arguments consistent?
2. Have I seen all the implications involved in using a particular concept?
3. Does my language drive my arguments in the direction I want them to go?
4. Is there enough evidence to support my conclusions?

Beyond this, there are probably two other reasons why suspending our judgement is so important. First, if we want to develop our thinking skills we must use them as we do any skill. But to use them, we must have the opportunity to think, and for this we must suspend our judgement: things must be up for grabs. As Paul Tillich once said, 'The passion for truth is silenced by answers which have the weight of undisputed authority.'[6] Once we accept something as true, there is nothing more to discuss and, therefore, no opportunity to develop our thinking skills.

Unfortunately, in our professional lives it's all too easy to assume that at all times we are required to be clear sighted and decisive. Not to have almost instant judgements on things seems indecisive, muddled, even timid. The executive who takes her time, weighs up the issues and comes to a measured judgement is not the modern hero we are persuaded to emulate. But most complex problems need careful reflection and delayed judgement, not instant decisions modelled on established patterns.

The second reason is not unconnected with the first. Coming up with good ideas is a continuous, unbroken process. Ideas, good or bad, breed other ideas. When we think about a problem we may produce an idea that clearly wouldn't work, but it is very likely to produce other ideas out of which solutions are likely to come. They are seeds that will bear fruit. Our minds process these ideas while we are preoccupied with other things, so that when we return we discover new shape and clarity to our thinking. Therefore, by suspending our judgement and playing devil's advocate, even developing ideas we may not think are workable, we are fuelling this creative process.

3 Think naïvely

The Ancient Greek philosopher Socrates characteristically professed an ignorance of any subject he discussed, even though this itself pointed to two of the most important convictions that underscored his own philosophical method: that human wisdom begins with the recognition of one's own ignorance and the unexamined life is not worth living. Reading Socrates's famous dialogues leaves you convinced of how important this is for training the mind's eye to see what needs to be seen, but is so often missed.

It is like an artist who learns to look at familiar objects naïvely, without preconceptions, until they seem strange and alien: until, that is, the artist begins *actually* to see them, instead of seeing them through the conventional lens as he has always seen them. Likewise in our thinking, we need to develop the habit not just of critical *thinking*, but critical *attention*. The first contact with a problem should leave us with as vivid an impression as we are capable of. The solution to many of our problems is hidden in plain view, so making ourselves naïve is a key condition to solving them.

4 Make room for reflection

Most of us go to great lengths to avoid the effort of thinking. Aldous Huxley once said, it seems, 'Most of one's life … is one prolonged effort to prevent oneself thinking.'[7] If the research is to be believed it is said that company executives do not spend more than ten consecutive minutes alone in any working day. As Charles Handy concludes, 'They have not had the time to think, even if they know what to think about and where to start.'[8]

It takes most of us a lifetime to realise that there is no room for serious thought in such a half-shut, cluttered mind. The thoughts may be there, full of insight and vision, but you can so easily pass through life without even knowing that they are there at all. To let good thoughts come through we must clear a space for them. There must be no irrelevant preoccupations prowling around, hijacking the mind.

4.1 Obsessions

But once we have cleared a space, what then? The simple answer is, don't overcomplicate. Keep constantly in front of your mind one object, one thought or problem, and let it take over your mind, engrossing it. This means working without a net: without the comforting support of a book or other people's ideas.

Solutions may come suddenly, but they are long preparing through a process of careful, sustained work. It's the sort of active reflection that involves thinking attentively about the same thing many times over. This is not mere repetition, rather it indicates the presence in the mind of one object that takes it over until the mind and all its subconscious activity brings it to fruition in a solution.

> *Examples: Newton and Einstein.* When asked how he went about his work Einstein answered, 'I think and think, for months, for years, ninety-nine times the conclusion is false. The hundredth time I am right.'[9] And when Sir Isaac Newton was asked how he discovered the law of gravitation he answered, 'By thinking about it all the time.'[10] He explained, 'I keep the subject constantly in mind before me and wait 'til the first dawnings open slowly, by little and little, into a full and clear light.'[11]

Like Einstein and Newton we need to learn the value of allowing ourselves to become obsessed by an idea, so that it never gives us rest. To find the answer to a complex problem we may need to keep it in our minds for days or weeks on end.

4.2 Clarify it

However, to use a phrase familiar to academic researchers, often 'the problem's the problem'. We fail to clarify it well enough, leaving the mind to make connections that send us off in the wrong direction. The mind has learnt through years of evolution that it must be quick to recognise a pattern. Important though this has been for our survival, it is a distraction for our thinking about complex problems. All too often the patterns it identifies are the nearest approximations; they are obvious and superficial.

For a complex problem, we must analyse it clearly so we present to our minds a full and accurate idea of it and then leave it to incubate in the subconscious. If we always want instant results, then our minds will take the easy way out. Defining the problem clearly in this way we set the agenda that our mind has to work on. Once we've done this we can safely leave it to our subconscious. It will continue its work without our conscious intervention and direction.

Example: Newton. When Newton worked he would concentrate his attention on a problem, thinking about nothing else, until he had made it clear to himself. Then he would put it aside. When he returned to it, he would make another leap forward. As his biographer, Peter Ackroyd, explains, 'He learned how to "husband" his mind ... to allow it to lie fallow before it became fruitful once more.'[12]

Example: Henri Poincaré. Henri Poincaré, the nineteenth-century French mathematician, recounts similar working experiences. When he was working to prove that there could not be functions like those called 'Fuchsian functions', he worked every day on a great number of combinations, yet without success. Then, one night, after drinking too much black coffee, he struggled to sleep. In his dreams he saw ideas chasing each other round and round, combining and recombining, with him as a mere spectator. The next morning, jaded and half asleep, the solution was there, despite himself. After two hours of concentrated work he was able to set out the proof that he was after.

A number of writers, philosophers and scientists from radically different backgrounds have spoken of the same thing, describing this 'fallow' period as the 'incubation' or 'gestation' stage. All of them describe much the same experience of leaving their work, having reached a stage where nothing appears to make sense and there seems nowhere to go.

Then, the solution might come to them suddenly when they least expect it, in the middle of the night, or more normally when they resume work the next day ready to confront the problem they were struggling with, only to find the solution staring them in the face. And, naturally, they wonder what it was that caused them to stumble the previous day.

Sleep

Recent studies have shown how important sleep is for the incubation of our ideas. Results show that it improves our creative ability to generate insights and uncover novel connections among seemingly unrelated ideas.

It seems that sleep helps us to process ideas by allowing the typical approaches we might adopt to solve problems to decay, so we can switch to more innovative alternatives. Dr Jeffrey M. Ellenbogen, one of the researchers who conducted the study at Harvard University, maintains that, if the incubation period includes sleep, people are 33 per cent more likely to infer connections between distantly related ideas.

Sleep brings a change of approach. Otherwise we are trapped within tunnel vision. This might not matter so much for the less important decisions, but for the really significant ones that involve what Dr Ellenbogen describes as the 'big picture' realisations, like those resulting in major scientific breakthroughs, sleep appears to play a decisive role. 'Inferences are abundant in the world,' he explains, 'Only a few are obvious. The rest need time and sleep to discover them.'[13]

Example: Elias Howe. Among the many stories illustrating the power of sleep is that of Elias Howe, the inventor of the automated sewing machine. The original model used a needle with an eye in the middle. One night Howe dreamt that he was being attacked by painted warriors brandishing spears with holes in the sharp end. He immediately patented the idea. When the patent expired in 1867 it had earned him 2 million dollars in royalties.

4.3 Solutions

After we've given our subconscious the problem to work on for a few days, we're likely to find our original ideas suddenly reappear further developed, if not fully formed as a solution to our problem. These are the moments when an idea we've been living with seems to have reached its final form and we're conscious of the need to get it down clearly. It's important not to resist the impulse or defer it till later. At times like these it seems we are doing our best work, yet doing it in such a way that seems to demand no effort from us. We're aware that our intellectual vision is sharper, keener than we ever realised. No matter how inconvenient, we need to write the idea out.

Simple systems

At this point it's not unusual for people to despair at finding the time for such reprogramming and the change in habits it involves. Yet creating the conditions necessary to think routinely in this way is a lot easier than we normally imagine.

There are problems that stalk our professional lives each day that we fail to solve, because we haven't sharply focused our thinking on them. To do this can involve something as simple as writing out our own ideas as to what we believe is the problem in a notebook or journal. Clarifying the details and laying out the problem simply and deliberately in this way we create the need to find a solution. In effect we give our subconscious clear instructions to set about finding one.

Good thinking starts with good organisation: simple things like creating a retrieval system out of notebooks, journals, card indexes and project boxes, to catch ideas that come when they're least expected.

Conclusion

In the following chapters you will learn simple techniques and strategies that you can use routinely. As you do, you will learn how to be an inventive thinker, someone who can not only identify key problems, but knows how to work towards a solution. In the process, you will give yourself a choice: you will no longer just have to do things because that is the way they have always been done. You will have the skills you need to look forward, not just back.

2
Asking the Right Questions

The eighteenth-century French writer and philosopher Voltaire is said to have insisted that we should judge a man by his questions rather than by his answers. The best minds see in any situation several distinct and interesting questions. They are good at defining them and analysing their internal elements and external implications.

Clear answers depend upon clear questions. Otherwise your mind will see only what it is prepared to see; what it always sees. By asking a clear question we point ourselves in the right direction to find the ideas and evidence we need: we set the controls on our thinking that will determine what's relevant and what's not. The clearer the question we set ourselves, the more dominant and effective are these controls.

What type of question is it?

But first we need to ask, what type of question is it that we are asking? Is it a question of fact, value or concept? If we get these wrong and confuse one with another, we can find ourselves producing a bewildering solution that fails to address the important issues.

A few years ago a local health authority decided to withdraw the dialysis treatment from a patient, who lived in a hostel for the homeless. Medical resources are limited, so these decisions have to be made. But the type of reason that is to count as a good reason depends on the type of question you ask. Unless you identify and separate the different types of questions involved, you could easily find yourself searching for one type of answer to a problem that really needs another: you might treat a problem as, say, a question of fact, when it is in fact a question of concept.

Listed below are the sorts of statements that were made to explain the decision. See for yourself the kind of traps we could easily fall into. Can you identify which are statements of fact, value and concept, and which are mixed? Can you see what they are a mixture of?

1. The patient is rude.
2. He is aggressive.
3. He has poor quality of life.
4. He should be denied treatment.
5. He is unemployed.
6. He lives in a hostel for the homeless.
7. The treatment should be given instead to someone else.
8. He is rootless.
9. He has no family.
10. He makes a mess which the nurses have to clean up.

Answer:

Mixed:	A. Fact/concept 8, 9, 10
	B. Fact/value/concept 1, 2
	C. Value/concept 3
Unmixed:	4, 5, 6, 7

Fact/concept

In group A, clearly these are statements of fact, but what is meant by 'rootless', 'mess' and 'family'? One person's mess might be another's everyday disorder; something that it is just not worth getting worked up about. As for 'rootless', the patient might not have a family, but he might have rich personal relations with his friends in the hostel. Even 'family' raises problems. He might not have many close blood relatives, but he might have many close friends he likes to regard as 'family'.

Fact/value/concept

As for group B, words like 'rude' and 'aggressive' are not just descriptions of a way of behaving, they are also evaluative: we usually don't approve of such behaviour. But, then, there are also questions of concept raised by these words. What do we mean by 'rude' and 'aggressive'? Do they just convey personal prejudices or is there an objective standard by which we can judge such behaviour?

Value/concept

Similar questions can be raised about the one statement in group C. Clearly, there is a question of value here with the use of the word 'poor', but we can also raise a question of concept about the 'quality of life'. We need to analyse this carefully before we allow ourselves to apply it to this sort of case.

1 Facts and values

It's not inconceivable that some people might argue, 'Of course his treatment should be withdrawn. He lives in a hostel!' To them it seems a simple question of fact. But, as you can see, it's more complex than that. Obviously, it is a matter of fact that he lives in a hostel, but the implication of this is that, as a result, his quality of life is not good enough to justify the treatment. So on this simple statement of fact hangs also a question of concept as to what is a satisfactory quality of life, and a question of value, that the failure to reach this standard justifies the judgement to remove the treatment from him.

The most obvious difference is that between a fact and a value. Put simply, a fact is a statement about what *is* the case, whereas a statement containing a value judgement is about what *ought* or *should* be the case. One is *descriptive*, the other *prescriptive*. A statement of fact purports to represent the way the world is and, therefore, it is subject to rational criticism: we can assess it in terms of its truth or falsehood as to whether it succeeds in representing the world accurately. In contrast, a statement of value is concerned about how the world should be. It does not purport to represent the way the world is and, therefore, cannot be assessed in terms of truth or falsehood.

Fact	Value
A statement about what *is* the case.	A statement about what *ought* or *should* be the case.
Descriptive	Prescriptive

Statements like 'He is unemployed' and 'He lives in a hostel for the homeless' are clearly statements of fact that can easily be proved true or false. Whereas statements, like 'He should be denied treatment' and 'The treatment should be given instead to someone else', state what *should* happen to the patient and his treatment. If we disagree with any of these judgements, unless we can show that they are based on inconclusive or contradictory evidence, or there is an inconsistency in the argument, we will be faced with a non-negotiable value judgement, a prescription, which is simply different from our own.

Although the difference between a fact and a value is not difficult to understand, it is still very easy to introduce a value into an argument without really knowing it. Often, when words are used in a different context or for different purposes they become mixed, both fact and value. Words like 'honesty', 'promise', 'heroism' and 'cowardice', used in a particular way in a particular context, represent both a description of the facts and a value judgement.

> *Example: Promise.*   The statement 'John promised to pay Sarah £30' is a simple statement of fact. But the word 'promise' means more than just an undertaking to do or to refrain from doing something. It also means it's 'good' to keep such an undertaking and 'bad' not to. In other words, there are both prescriptive and descriptive elements to the meaning of the word. Consequently, from the statement of fact that 'John promised to pay Sarah £30', we can deduce the value judgement that 'John *should* pay Sarah £30'.

2 Concepts

Questions of concept can also hide unnoticed within a simple statement of fact in a similar way. In each case where concepts are used we're asking a unique sort of question: 'Yes, but what do you mean by X?' In a probing, self-reflective way we are questioning our own use of these quite ordinary words. We are saying that these can no longer be taken for granted; that there are implications to our argument that are concealed by our use of these words.

In some discussions we have to step back and ask questions like these. In the statements about the dialysis patient we would have to ask, 'What do we mean by 'rootlessness', 'aggression', or even 'family'?' Often our discussions turn on the meaning of such concepts. What seems like a discussion over a difference of fact turns out to be a difference of concept with both sides using it in different ways.

> **The problem ...**
> The precision needed to argue consistently is at odds with the flexibility of language.

One reason we have this problem is the flexibility of language. Words have a capacity for holding many shades of meaning, or even several separate meanings, which compounds our problems in communicating well-reasoned arguments and ideas. While the essence of reasoning is precision, language normally tends toward imprecision. Two opposing forces are at work. The sharpness, clarity and constancy of meaning, that are important to consistent reasoning, are at odds with the ambiguity of language, the lack of sharp and stable definitions.

Is there a better question?

Now that we are aware of the particular problems posed by these different types of question, we are able to ask a better type of question: one that is more relevant to the problem and avoids many of these complications.

Moreover, after analysing the concepts used to pin the problem down, we will know whether there are different solutions on different levels. A more effective solution may be one that comes from stepping back from the problem to see it more objectively. By questioning concepts we step outside the question and ask self-reflectively, 'But what do we mean by X?' If we can do the same with the question and step outside the immediate situation, we may be able to design a solution not just for this problem, but for similar problems in the future.

> A better question:
> 1. Avoids complications: fact, value, concept.
> 2. Is more relevant to the problem.
> 3. Answers it on different levels.

Whistleblowing

To illustrate this, think about the problem of whistleblowing. Over the years those who feel they have no choice but to do this have taken on the mantle of modern professional heroes, willing to put their own interests at risk to expose companies who pursue profits at the expense of the public.

They include people like Loretta Lynch, the president of California's Public Utilities Commission, who helped expose corrupt practices at Enron in May 2002; Gary Brown, an employee of a well-known British building society, who became suspicious of advertising contracts that were awarded to a company employing the boss' sister; and Dr Stephen Bolsin, the consultant anaesthetist at Bristol Royal Infirmary, who blew the whistle in 1995 when he became convinced that the death rates for children undergoing heart surgery were higher there than in most hospitals.

> *Example: Dan Applegate.*   One person who was placed in exactly this position was Dan Applegate, a senior engineer with Convair, a company subcontracted to work on the DC-10 plane for McDonnell-Douglas. In 1972, as the project director, he wrote to his vice-president detailing design faults in the fuselage of the plane. He believed that the cargo doors could open during flight, which would depressurise the cargo bay, causing the floor of the passenger cabin above to buckle. This, in turn, would affect the plane's control lines, which were housed in the floor, with the very high risk that the plane would crash, unless modifications were made to the design of both the doors and the floor.

Rather than deal with the technical risks, Convair's response was to emphasise the financial risks to the company if McDonnell-Douglas were informed of these problems. The management argued that the company would be placed at a competitive disadvantage because of the high costs of delays and rectifications. Two years later in 1974 a fully loaded DC-10 crashed on the outskirts of Paris with the loss of 346 lives. [1]

Dan's concerns were on the one hand to be loyal to his company and cause it no harm, while on the other to protect the public. On the personal level this is a difficult, complex problem. But, if you were the CEO of the company, looking at this problem after the event, in addition to Dan's personal dilemma you would also have concerns on another level. You would have to step back from Dan's problem and look at the causes of whistleblowing to see what could be done to make it unnecessary. You would need to ask whether the question can be changed or represented in a different way.

You might conclude that two things should be done. First, the lines of communication within companies could be strengthened and made to work effectively, so that employees like Dan would no longer need to go public with their damaging revelations to get their concerns addressed.

And second, there could be more transparency within companies and more effective public participation, thereby reducing the number of abuses that whistleblowers report. By re-designing the question in this way we can design a better solution that deals with the wider problem.

Bribery

Consider another example: the problem of bribery facing foreign business people and professionals working in countries where it is endemic.

Example: Bernard Fleming. In 1989 Bernard Fleming set up a training college in a large town in Southern Europe. The college was running courses that were designed to train the employees of local businesses and anyone who wanted to retrain or gain promotion by getting better qualifications. Six months after the college had opened, it was struggling to survive with very low student enrolments. Then Bernard had a visit from the local mayor, who explained that for a 'consideration' he would tell his employees that they must come and enrol on courses. Then he would tell other employers to follow his lead and send their employees to be trained. Each year, for a similar 'consideration', he would make sure that the enrolments kept growing.

Bernard knew that if the college were to survive he needed to get more students enrolled. He had tried everything. The mayor's offer now explained why all his efforts had come to nothing. Indeed, local businessmen told him that nothing happens there without the mayor's approval. He could even close the college down if Bernard refused to go along with his plan.

If you were working in your home country the solution might be simple: it is against the law and is always wrong, so don't do it. Exporting these principles abroad might lead you to conclude that if you can't do business without doing it, don't do business in that country. If Bernard had gone to his embassy for advice, this is what he would probably be told. But Bernard was working in a different environment, in which he may not have been able to survive without engaging in it. This sort of advice is not helpful for someone who has invested his life savings into a project and whose employees and their families are all dependent on him finding a solution to the problem.

1 Questions of fact, value and concept

So we need to analyse the question to see if it can be changed or represented in a different way. This means looking at the nature of the question – whether it is a question of fact, value or concept, or a mixed question – and then looking at it on different levels.

Analyse the question:

1. Nature of the question – fact, value or concept.
2. The different levels.

First, there are certain questions of **fact** we need to answer. Why are bribes routine and unavoidable in some cultures? Is it because officials are poorly paid or are such 'gifts' commonly accepted within the local culture as just an expression of respect?

Second, there are questions of **value**. Should we conduct ourselves in accordance with our own conscience, which tells us that bribery is wrong, or should we be more pragmatic? Are we right to insist upon working in accordance with the ethical values imported from a different cultural environment, or, as we have chosen to work within that culture, should we just accept the ethical norms of that society?

Then, third, there is a question of **concept**. What is a bribe and how does it differ from gifts, like the tips we leave for those who wait on our table in a restaurant, or commissions, like the incentive packages negotiated with workers to increase their productivity?

Bribery in business – is there a better question?

1. **Questions of fact:**

    1.1 Are they routine and unavoidable?
    1.2 Are officials poorly paid?
    1.3 Are they an expression of respect?

2. **Questions of value:**

    2.1 Should we obey our conscience or be more pragmatic?
    2.2 Should we just accept the ethical norms of that society?

3. **Questions of concept:**

    3.1 What is a bribe?
    3.2 How do they differ from gifts and commissions?

---

2 Levels

Now that we have been able to separate out the different questions that hide within the problem, we can see more clearly the issues that need to be considered on different levels.

2.1 General level

On the general level there is the question, what needs to be done to make bribery unnecessary so that business can be conducted between different countries and by people of different nationalities without their values being compromised in this way?

Your analysis of the concept of bribery might have revealed that there is a distinction between bribes on the one hand, and gifts and commissions, including tips and incentives, on the other. You might now conclude that gifts and commissions are part of the system: they are public, openly accountable and known to all who do business. They are incentives for working harder and more efficiently; for providing a better service. In contrast, bribes are private and secretive. They sidestep the ethical norms of the market, which attempt to ensure equal opportunity, free enterprise and perfectly competitive markets. In effect, they amount to an attempt to gain some advantage over your competitors which you don't deserve.

Different solutions

This now reveals quite clearly different types of solutions on the general and personal levels. On the general level, in answer to our question of how we can change the situation to make bribes unnecessary, we might argue for international pressure, like sanctions, to bring about political change within the country to root out the culture of corruption. It might need social and economic reform to improve the pay of officials and introduce a better system of regulation and accountability.

2.2 Personal level

Perhaps even more important, having separated out the general problem we can now be clearer about the questions on the personal level as it affects Bernard and individuals like him, who must do business and survive in an environment where it may be unavoidable. The question is clearer, sharper, and the possible solutions are much more obvious.

It's clear we can't avoid the problem. So now our question is, can we limit our involvement in this activity to gifts and commissions, which are ethically acceptable? For Bernard this may mean renegotiating with the mayor to place their relationship on a different footing. Even so, this still may involve difficult ethical decisions if you are working in an environment where the demand for 'gifts' is backed by threats. But at least now we understand more clearly the different elements raised by the question.

As this shows, analysis of the problem in this way not only separates out and distinguishes questions of fact, value and concept, but makes us more aware of the different levels on which the problem has an influence.

Conclusion

Now that we have found the right questions we need to answer, we can begin to turn our attention to the processes involved in genuine thinking. We like to think that most of our solutions come through a straightforward step-by-step process of logical reasoning. But this is the way the story of discovery is told after the event, rather than how it actually happens. In fact it is a much more creative process, which starts by revealing the underlying structure that organises our ideas, so that we can work with it, adapting it to find the solution we're after. As we'll see, this is conceptual and creative thinking. But first, we must learn to generate our ideas.

3
Generating Ideas

An important part of any professional training involves developing an understanding of how people think in that profession. To be a lawyer we must learn to think like a lawyer, as we must learn to think like a doctor, teacher, architect, auditor or police officer if we want to enter any of these professions. We learn certain organised strategies and principles, which seem to define thinking as an ordered process like logical and mathematical thinking.

Scientists, too, describe their work in the same way. In their accounts of major discoveries, they describe the same assured logical steps taken with a clear view in sight. And yet, in reality more often their discoveries are like stabs in the dark, followed by false dawns and disappointments, until a sudden intuition finally lights their way.

Sir Peter Medawar the British immunologist and Nobel prize winner argues that it only seems to be logical in character, because 'it can be made to appear so when we look back upon a completed episode of thought'[1]; it is 'simply the posture(s) we choose to be seen in when the curtain goes up and the public sees us.'[2] In fact, he argues, it is a much more imaginative and intuitive process.

Good thinking involves more than just logical and critical thinking. Although essential to check that our arguments and ideas are consistent, on its own this type of thinking will not generate one new idea. When we use our logical and critical thinking skills we work with what we're given, either to produce a better form of the idea, or to show grounds for rejecting it altogether. We seek out the faults and repair the line of reasoning.

To generate our own original ideas in the first place we need to learn the skills and techniques of creative and imaginative thinking. In contrast to logical and critical thinking, this involves using our intellectual skills in quite a different way and with radically different assumptions as we approach problems. In what follows two principles are worth remembering:

- We don't have to be right at each step.
- There is no single way of getting to where you want to be.

Questioning: a structured approach

The problem is, when anybody tells you to generate your own ideas, they mostly end up just giving you vague, unhelpful advice. They might tell you to 'Think for yourself' or 'Ask yourself questions', which doesn't tell you exactly what you should do. You might be advised just to lower or remove altogether your inhibitions, as if there is a torrent of ideas just waiting to cascade before you, if only you could overcome your fears about appearing to be foolish by saying things that seem naïve. Either that or we are assembled into groups and told just to throw out the first thought that comes into our minds.

In fact we can do this in a much more organised, systematic way. Indeed, this is exactly what most of us do all the time without knowing it. We ask ourselves certain routine trigger questions through which we assemble the ideas and facts we need to make a decision.

Most of us who have struggled unsuccessfully to start our cars know exactly what we mean by this sort of organised thinking. Well-meaning neighbours and passers-by gather around giving you advice as you vainly try to get the car started. Then the mechanic arrives and you know at once that you're in the presence of a thinking, intelligent brain. He quietly goes over the engine, asking questions, testing and eliminating hypotheses until he arrives at the solution. It's clear he is using an ordered series of questions as he gathers information and eliminates one hypothesis after another.

> *Example: Doctors.* In the same way, a doctor will systematically work through her questions, gathering evidence of symptoms and matching them to patterns suggesting various causes.

> *Example: Teacher.* A teacher, who finds one of his strongest students is suddenly producing poor work, will have a similar set of questions to work through, systematically gathering the evidence before he can come to a solution.

Routine questions

We all do this; for some of us it's more obvious than for others. So, the first thing we must do is look carefully at the series of questions we routinely ask ourselves: a trigger list we work through in the same way. Most creative thinkers are constantly refining and adapting them, adding new ones they might hear elsewhere. Those whom we describe as geniuses, who solve problems by seeing something no-one else can see, come to their solutions in exactly this way. They ask questions nobody else asks. They approach the problem from a different direction with different classifications.

> Genius: someone who asks questions nobody else asks.

Consider, for instance, the unique classifications of human beings invented by creative thinkers in the past. In the nineteenth century William James, the American psychologist and philosopher, classified people as 'tough-minded and tender-minded'. The Swiss psychiatrist Carl Jung invented the now common classification of people as 'introverts and extroverts'. Developments in psychology and behaviourism brought us 'convergent and divergent' thinkers. The point is that such new classifications, and the questions they evoke, can completely change our attitudes and thinking.

Combine them and you get structures for generating all sorts of unexpected, interesting ideas and ways of freeing us from routine, predictable responses. We can now talk about 'divergent introverts', 'divergent extroverts', 'convergent introverts', and 'convergent extroverts'; classifications that can help us explain all sorts of behaviour, which we would otherwise find difficult to explain.

Example: Hotel guests. Recently, researchers at Cornell University examined the attitudes of hotel guests. They broke them down into four research categories by combining four concepts: 'satisfied' and 'dissatisfied' and 'stayers' and 'switchers' to get 'satisfied stayers', 'dissatisfied stayers', 'dissatisfied switchers' and 'satisfied switchers'. Of course it would have been obvious to think about satisfied stayers and dissatisfied switchers, but without combining the concepts in this way it would have been difficult and counter-intuitive to think there may be dissatisfied stayers and, even more, satisfied switchers.

So, ask yourself what questions you routinely ask in your subject: write out a list. And be alert to every new question and classification you think might be useful and add it to your list.

Trigger list of routine questions:
1. Make a list.
2. Be alert to every new question and classification.
3. Add them to your list.

Compiling a trigger list

So what sort of questions should we expect to find on our trigger list? Although the following are not specific to any particular profession, you will probably find some of your questions take a similar form.

1. What do we mean by X?
2. Why did that happen?
3. What is the connection between A and B?
4. How do we know that?
5. What evidence have we got for that claim? Is it reliable?
6. If that's the case, what follows?
7. How is it that A is the case when B is or is not the case? Is there an inconsistency?
8. What other examples are there for this sort of thing happening? Are there grounds here for a general rule?
9. What is the history, the background, to this?
10. Is it something quite unique, or has it developed out of something else?

As you think about your own trigger list, it will probably help to keep in mind four useful rules:

1. Generate as many questions as possible.
2. Make them as clear and specific as you can.
3. Then pursue them as far as they will go.
4. If all this comes to nothing, ask another one.

Example: Police officer.   If you were a police officer investigating a suspicious death, you might find yourself working through an alphabetical list of routine questions. Each one would remind you to gather evidence on a particular feature of the person who has been found dead:

1. Age
2. Build
3. Clothes
4. Distinguishing marks
5. Ethnic origin
6. Face
7. Glasses
8. Hair
9. Items he or she had with them.[3]

Example: Marketing manager.   If you were responsible for marketing a new product you might routinely ask questions like the following:

1. What is the primary market for the product?
2. What is the size of this market?
3. Are there notable characteristics to this market?
4. What are the key characteristics of the typical consumer?
5. Are there important secondary markets?
6. How large are these?
7. What are the main competitors?
8. What key advantages does the product have over its competitors?
9. What are its key selling points?
10. When will the product be ready to go into production?

If you were an investment manager thinking about whether to invest in a particular fund, your concern would be to get a clear idea of when demand will be greater than supply, causing a price spike: the maximum point of profit. You might assemble the ideas and information you need by asking questions, like the following.

Example: Investment manager.

1. Will the price of commodities rise (oil, wheat, corn, industrial and precious metals etc.)?
2. Are the factors that cause the price rises in place?
   2.1 Is there strong demand? Are the inventories high?
   2.2 How are the factors influencing supply? Are suppliers cutting production (OPEC, mining companies, farms)?
3. Are governments implementing policies that will affect supply or demand?
   3.1 Subsidies e.g. biofuels?
   3.2 Low interest rates stimulating consumer purchases and investment to increase production?
   3.3 Tariffs?
4. Geography – where are commodities produced? Transport and the price of oil are underlying price components.
5. Are there significant changes in social and economic behaviour? For example, changes in the nature of populations and consumption habits bringing about increased demand for certain products, e.g. cars, consumer goods, etc.
6. What are the movements in price?
   6.1 If prices are falling, investors will sell in the hope of buying back in at a lower rate in the future.
   6.2 If prices are rising, they will buy in the hope that they can sell at a higher price in the future.
7. Are there significant currency fluctuations? Most commodities are priced in dollars, so the strength of the dollar affects demand.
8. What are the risks and rewards?
   8.1 Is the increase in demand/price sustainable?
   8.2 Is supply at full capacity?[4]

If you think back to when you were at school or university, for each subject you studied you will have learnt the most relevant, routine questions to ask of each topic you studied. If you were studying history, a well-designed course would teach you not just the facts of history, but how to think like a historian. So the sort of routine questions you would have learnt to ask might include:

1. What was the cause of the event?
2. What was his motive?

3. Is there sufficient evidence to justify that explanation?
4. What were the effects?
    4.1 How large?
    4.2 How significant?
    4.3 Who was most affected: individuals, groups, social classes?
    4.4 What type of effects: economic, social, political, intellectual?
5. Who was involved: social classes, individuals, groups (religious, professional, military)?

If you were studying literature, you would no doubt have questions about the possible influences on a writer's work, comparisons with other writers and questions on plots, atmosphere and background, common themes, characters, style, dialogue, pace, suspense, humour, tragedy, and so on. The point is that for every subject and profession there is a routine set of trigger questions that we use to generate and marshal our ideas – things we routinely look for.

The power of questions

If you doubt the power of these questions to generate a wealth of ideas you need to tackle a problem and make a decision, consider the following. In *The Art of Clear Thinking*[5] Rudolf Flesch reminds us of the extraordinary power of a popular 1950s TV game to negotiate, through a series of questions, the vast territory of possible answers to a problem and come up with the answer we're looking for.

The programme, known as 'Twenty Questions' or 'Animal, Vegetable, or Mineral', would set four panellists a problem. To find the answer they would be given between them 20 questions, which could only be answered by yes or no. In most cases, in a surprisingly short time, the answer would be found by a series of well-crafted questions. Why is this so extraordinary? Well, as Flesch reminds us, asked by a perfect player these 20 questions would cover a range of 1,048,576 possible solutions. In other words, in the space of five minutes, the time taken to ask and answer 20 questions, you can narrow it down to one answer in a million.

> Using a set of routine questions you can find that one in a million original idea.

Moreover, this is not just the stuff of TV games. Prior to the computer age, police sketch artists would use the 'Identikit' system to help witnesses put together a likeness of a suspect. The face would be divided up into, say, 10 building blocks: the hairline, forehead, eyes, nose and so on down to the chin. Each would be represented on transparent strips with a variety of options to choose from. Let's say there were 10 hairlines, 10 foreheads, 10 eyes and so on, amounting to a total of 100 transparent slips. Using this it would be possible to create 10 billion different faces, out of which the witness could produce a very close likeness of the suspect quickly. So here you have a problem with 10 billion possible solutions, yet using this simple system, composed of a routine set of questions, it is possible to arrive at a solution in no time at all.

Exploring different perspectives on different levels

1 Different perspectives

The reason this works is that we routinely remind ourselves to ask questions that we might otherwise forget or assume are irrelevant. But, then, beyond this, as we've said, original thinkers take one further step: they invent new questions to open up new perspectives others have not seen. Therefore, in addition to these routine trigger questions, we need a method that gets us to think outside our own limited perspective to ask questions we might otherwise dismiss as irrelevant and unthinkable.

In the Cornell research it was counter-intuitive and unthinkable to believe there are actually such people as 'dissatisfied stayers' and 'satisfied switchers', who would do something against their interests. Not until we change perspectives are we likely to think the unthinkable and consider the counter-intuitive.

Unfortunately, our routine patterns of thought and behaviour can leave us blinkered to these other perspectives. We are so used to thinking in one particular way that we find it impossible to change our perspectives and approach a problem as others are approaching it. In all professions this has a serious impact on our performance. A teacher who can no longer see how difficult it is for his students to understand a topic in the way he presents it is unlikely to get the best out of his students. A business person who goes into negotiations with a customer unable to put herself in the other side's position is going to find it difficult to get the business.

Example: Business in Japan. Edward de Bono argues that when western business people first started doing business with Japanese companies they were confused about what was going on in their negotiations. To the Japanese executives, the information and values that were expressed were put forward not as the basis for argument, but as inputs, which gradually came together to form an outcome or decision.

The western business executives were confused by this because they deal in arguments and propositions first and these determine what's relevant to discuss. They complained that at a meeting the Japanese executives would seem to hold back and make no proposals at all. But the Japanese were not holding back; they simply didn't have a position or an idea at that stage; these emerged only later.

In some professions, of course, like nursing and social work, learning to change perspectives in this way, so you can see more clearly the situation from your client's or patient's perspective is an important part of the job. But to be successful all professionals have to learn to place themselves in the other person's position and vicariously experience their feelings, anxieties, hopes and beliefs.

In business education, modern stakeholder analysis involves thinking about a problem or situation by placing yourself imaginatively in the position of each stakeholder who affects or is affected by the decision you make: employees, customers, suppliers and shareholders. Failure to do this can lead to poor decisions.

2 Different levels

Then, once you've done this, think about the problem from these different perspectives on different levels. Traditionally, professionals, like doctors and lawyers, worked in one-to-one relationships with their clients, engaged in relatively simple activities, and this shaped our concept of professional skills and responsibilities. But today we live in much more integrated societies where professionals, like doctors, play an important role in a complex pattern of interrelations. Their influence is felt on different levels, not just on the individual level (biological, psychological, moral, intellectual), but on the physical (material needs, transport, climate, food and shelter, and the environment) and social (cultural, political, economic) levels.

Example: A local doctor.   Today a local doctor is not just responsible for her patients individually, but with the prevention of illness generally in the community by promoting healthier lifestyles, even influencing planning decisions that might adversely affect the environment in which her patients live. She is, therefore, publicly accountable for the values she promotes, which have a significant impact in redesigning our communities. Her responsibility is not just for her individual patients, but for the whole community.

The same is true of other professionals.

Example: Accountants and investment managers.   An accountant is no longer just a bookkeeper, but an auditor, a financial adviser, a credit controller and a tax adviser. He will draw up financial projections for his clients and business plans for small businesses. He can exert a diverse and significant influence on people's lives. An investment manager controls the saving of thousands of families, the product of their life's work and their security for the future.

The effects of our decisions are felt not just on the individual level as they affect particular self-interests, but on the values and well-being of society and the physical conditions of life in our communities. A decision to invest in a new manufacturing plant not only improves the lives of individuals by creating jobs, but has an impact on the local community by increasing the demand on local shops and businesses. The local council might need to invest in new schools and roads to relieve traffic congestion. The environment might be affected as local residents suffer noise and air pollution. Wider still, it may have an impact on the national economy and even climate change.

No matter what your business or profession, it is not difficult to think in this way routinely. After you've answered all your trigger questions, do two things:

1. Examine your topic from the perspective of all those involved;
2. As you do this, think about each one on different levels;

2.1 Physical (material needs, transport, climate, etc.,),
2.2 Individual (biological, psychological, moral, intellectual),
2.3 Social (cultural, political, economic).

Levels:	
Physical	1. Material needs
	2. Transport
	3. Climate, etc.
Individual	1. Biological
	2. Psychological
	3. Moral
	4. Intellectual
Social	1. Cultural
	2. Political
	3. Economic

Of course, not all these levels will be relevant for each perspective and for each decision, but a routine that gets us to explore them before we reject an idea makes it less likely that we will miss the sort of idea that the Cornell researchers found so useful. When Paul Moore warned that HBOS was taking risks that would jeopardise the survival of Halifax and the Royal Bank of Scotland, his warnings seemed to go unheeded and he was sacked as head of risk at HBOS. Despite the significance of the decisions that were being made, there seemed to be a reluctance to think freely from different perspectives on different levels. As a result, it appears some things were taken for granted, while others were overlooked.

Conclusion

We began this chapter by drawing attention to the difference between logical reasoning and critical thinking on the one hand and creative thinking on the other. Creative thinking presents us with a different style of thinking altogether: one that is open, divergent and far less controlled by its own internal laws. As we've seen, we don't have to be right at each step and there is no single way of getting to where we want to be.

In this chapter we've learnt ways of generating our own ideas from different perspectives and on different levels. Rather than a simple linear account of what we already think, we will end up with a multi-layered structure of new ideas that we will now need to think about. It will be broken up into sub-issues and sub-questions. The clearer these are, the better. That way, we will be able to see how they combine and inter-relate; how some reinforce each other, while others are irrelevant to the overall issue we need to think about.

In the following chapters, we will structure these ideas into patterns and hierarchies to reveal their interconnections. This will give us a clearer idea of how our ideas are organised. Then, with this structure in front of us, we will work with it to design the best solution.

Part 2
Structuring Our Ideas

Now that we have generated the ideas, the next step is to reveal the underlying pattern or structure into which they are organised. To understand what appear to be just unconnected facts and ideas we organise them by classifying them in general terms. This ties them together in causal or logical relations: either we understand them as parts of a causal sequence of events or as the internal elements of a concept, which are bound to each other logically. By revealing how our ideas are interrelated in this way we come to understand their meaning and significance.

Over the next four chapters we will learn ways of analysing these patterns of interrelations, revealing the different types of relationships that make them up. Some ideas are related as convergences or divergences, comparisons or just as examples. Some are linked as cause and effect. Others complement, supplement or reinforce each other. But whatever they are, they reveal the meaning and significance of our ideas by structuring them into a hierarchy. These patterns are the scaffolding of our understanding: the way we make sense of the world around us.

But unfortunately, as we saw in Chapter 1, they are not always the most useful ways of understanding the facts and ideas that relate to a problem or situation. The relevance of our routine approaches to problems can be undermined by circumstances that have changed or are changing. Yesterday's solution or pattern of expectations may lead us to unwise decisions, as we saw when the board of the Royal Bank of Scotland decided to acquire parts of ABN Amro with the credit crisis well underway.

A better solution appears sometimes just by analysing a concept, which reveals the problem in a completely different way. Like a crime novel, we find that the key fact pointing towards a solution has been hidden in full view all the time. This willingness to question what seems obvious, like a concept we use everyday without thinking, has led to some of the most important breakthroughs in modern science, as the work of scientists, like Copernicus, Galileo, Darwin and Einstein, illustrates.

Galileo and Copernicus both questioned the assumption, which seemed obviously true to all sane people, that the Earth was still and the universe rotated around it. Einstein questioned the deeply held intuitions of absolute space and time to arrive at his theory of special relativity, which overthrew the Newtonian physics that had dominated thinking for two centuries.

Normally, though, as we will see in Part 3, we will have to work with these structures, changing them and approaching them differently to find a solution. Again, some of the most significant breakthroughs in modern science have come about in just this way, not as a result of new discoveries or new empirical evidence, but because a scientist has looked at the problem differently.

4
Causal Thinking

Beyond the simplest operations, thinking is all about creating connections between ideas. On their own, ideas have little value or significance; it is only when we make connections with other ideas that they become useful. Although the idea, 'The object in front of me is red', makes sense, it has very limited value or significance. But connect it with other ideas, like 'The object is a person' and 'The red is blood', and it becomes altogether more significant.

Hence, the quality of our thinking is determined not by the strength of our ideas, but by the significance of the relations we find and the connections we make. Now that we've generated our ideas, we must look at their relations, mapping them out in simple patterns or structures.

> The quality of our thinking is determined not by the strength of our ideas, but by the significance of the relations we find and the connections we make.

The structure of our ideas

As we've seen, much of our thinking is done in patterns or structures. Out of our experience our minds create certain patterns of behaviour, retaining only those that have been successful in dealing with the routine situations we confront. These are patterns of interrelated beliefs, values and preferences. They are mental short cuts so that we can avoid having to make lengthy and involved calculations every time we have to decide what it would be best to do.

Over the years our thinking has been extensively programmed in this way. We use these patterns of behaviour routinely and without deliberation to help us navigate the immense space of possibilities open to us. In this way we can interpret experience, reduce our confusion to manageable levels and predict what is likely to happen if we choose one thing rather than another.

> *Example: Consumers.*   As consumers we are presented with such a bewildering range of choices that we cannot hope to evaluate each one before we decide. Instead, we take short-cuts: we form patterns into which we organise our beliefs, values and preferences, which then act as standard operating procedures to guide us routinely as we make these decisions.

Most of our problems we solve in exactly the same way. We take the same route to work each day and we have in our minds the same list of things we need, representing the pattern of our consumption habits, each time we go to the supermarket. Faced with a bewilderingly large number of TV channels we program into our receiver a template of our favourite channels.

But the problem is that the most familiar patterns are not always the most useful. And in most cases we're not likely to be aware of this. Once we've formed them, we tend not to second guess them. To do so would be to sabotage them. We choose what we have become used to choosing because it is easier to navigate the immense space of possibilities that way. Accordingly, we tend to ignore anything that might seem to contradict and throw into doubt our choices and established patterns of behaviour. In the 1950s, studies of cognitive dissonance found that consumers would continue to read advertisements for a new car after they had bought it, but would avoid information about other brands, fearing post-purchase misgivings.

So, now that we've generated our ideas, the next step is to bring to the surface the patterns into which we've organised them. We can then test and develop these to create a pattern that reflects a more complete and nuanced understanding of the topic. This, in turn, will give us a better chance of arriving at the best solution.

These patterns take a familiar form with a hierarchy of ideas in which a few main points are broken down into subpoints, and these into sub-subpoints. Recreating the pattern of our ideas in this way helps us lay out the problem. Once it's in front of us, we can begin to work with it by testing and adapting it.

Structuring our ideas

Like most of our thinking skills, structuring our ideas seems difficult and complex, yet we do it a lot of the time without even thinking. Patterns or structures are the scaffolding of our understanding, so they lie at the heart of almost everything we do. Without them, we would struggle to see the point of a witty or humorous comment, and we couldn't even start to tackle a crossword puzzle without recognising, comparing and adapting them.

A typical cryptic clue might be split in two with both parts leading to the same word. As you compare the structure of ideas represented by both words your aim is to find a similarity, which points to the answer. The clue might be 'Savings book (7)' and the answer is, of course, 'Reserve'. Your savings are a reserve and you can book or reserve a table in a restaurant or a seat on a train. Some clues expect you to adapt the structure of the clue as you can see in this one: 'H, I, J, K, L, M, N, O (5)'. The answer: 'Water'. The solution comes from adapting the structure, reducing it to 'H to O', which then translates into the atomic composition of water, 'H_2O'.[1]

As for wit and humour, Sir Peter Medawar, in his book *Induction and Intuition in Scientific Thought*, gives us this one. He explains:

> The Rev. Sydney Smith, a famous wit, was walking with a friend through the extremely narrow streets of old Edinburgh when they heard a furious altercation between two housewives from high-up windows across the street. 'They can never agree,' said Smith to his companion, 'for they are arguing from different premises.'[2]

As he points out later, in this and similar examples there is a real or apparent structural similarity between two or more schemes of ideas and it is this that makes it witty. We instantly recognise that the word 'premises' can be used in two ways.

It's interesting to note that moving in this way, from the concrete to the abstract, produces wit; moving the other way, from the abstract to the concrete, produces humour. The first involves synthesis as you generalise, turning the concrete and particular into general ideas. The second involves analysis as you particularise, turning general ideas into particular people, things, characters and situations.

Wit	Synthesis: Concrete	$\longrightarrow$	Abstract
Humour	Analysis: Abstract	$\longrightarrow$	Concrete

More significant, when this similarity between structures of ideas is real, we experience those wonderfully insightful moments of sudden clarity, when we understand a difficult principle or idea for the first time. A teacher might give you an analogy which suddenly makes a difficult subject clear. This sudden insight and the clarity it brings comes from instantly apprehending the structural similarity between the two sets of ideas: the subject and the analogy.

Insight is the sudden recognition of the structural similarity between two sets of ideas.

To make sense of isolated facts and ideas, then, we must reveal the connections between them and map out their interrelations. The two most effective means of doing this are by analysing the causal and conceptual relations between ideas.

Structuring ideas
1. Causal relations.
2. Conceptual relations.

Causal relations

Many of the problems we have to solve have arisen as a result of the change in causal relations between individuals, within an organisation, or wider still in society and the economy. So, the first step is to map out these causal relations. Otherwise, we will not know whether we are looking for a single cause or a pattern of causes; whether the problem is the result of the emergence of a factor that has had a significant impact on things, or whether the pattern of influences has shifted and self-organised to form a different pattern.

Example: Estate agent. An estate agent might experience a sudden fall in the number of enquiries he is getting. Properties that were being sold within a few weeks of going on the market might now be taking months to sell. The first thing he must do, therefore, is map out the factors in the market that influence buyers' decisions. He may discover a single local cause. There may be lay-offs in a few local businesses. Hearing about them one by one, he may have underestimated the total number. Or he may see a pattern of causes all reinforcing each other: an increase in interest rates may have been compounded by a rise in food and utilities costs and by tighter regulations on mortgages.

Once he has mapped out the causal pattern he will be in a much better position to design an effective solution. He will certainly be less likely to fall back on a pattern of behaviour that has worked in the past, but may no longer indicate the most effective response in these changing circumstances.

Complex decision-making of this kind calls for a different type of thinking from routine pattern compliance, one that involves analysing the pattern and evaluating the relations between ideas that it represents. In this way we identify and eliminate false and misleading inferences and assumptions. Then we can either adapt our routine patterns of thinking or search for new ones.

Practical knowledge

Unfortunately, our education and training largely ignores this type of practical thinking. This encourages us to believe that knowledge in business and professional life is exclusively theoretical knowledge derived from academic research and then applied in our work.

But of equal importance is practical knowledge, represented in the patterns of ideas and behaviour that we create from this sort of reflective thought in the actual situations we confront each day. From this, we create and learn to use an accumulated bank of predictive patterns, which help us decide what to do each time we are presented with difficult problems. Our practical knowledge is acquired on the job as we adapt these patterns to help us understand more effectively the situation we confront.

Lisa Tsoi Hoshmand and Donald E. Polkinghorne (1992) describe these as 'practical paradigms'. They insist that we should learn to use both types of knowledge: the theoretical and academic on the one hand, and the practical on the other:

> In actual practice, at least *two* types of knowledge are available: one contained in the theoretical and research literature ... and the other derived from the experience of actual practice (usually in the form of interpretative patterns derived with practical reasoning). There are indications that the use of both types of knowledge is more effective in practice than is either alone.[3]

Each time we confront a difficult problem, our starting point in devising a structured understanding of the situation is to call upon routine responses we have learnt by trial and error. Positive feedback reinforces those that are the most successful, with the most effective patterns getting stronger and the least effective getting weaker. We then test and modify them, fitting our routine causal patterns to match the complexity of the situation, until we finish up with practical paradigms.

These appear to lie at the heart of practical thinking. Created from the working experience of business people and professionals, they reflect both the local and historical character of practical knowledge. They not only map out the social realities in which we do our work, but give us a way of predicting what is likely to be the most effective action to take.

Discovering causal relations

There are simple steps we can take to identify the pattern of causal relations in any problem situation.

1 Lay out a complete account

The first thing to do is lay out as complete an account as you can of the key ideas and facts as you see them. Often we take it for granted that we are aware of everything, so we see no point in doing this. As a result, we not only miss obvious things, but we fail to register possible solutions and questions we need to ask. So try to be naïve, take nothing for granted, and set down all you know. Often you will see for the first time interpretations you've never considered. Things will simply jump out at you because they are no longer obscured by the veil of your routine thinking.

2 Revealing the hierarchy

Along with the ideas, you will, of course, also begin to map out the relations between them. The pattern of your ideas will reveal itself as a hierarchy. Some of your beliefs will be more important than others. Some will be a deduction from more fundamental beliefs, while others perform a supporting role as evidence or illustration. The same will be true of your preferences and values. Certain preferences you may not want to compromise on and some values may be non-overridable.

But you will also discover that some conflict with others. When beliefs conflict it indicates that our understanding of the situation is inconsistent, that we've made a mistake and we need to review them. When preferences and values conflict it means that we must consider again the relative importance we attach to them. To hold one value as non-overridable might mean that we will have to be prepared to compromise on another. Similarly, it may become clear that we can no longer satisfy two conflicting preferences. As a result, we will begin to see not just how our ideas are organised, but ways in which we can adapt the structure to find different solutions to the problem we're trying to solve.

Of course for some of us, mapping out clearly the pattern of beliefs, values and preferences that we claim guide our choices may still not produce better decisions.

> *Example: Smokers, drinkers and overeaters.* For many of us there are parts of our lives, particularly involving risk-related behaviour, in which we routinely make decisions that not only fail to reflect our beliefs and values, and optimise our preferences, but threaten our lives. Many smokers, drinkers and overeaters continue to make the same decisions, even though they know and regret the effect it has on their health. Indeed, many are even willing to pay fitness trainers, psycho-therapists and others either to help them make better decisions or make the decisions for them. Their representation of this behaviour seems to be blighted by an addiction, which blinds them to the longer term consequences.

But for those of us who are not driven by the compulsion of an addiction, mapping out our patterns of ideas in this way is likely to make it easier for us to see the decisions we need to take, particularly when the problems we face involve complex issues.

3 Convergences and divergences

However, if nothing suggests itself as a possible solution, you will have to take more deliberate steps to interpret the structure.

Interpreting the structure:
1. Convergences.
2. Divergences.

Think about how you would set about finding a solution to the following problem.

> *Example: Health inspectors.* Some years ago in Quebec City, over a short period 50 cases of illness occurred all with the same symptoms: nausea, shortness of breath, a cough, stomach pains, loss of weight and a marked blue-grey coloration. This all suggested severe vitamin deficiency, but there were too many cases in too short a time for this to be the explanation. What's more, the post-mortem results on the 20 who had died revealed severe damage to the heart muscle and the liver. Both features were inconsistent with vitamin deficiency.[4]

3.1 Convergences

The first thing to do is try to identify all those things that converge with each other. Some will *reinforce* each other: they will act in similar ways, perhaps providing the evidence that supports a particular interpretation. Others may *complement* each other: you may find that if A is to be true, there must also be B – one cannot be present without the other. Alternatively, you may find that in the relationship between two elements one is *supplementary* to another.

Convergence:
1. Reinforcing.
2. Complementary.
3. Supplementary.

Example: Health inspectors. Having mapped out the structure of everything they knew about the case, health inspectors started to search it for convergences, a commonality between all the sufferers, which might indicate a possible cause. Eventually they found it: all 50 were prodigious beer drinkers, and they habitually drank one particular Canadian brand. So it seemed obvious that it was in some way connected with this beer, which was brewed in both Quebec and Montreal.

3.2 Divergences

However, often divergences are even more useful in suggesting the solution to a problem or the sort of questions that it would be most helpful to ask.

Example: Health inspectors. In this case, to test the tentative solution suggested by the convergence that they had found between the symptoms and the consumption of this particular beer, health inspectors searched for divergences. They soon found that those who drank the beer brewed in Montreal shared none of the symptoms. So it now appeared there must be a significant difference in the brewing process at the two plants. And so it proved: the Quebec brewery had added a cobalt compound in order to improve the head of the beer, but the Montreal brewery hadn't. What's more, the compound had been added only a month before the appearance of the first victims and as soon as the brewery stopped using it, no more victims appeared.

So the reasonable conclusion was that the cobalt had caused the illness, which was substantiated a short time later when 64 beer drinkers in Omaha manifested the same combination of symptoms and it was discovered that a local brewery was using the same cobalt compound. When it stopped using it, no more cases appeared.

Nevertheless, the inspectors were still cautious, because the amount of cobalt in the beer was not sufficient to kill a normal person. That it killed so many (30 in Omaha in addition to the 20 in Quebec) seemed to be due to the victims' heavy drinking that had reduced their resistance to the chemical.

As you can see, in this case, as in so many, the solution came from identifying the important convergences and divergences:

Convergences	1. All the victims drank large quantities of beer.
	2. All drank one particular brand.
	3. Only drinkers of beer were affected.
Divergences	1. While drinkers in Quebec were affected, those in Montreal were not.
	2. Moderate drinkers were not affected.

Case study

The following case study illustrates the sort of problem that an editor of a local newspaper might have deciding whether or not to cover a story and how the method we have described might help her come to a decision.

Case study: The editor of a local newspaper. The paper is told that a local man is setting out that morning to swim the ten treacherous miles across the local estuary. As he is raising money for the children's ward of the local hospital, which is threatened with closure, he is inviting the paper along to cover the story with a photographer. He is being sponsored by a large supermarket that advertises with the paper. So the editor must decide whether she should run the story.

Of course, we need to know what other stories are competing with the same space that day, but still we can see the sort of thinking the editor needs to do to make her decision. And although most editors are probably guided by a set of intuitions, these intuitions themselves are likely to be shorthand for exactly this type of thinking.

1 Generate ideas

The first step is to generate ideas from the different perspectives of all those involved: the local community, readers, advertisers, the charity and, of course, the paper. The sort of ideas she might list include:

1. the community approve of those who support campaigns to improve local amenities;

2. readers want to read local stories;
3. advertisers want positive publicity;
4. the charity would welcome publicity for its cause;
5. and so on.

2 Reveal the structure

She will give a certain relative importance to each of these ideas. Over the years her beliefs, values and preferences will have helped her form a hierarchy of normative principles that guide her judgement as to which stories are worth pursuing and which are not, principles like:

1. all stories must be local;
2. always keep advertisers happy;
3. the names of local people sell papers;
4. photographs always sell a story;
5. and so on.

Her years as a local journalist have shown her that good, local stories sell papers and, when you lose sight of this, circulation begins to fall off. So, one of her key normative principles is that all stories must be local. And the same is true of the other principles.

All of them help her prioritise the ideas into a hierarchy, giving them structure. If the story ticks all these boxes and is a perfect match for this hierarchy, then she has a simple decision to make. But if it doesn't, she will have to search for convergences and divergences.

3 Convergences and divergences

This means comparing the story with the similar structures of other stories competing for the same space. Each story will have its own structure. Once revealed, the editor will compare them and decide which matches up most closely to the hierarchy of normative principles and, therefore, is most likely to be best for the paper and its circulation. The decision she makes will reflect the significance of these different convergences and divergences.

Conclusion

In this chapter we have seen how to map out the structure of our ideas by analysing their causal relations. The alternative method is to analyse their conceptual relations. In the next two chapters we will learn how to do this using a simple method.

5
Conceptual Thinking – Analysis 1: Second-Order Thinking

If university education is about any one thing, it is about developing our ability to think conceptually: to lift ourselves above our normal dialogue and examine it from a distance; to think about our thinking.

Second-order thinking

This is second-order thinking or 'metacognition'. We step back from our arguments and ask ourselves, 'Have I seen all the implications of using this concept in this way?', 'Can I synthesise these ideas and bring them together under one concept to see something I haven't seen before?' and 'If I use this concept in this way, will it be pushing my arguments in a direction I don't want to go?'

Unfortunately, at university few of us were ever taught these skills. We learnt something about them in those rare moments when we saw our tutor analyse a concept or pull ideas together into an original synthesis to create a new way of looking at a problem. If we were able to recognise the significance and meaning of what had happened – and, sadly, most of us weren't – we might have had a chance of retaining a small inkling of what went on so that we could try to do the same ourselves.

1 Analysis

As a result, most of us leave university unsure even about what we mean by conceptual thinking, let alone how to do it. One important aspect of it is the ability to stand back from the concepts we use and analyse them by asking questions about how we use them; 'What do we mean by authority?' or 'freedom', 'bribery' and so on. Nevertheless, this is just one aspect of thinking conceptually; perhaps the most obvious, even though many of us go through our lives without knowing we're doing it.

2 Creating new concepts

A second aspect is the ability to create new concepts. As ideas come together we see them form a configuration that we cannot describe using any existing concept, so we have to invent a new way of representing that structure of ideas.

3 Synthesis

The third aspect is the ability to synthesise our ideas under concepts, so that we see things in a new and insightful way through them. This is the source of some of our richest insights as we will see. We use our concepts in a new and interesting way to see things we have never seen before.

Conceptual thinking:
1. Analysing concepts.
2. Creating new concepts.
3. Synthesising ideas using concepts.

In this and the next chapter we will explore the first of these, leaving the other two to Chapter 7. So far we have shown how we can reveal the structure of interrelations between our ideas by analysing the way we think they are causally related. The other way of revealing this structure is through conceptual analysis. Indeed, any attempt to map out the organisation of our ideas will almost always involve analysing the concepts we use to express them. Analyse any concept and you will see a structure appearing.

What is a concept?

A concept is a general classification of particular things. It is a universal: it groups 'all' things that share particular characteristics under one idea or principle. All occupations that share particular characteristics are grouped together and classified as 'professions'. When we conceptualise from our experience we abstract the general concept from the particular concrete experience. Underlying these concepts or general classifications are patterns, through which we group and organise experience, and which allow us to see things in a particular way. The philosopher Bertrand Russell explains, 'Awareness of universals is called *conceiving*, and a universal of which we are aware is called a *concept*.'[1]

Effects on our thinking

The importance of the patterns that concepts bring to our thinking generally goes unnoticed. We have already seen how these patterns give us the capacity to interpret the world, to reduce the confusion of life to manageable levels. Concepts represent our most effective means of doing this. Each time we use them we bring the under-standing we have gained from past experience to bear on the present and to shape the way we act in the future. In this way they reduce the complexity of our environment, making it easier for us to make our decisions.

They also serve a similar function to that of a modern library's classi-fication system by giving us instant access to the impressive amounts of useful information we have stored under them. Indeed, our survival in the past has depended on this. Recognising that a certain configuration of colours and movement represents a dangerous predator has been the difference between life and death.

> *Example: Insurance claims assessor.*   In the famous 1944 film *Double Indemnity* the claims assessor, played by Edward G. Robinson, tells his boss how mistaken he is to assume that a man's death is due to suicide from falling off the back of a train. He quickly runs through the concepts that make up the general classification sys-tem for organising the actuarial evidence for every type of suicide to locate rapidly the evidence that shows the man's death could not have been the result of suicide by this means.

Using these powerful tools of thought, we seem to come to our judge-ments almost effortlessly. An accountant can interpret a balance sheet; a teacher, an essay; a barrister, a brief; and a journalist, a list of isolated facts. Each one, by bringing to bear their conceptual understanding, can interpret their material and make sense of it.

But in this lies not just the importance of conceptual thinking, but the dangers too. Its creative power allows us to think imaginatively about all the possibilities; not just about what is at present a fact, but about how things might or should be. When we think conceptually we abstract the general concept or principle, which applies to all circumstances (past, present and future), and divorce it from the concrete circumstances embedded in the present.

By abstracting the universal from the particular we reveal a general pattern through which we can predict the likely effects of doing one thing rather than another. We create patterns that map out the environment, helping us predict what is likely to happen when we act.

But while they liberate us from the tyranny of an uncertain future in this way, concepts can also trap us in the comfortable predictability of routine thinking. They can influence our behaviour quite independently of our rational evaluation by setting off a train of thought which we follow routinely.

When we use them they allow us to see things in a particular way. We interpret experience, organise it and advocate a certain type of action as a result. The basis of a concept is a readiness to respond in certain ways rather than others. It is this that makes it so important that we analyse them so we know, when we use them, which way they are pushing our thinking.

> We need to analyse the concepts we use, so we control them, rather than the reverse.

This explains why learning the key skills involved in conceptual analysis is so vital in business and professional life. It enables us, and the organisations we might work for, to see what needs to be done in the future, rather than just repeat the past. If organisations are to survive, they need to avoid the threat to their survival that comes from the tendency to manage themselves as they have always managed themselves in the tried and tested ways.

Concentrating exclusively on the concrete here and now draws on the assumption that the future will provide more of the same. We can easily get trapped in our own culture, believing that this is the way we've always done things and, as it has always brought success, we ought to keep doing it this way. As Charles Handy warns, it is tempting to train

---

Concepts:
1. Interpret and organise experience.
2. Give instant access to vital information.
3. Help us predict the effects of our actions.
4. Advocate a certain type of action or attitude.
5. Make our decisions easier.
6. Allow us to think imaginatively.

people for yesterday's work.[2] Organisations must prepare their staff not for the past but for the future. To do this we need to start thinking conceptually, so that we can rise above the day-to-day administration and think strategically.

Solving the most difficult problems

Many of the most significant breakthroughs in our understanding have come about not because researchers have new or better data, but because of the quality of their thinking and the concepts they create. In many cases, faced with problems that defy solution, the answers have finally only come as a result of being able to think outside accepted concepts and methods. Once we've revealed the structure of our concepts and the way our understanding is organised, we can then manipulate it and form new structures as we saw with humour, wit and the answers in crossword puzzles.

We like to think that most of our solutions come through a straightforward process of logical reasoning. But this is the way the story of discovery is told, rather than how it actually happens. For this we need first the ability to analyse concepts and, out of them, create new structures, through which we can look at the world differently and organise our information about it.

> Original ideas come from stepping outside our concepts and the routine thinking they dictate.

Example: Semmelweis and puerperal fever. In 1847, at the height of the outbreak of puerperal, or childbed, fever at the General Hospital in Vienna, everyone had access to exactly the same information as Ignaz Semmelweis, but only he was able to make connections between the different bits of information and create a concept that led to the solution. Even so, like many who make such original breakthroughs, his idea that minute particles, too small for the naked eye to see, entering the bloodstream were responsible for the deaths in pregnant women seemed ludicrous to his colleagues – not much short of witchcraft. Today, of course, we accept it as common sense.

In fact, for many scientists such theory, and concept, creation seems to be all they do for much of the time.

Example: Watson, Crick and DNA.   In 1953 Francis Crick and James Watson together discovered the 'double helix', the structure of DNA, for which they were later awarded the Nobel Prize. In his account of his work with Crick, Watson admits that, 'The idea of Francis and me dirtying our hands with experiments brought unconcealed amusement.'[3] He says of his collaborator, Francis Crick, that he was easily bored with experimentation and immersed himself for much of the time in theorising. He was an unpredictable, inspirational thinker, who would suddenly be consumed by an idea that had been long fermenting in his mind.

One day on a train journey to Oxford, Watson describes how Crick suddenly saw a key part of the solution:

> Soon something appeared to make sense, and he began scribbling on the vacant back sheet of a manuscript he had been reading. By then I could not understand what Francis was up to and reverted to *The Times* for amusement. Within a few minutes, however, Francis made me lose all interest in the outside world .... Quickly he began to draw more diagrams to show me how simple the problem was.[4]

By the end of the hour-and-a-half journey, he explains, it was clear what they had to do.

Examples like this show that it's not the quantity of information alone that yields good decisions, but the quality of our thinking and the type of concepts we use. We hear a lot about the 'information age' and how important it is for us to be kept constantly up to date. But more important is how we use this information. If we fail to analyse and evaluate the concepts we use, we might only be coming to conclusions that repeat the mistakes of the past.

Analysing concepts

However, the problem we all face is that analysing the concepts we use every day just seems a rather unnecessary thing to do. It seems obvious: we all know what's meant by words like 'needs', 'privacy', 'bribe' and 'authority', or phrases like 'quality of life'. So we have to learn to ask that characteristically philosophical question, 'Yes, but what do we mean by X?', particularly when the meaning seems obvious to everyone. In a probing, self-reflective way we are questioning our own use of these quite ordinary words, which can no longer be taken for granted.

The first step is to realise that words have more than one meaning, depending on the context and purpose for which they are used. They have no meaning in their own right. Therefore, our concern should be for their actual and possible uses. If we were to look up their meaning in a dictionary, we would find just somebody's picture of what they mean in a particular context, or a mere snapshot, a still in the moving reel of images, each one recording what the concept meant at a particular time and how it has changed and is still changing. Our task, therefore, in analysing a concept is to map out all the different ways in which it is used.

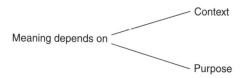

Most of the concepts we use are constantly changing, both because of cultural and social change and because the purposes for which we use them change. The meanings of concepts, like 'progress', 'success', 'luxury', 'necessity', 'poverty' and 'prosperity', are all relative to who uses them and the context in which they are used.

> *Example: Poverty.*   We might be able to agree that in the 'absolute' sense the concept of poverty means someone who has no means of sustenance or permanent shelter from the elements. But in its relative sense, it means different things in different circumstances to different people. In some societies today poverty is more like being without a colour TV, a refrigerator or even a second car. In this sense, someone suffering from poverty is anyone without the means of maintaining themselves at an average level of comfort typical of the social class to which they belong.

Open and closed concepts

1 Closed concepts

Even so, with some concepts analysing them is, indeed, as straightforward as looking up the word in a dictionary. They are what you might describe as 'closed concepts'. They usually have an unchanging, unambiguous meaning. Words like 'bicycle', 'bachelor' and 'triangle' each have a structure to their meaning, which is bound by logical necessity. We all agree to abide by certain conventions that rule the meaning of these words. So, if you were to say, 'This bicycle has one wheel' or 'This triangle has four sides', no-one would be in any doubt that you've made a logical mistake. When we use them according to their conventions we are, in effect, allowing our understanding of the world to be structured in a particular way.

> Closed concepts: their structure is bound by logical necessity.

2 Open concepts

But with 'open concepts' it's the reverse: our experience of the world shapes our concepts. Their meaning is not governed by a complex set of formal rules, like closed concepts, so they cannot be pinned down just by looking them up in a dictionary. Their meaning responds to, and reflects, our changing experience. As we saw above with the concept of poverty, they change through time and from one culture to another.

> **Closed and open concepts:**
> 1. Closed concepts are governed by complex sets of formal rules, while open concepts adapt to changing circumstances and experience.
> 2. Closed concepts structure the way we understand our experience, while open concepts are structured *by* it.

Our concern, therefore, is rarely with the words and their meaning, but with the context in which they are used. If I say about the dialysis patient that 'He has a poor quality of life', you know the meanings of the words I use, yet you can still ask, 'But what do you mean by "poor quality of life"?' Though we understand the words, the question of the concept remains.

> *Example: Family.*   The word 'family' is not difficult to understand, but the concept can be. In some societies and at some times 'family' and its related concepts, like 'aunt' and 'uncle', have a fairly unambiguous, unchanging meaning: narrow definitions exclusively grounded in relations by blood and marriage. But in other societies they are more open, encompassing not just relatives in the strict sense, but also older, long-standing friends of the family.

This is likely to be a reflection of the social practices prevalent in different societies and at different stages in their development. A predominantly rural society with limited social mobility might use them in the narrow sense. In contrast, in a society undergoing rapid industrialisation, with greater social mobility and less permanent communities, the concepts are likely to be applied more loosely to close friends of the parents of a child. A young family, which has recently moved to a city some distance from their parents' homes, may seek to reconstruct the security of an extended family by including close friends as aunts and uncles to their children.

In fact, some open concepts seem more open than others: there seem to be no core elements at all to the concept, even though all the examples we come up with we still call by the same name.

> *Example: Games.* In *Philosophical Investigations,* Ludwig Wittgenstein cites the example of 'games' and concludes that there is no core set of characteristics: nothing that you can say that is common to them all. As you move from one type of game to another some common features appear, while others drop out. Some involve competition, while others involve just one player. Some require skill, while others require just luck. All that we have, he argues, is just 'a complicated network of similarities overlapping and criss-crossing'.[5]

Try it for yourself. List every game you can think of and try to find a core set of characteristics that is common to them all. Who knows, you might be more successful than Wittgenstein.

Conclusion

Concepts have a hidden nature, a set of assumptions that can dictate our thinking, persuading us to think and act in particular ways without us making any deliberate choice. Therefore, it's important to learn how to analyse them well. In the next chapter we will work through a simple set of steps you can use to develop your abilities to do this.

6
Conceptual Thinking – Analysis 2: The Three-Step Technique

No doubt some people reading this book will think that talk of abstract concepts is more a subject for intellectuals and academics than practising professionals. Yet none of us escape the need to use and analyse them in our work. A businessman trying to find a niche for his service, an advertising executive searching for new ways to promote his client's product, or an engineer with a groundbreaking invention or design; they are all analysing concepts to see how they can place their work to meet the strongest demand.

Everyday new concepts are created: an idea of a product or a service that will meet people's needs. We are told that we lead busy lives, constantly on the move, so we need to be constantly in touch. With this idea, the mobile phone was born. Someone sat down and analysed the concept of the telephone to see how this could be reshaped to provide new business opportunities. Applying the idea of mobility to radios, televisions and computers as well as telephones has produced new concepts that have, in turn, spawned thousands of new products.

> *Example: Estate agent.* If you were an estate agent suffering from the downturn in the property market, to survive you may have to analyse your concept of an estate agent to see if there are ways of remodelling it to give you new opportunities to generate business. You might find that there are opportunities for you to go into the rental market or into estate management, which you hadn't noticed before.

Indeed, it affects us all, not just those in business. To be a good teacher, nurse, dentist, optician or physiotherapist, you will have to stand back from your concept of the role of someone in your profession and ask yourself, 'What is this sort of professional supposed to do? Can I do more for my patients or clients?'

> *Example: A local doctor.*   In Chapter 3 we saw how the concept of a local doctor has changed over recent years. Today she is not just responsible for her patients individually, but for the prevention of illness generally in the community by promoting healthier life-styles, even influencing planning decisions that might adversely affect the environment in which her patients live.

There will be concepts at the heart of your work that you are constantly wrestling with to make sure you do a good job. A nurse, a doctor and a hospital administrator, all will have to be clear about their concepts of 'patient care', 'quality of life' and 'patient autonomy'. A teacher will have to be clear about the concept of 'duty of care': where it begins and ends. A journalist and an editor will have to know what's meant by 'privacy' and 'public interest' and at what point one can no longer be an excuse for invading the other.

> *Example: A teacher's 'duty of care'.*   The world over, it seems, teachers have to struggle to meet their professional obligations on limited budgets. Over recent years commercial organisations have seen in this an opportunity to get their message across to the next gene-ration of consumers while helping teachers with the funds they need to improve the quality of education. Large corporations, like Exxon, have sponsored education materials to be used by children in schools, while others have given vending machines and equip-ment, all in return for some commercial exposure in the school.

But what is the teacher's 'duty of care' and how far does it go? While it carries the responsibility to protect students from physical harm, does it extend as far as intellectual harm? Do teachers have a responsibility to protect students from the advances of a commercial organisation whose intentions might be to persuade them to believe something that might not be true, or which makes an emotive appeal that by-passes their intellectual capacity to evaluate what they are being told?

When the US Consumers' Union assessed over 200 examples of sponsored education materials, it found that nearly 80 per cent contained 'biased or incomplete information promoting a viewpoint that favours consumption of the sponsor's product or service or a position that favours the company or its economic agenda'.

Conceptual analysis – the three-step technique

So, no matter what our business or profession, we all need to develop the skills to analyse concepts to reveal the underlying structure of our ideas. We can then work with this, adapting and changing it until we find the solution to the problem we face. In what follows you will learn a simple three-step technique, which you can use routinely. As you work through it, think about the concepts you come across in your own profession, concepts like 'bribes', 'authority', 'privacy', 'needs' and 'duty of care,' and ask yourself, 'What do we mean by this?'

Step 1: Gather your typical examples

First, spend some time gathering the evidence: say, five or six examples of the way you use the concept in your everyday life. Try to make them as different as possible. In this way you'll be able to strip away their differences to reveal more clearly their essential similarities.

> *Example: Authority.* You might be a lawyer or a juror in court and you hear a defendant argue that his life of violence has been justified by the authority he commands on the streets of his local community, which he uses to settle disputes and keep order. What are you to make of this?

To analyse this concept of authority and see clearly the implications of his claim, you need to summon up a few examples of situations in which you might use the concept, say, in your family, in your local and then the wider community, and then in the schools, colleges and universities you may have attended. These might involve figures of authority, like police officers, judges, teachers, and other people, who have the power and influence to get you to do what you might not otherwise want to do.

1 How do I use the concept?

If you find it difficult to come up with examples, start by asking yourself three questions. First, 'How do I use the concept – do I use it in more than one way?' If you find you do, then you have a structure emerging: each way needs to be explored and its implications unwrapped. The prepositions we use with concepts are in many cases a very useful indicator of different meanings. For example, we use the concept 'authority' in two different ways when we say that someone is 'an' authority and when we say they are 'in' authority.

Example: Freedom. The same can be said about the concept of freedom. We tend to talk about being free *from* things, like repression, constraints and restrictions of one form or another. I might say with some relief that I am finally free from pain having taken tablets for pain relief, or that a political prisoner has at last been freed from imprisonment. In both cases we're using the word in a negative way, in that something is being taken away, the pain or the imprisonment.

But we also use the word in what we might describe as a positive way. In this sense the preposition changes from being free *from* something to being free *to do* something. We often say that, because a friend has unexpectedly won a large amount of money, she is now free to do what she has always wanted to do – to go back to college, or to buy her own home. Governments, too, use the concept in this way, arguing that the money they are investing in education will free more people to get better, more satisfying, jobs and to fulfil more of their dreams.

2 What sort of thing am I referring to?

If this doesn't help, ask yourself a second question, 'What sort of thing am I referring to when I use the concept?' This means recalling simple everyday situations in which you might find yourself talking about, say, 'authority', even if you don't actually use the word. When you use the word 'bribe' or 'privacy' or 'need', what sort of thing are you referring to?

3 How does it differ from similar things?

To help you with this question, it's often useful to ask a third: 'How does it differ from similar things?' When I use the word 'bribe', how does it differ from other things like commissions, gifts, tips and incentive bonuses?

When I use the word 'authority', how does it differ from things like power, force, legitimacy and influence?

Questions:
1. How do I use the concept – do I use it in more than one way?
2. What sort of thing am I referring to?
3. How does it differ from similar things?

Step 2: Analyse your examples

Now, using these examples, create your concept: use your conceptual skills to abstract the general from the concrete. In other words, identify the common characteristics in each of your examples, isolating them so that you can then put them together to form the concept. This is one of those things we all know how to do, but most of us would be hard pressed to explain just how we do it.

In effect, it's simple pattern recognition. By recognising the common pattern of characteristics that each example possesses, we visualise what the concept might look like that underlies all the examples. Sometimes you may find you have, say, seven examples, four of which have the same core characteristics, while the other three fail to match them in all respects. That's OK, in these cases you need to corral the four similar examples, using these to create your concept, and then use the remaining three to test it.

Creating your concept – pattern recognition:
1. Identify the common characteristics in your examples.
2. Isolate them and put them together to form the concept.

Example: Authority. From your examples of 'authority' you might conclude that we talk about somebody being *in* authority, somebody like a police officer or a judge. In cases like these the word 'power' is used to describe somebody as having force, the capacity to compel us to do something against our wishes. A police officer has this sort of power. So, when someone is *in* authority we might not respect the *person* or the *reasons* they may give us for doing as they demand, but we might respect the institution they represent, or we might just comply with their orders because we fear the consequences of not doing so. Police officers have powers at their disposal that can seriously affect us, even denying us our liberty.

72

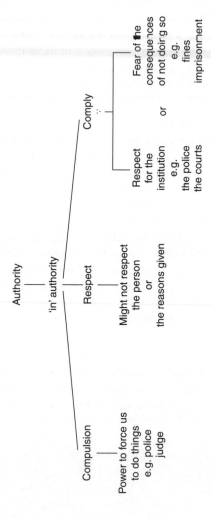

Structure 1

Step 3: Test your concept

In most cases you will find you have the overall structure right, but there may be details that are wrong or subtle distinctions you haven't seen. So, by testing your concept you will identify those characteristics that are essential, while you ditch those that are only accidental to it. In the process you will sharpen up your understanding of the core characteristics.

To test it in this way you need only take some simple, but quite deliberate steps. Our aim is to set up mental experiments to test our concept; first, against those examples that are borderline cases of it, then against those that are contrasting cases and, finally, against those that are doubtful cases. At each stage we will refine it until we have it right.

1 Borderline cases

First, with your structure in front of you, try to think of a borderline case, an example of your concept that doesn't fit comfortably within your structure. It may lack features that are in your structure, or have other features that are absent from it. Then analyse its characteristics to see if, in fact, it does fit after all. You may find there's more to this form of the concept than you first thought and it does, in fact, fit within the structure. Alternatively, after thinking through all the possibilities, it may become clear that it doesn't fit and you will have to adjust your structure to take account of it.

> *Example: Authority.* A borderline case for the concept of 'authority' might be a mugger, a local gang leader, or someone like the defendant who claims to have authority on the streets. All of these might be able to compel us to do things in the same way, through force or threats of force. But while they have this sort of power, it still seems odd to say they have authority.
>
> This suggests that authority doesn't simply amount to the possession of power alone: the defendant has no authority, in the usual sense, to command us to do anything, unlike the police officer, who has been appointed by representatives to parliament or the local council, whom we have elected. In this sense the representatives and, in turn, their officially appointed officers are said to have democratic legitimacy.

The result of this test can go in one of three ways: you will have confirmed that your borderline case is not an example of the concept; or that it is and it does fit into your structure; or that it is and it doesn't fit, which means that you will have to adjust your structure. Whichever is the outcome, you will have confirmed important parts of your structure.

> *Example: Authority.*   In this example the borderline case didn't fit comfortably within the structure, because it lacked an important feature. While the defendant had the power to make people do things they might not want to do, he had no authority to do so: he had no right. So this test has shaken something out, which appears to be merely accidental to the concept: the appearance that authority amounts merely to the power to force others to do things they would otherwise not want to do.

2 Contrasting cases

As a result of this test you will probably feel more confident that you have now got it just about right. So it's time to put this confidence to the sternest test you can find, this time by imagining an example that presents a clear contrast to your concept. Think of the strongest example you can find that clearly doesn't fit within the structure of your concept. The best examples fail to share one or more of the core characteristics of your structure. Again, test your structure against this example to see if you need to make any adjustments to the components and the way they interrelate.

> *Example: Authority.*   Authority seems to possess other qualities than mere power. To identify these qualities, which seem to be core characteristics of authority, we must compare our concept with an example that doesn't seem to share one or more of the core characteristics we have already identified.

> *Example: Art collector.*   Take, for example, an experienced art collector. In her field she is *an* authority, so we are right to be persuaded by the arguments she presents because she knows what she's talking about. No force or compulsion is needed here. She doesn't have the power to force me to do something against my wishes. We 'respect' her point of view and advice, which throws into relief the way in which the defendant in court was using the concept of authority to suggest he had respect on the streets. In his case it seemed more like fear, rather than the sort of respect we show to the experienced art collector.

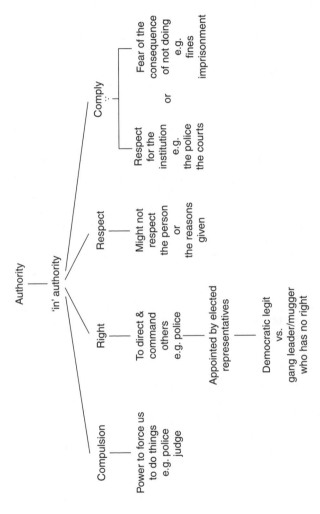

Structure 2

Power and force

Nevertheless, she does have a certain 'power' and 'force' that she can bring to bear. We use phrases, like 'the power of persuasion', in which the force involved is the 'force of an argument', to describe the sort of power that such authorities possess. In the case of the art collector she has the ability to persuade us to do something we would not otherwise do, by giving us good and persuasive reasons for doing it. Through the force of her arguments and her power of persuasion, she has the ability to secure voluntary compliance to her way of seeing things without the use of threats or force in the other sense, because she has earned her authority.

Right

We could say she has a 'right' to her authority, although it's a different sense of 'right' from that exercised by the police officer. It's the right that has been *earned* rather than been *given*. It's also different from the authority of the elected representative, although they can both be described as being 'an' authority. The difference is that the art collector's authority has been earned as a result of her study and devotion to her work, whereas the elected representative's authority has been earned as a result of putting himself up for election and campaigning for votes. Both have authority and exercise legitimate influence, because of the respect they have earned.

Once you have done this you will find that you have sharpened up your concept considerably. You will have identified one or more core characteristics that might not have been sufficiently clear in your original analysis.

3. Doubtful cases

Both of these two tests will probably have brought you to a point where you now know the core characteristics of your concept and the structure that defines their interrelations. If you are not this certain, you will have to test it with one or more additional contrasting examples, but it will rarely take more than this. In most cases you will have identified the core characteristics fairly clearly by now.

If this is the case, it's time to move to the next stage and test the consequences of adopting these as your core characteristics. We need to imagine cases in which it would be difficult for you to accept these consequences. Either these are not, after all, examples of the concept, or we have missed something.

Unlike the previous stages, in this one we are neither identifying core characteristics, nor others that we need to ditch because they are merely

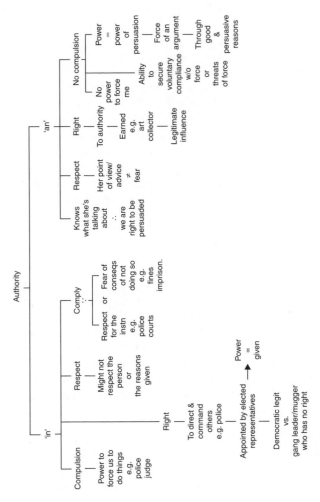

Structure 3

accidental to the concept. We have our core characteristics now and their interrelations that define the concept. In this stage we are refining the distinctions that are in our analysis, so we get a clearer, sharper understanding of the core characteristics and their interrelations. As a result we inject more subtle shades of meaning into our distinctions.

> *Example: The elderly.*   For example, there are some categories of people, like the elderly in our communities, who exercise the same legitimate influence, but who haven't earned their authority, either by being given it, as with the police officer, or having earned it, in the sense of 'an' authority, like the art collector. Nevertheless, we might argue that they, too, have earned their authority, only in a different way. The elderly in our communities have earned respect as a result of their years of experience and the wisdom this has brought. Others have certain personal qualities that have given them a reputation for integrity and honesty; people we might go to for advice and support.

Moral reasons

We could say that we have good 'moral' reasons for complying with this sort of authority: that is, we have reasons that convince us to act in this way as a matter of our own free will. Whereas, when we comply with orders of those who are *in* authority, we do so not necessarily because we have any moral reason, that we respect them as individuals, but because we know that it would be prudent to do so. Otherwise, we might suffer in one way or another as a result of the sanctions they can bring upon us. The threat of this is likely to force us, against our will, to comply with their orders.

Obliged/obligation

In this sense, we may be 'obliged' to obey if the local gang leader or the mugger is threatening to harm us, but we have no 'obligation' to obey, because such threats are not backed by any right to make such orders. Whereas the art collector has earned the right through many years of study, and the police officer, while he hasn't earned the same respect for himself as a person, has been given the 'rightful', legitimate authority by our elected representatives. In the same way, we could say that the elderly, with their years of experience to draw upon, have a similar authority and a right to exercise an influence.

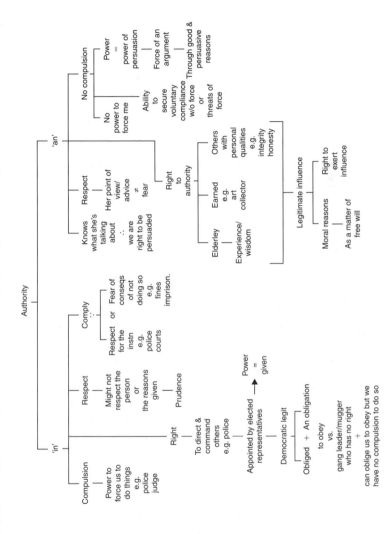

Structure 4

General structure: The three-step technique

Activity	Objective
Step 1: Examples List five or six of the most typical examples that are as different as possible	To get material that will illustrate similarities and differences
Step 2: Analyse Pattern recognition — identify the common characteristics and their interrelations	To form the hypothesis: the prototype concept
Step 3: Testing **1. Borderline cases** Compare our concept with an example that either lacks features that are in our structure, or has others that are absent from it	To identify all those features in our structure that are merely accidental
2. Contrasting cases Compare our concept with an example that doesn't share one or more of the core characteristics of our structure	To identify the core characteristics and their interrelations
3. Doubtful cases Test the core characteristics by examining a case in which it would be difficult to accept their consequences	To refine the distinctions in our analysis to get a clearer, sharper understanding of the core characteristics and their interrelations.

As we have worked our way through each of these stages we have deliberately asked awkward questions to test and refine the distinctions we made in our original analysis. In the table above you can see each stage clearly set out, so you can use it step by step in your own work.

Conclusion

For much of the time our thinking is guided by routine assumptions and intuitions. But our most difficult problems, those strategic decisions on which a lot rests, call for more than just routine, intuitive responses. Analysing the key concepts involved in a problem, deliberately and imaginatively, step by step, using this technique, will reveal the central issues we must take into account. As a result, in some cases the solution to the problem will become clear. If not, we will have a clear structure to our ideas that we can take into the next stage in Part 3, where we will work with it to find a solution.

Once you've used the technique a few times you will no doubt develop your own shortened version. But one thing should not be lost: genuinely thinking about concepts we take for granted, which will otherwise direct our thoughts into routine patterns. If there is one thing that all original thinkers have in common, it is the courage to question those ideas they and others have long accepted, no matter how unsettling and disturbing this questioning may be. Their brilliant insights and solutions to problems that have long dogged their progress more often come not from gathering new or more evidence, but through changing the concepts they use or the way they use them.

7
Conceptual Thinking: Synthesis

Most of our thinking goes from the general to the specific: from the abstract to the concrete. This is the way we find explanations for things. In the last two chapters this is what we have done: we have analysed concepts to reveal their underlying patterns of ideas, so that we can see how they structure our understanding of the particular problem we are trying to solve.

Now we turn to move in the opposite direction: from the specific to the abstract. If the first direction is the way we find explanations for things, this is the way we come to understand them. We do this either by creating a new concept out of the specific ideas and facts we have generated, or we synthesise them under an existing concept.

These are the remaining two aspects of conceptual thinking that we described in Chapter 5. As ideas come together we see them form a configuration that we cannot describe using any existing concept, so we have to invent a new way of representing that structure of ideas. Alternatively, we can understand things and reveal fresh insights by using concepts in a new and interesting way to see things we have never seen before.

Conceptual thinking:

1. Analysing concepts.
2. Creating new concepts.
3. Synthesising ideas using concepts.

In this chapter we will learn how to do this routinely as part of our normal habits of thought. Some of the methods will be similar to those we learnt in Chapter 4, but the relations we learn to uncover in this chapter are logical rather than causal. Ideas will be interrelated in similar ways: we will search for convergences and divergences; some will complement, supplement or reinforce each other. But they will be related conceptually in a logical network of ideas, rather than as cause and effect.

Creating new concepts

Although, like many of these thought processes, this sounds complex and demanding, it is done by ordinary people almost effortlessly every day. From those in PR and advertising, who think up novel ways of promoting a product, to inventors and designers, who create new types of product or service, like those who first thought about ways of helping people find new friends by creating networking sites on the internet, all are attempting to design new concepts. It starts with evidence of individual behaviour and moves to the general: from the particular to the universal. We see general patterns through which we can predict the likely effects of doing one thing rather than another.

Example: 2001: A Space Odyssey.   In a chilling scene at the start of Stanley Kubrick's 1968 Oscar-winning film *2001: A Space Odyssey*, an ape picks up a bone from the bleached skeleton of an animal and strikes the skull, smashing it into pieces. Then, in the moments that follow, quiet and motionless, with the bone held in both hands high above his head, he forms a concept. This is no longer just a bone to smash this bleached skull before him, but a 'weapon' to strike all the skulls of all his enemies.

Synthesising ideas under concepts

When we create a concept it's often easy to recognise that this is what we have done, but synthesising ideas under a concept often isn't. As we have said so often, we are not taught these skills even though at universities students are routinely assessed on the basis of them. In effect, we learn them in passing, if we know what we are looking for and we are perceptive enough to recognise it when it happens.

Example: Renaissance seminar. As an undergraduate I can remember it happening just once. I was in a seminar on the Renaissance with about ten other students. It was being run by two teachers, although one of them, a well-known Renaissance scholar, said nothing for the first hour. He just listened to us all very attentively. Then, in the middle of our discussion, to the surprise of us all, he intervened giving us a Hegelian interpretation of our ideas, which organised them into a structure of four different types of idea.

In other words, he drew upon the concepts developed by the nineteenth-century German philosopher G. W. F. Hegel to open up new ways of looking at what we had been discussing. The insight was blinding, although I wasn't sure exactly what had happened and knew even less about how to do it myself.

Bringing things together under a concept or synthesising different concepts can open up new insights, allowing us to see things in a new, unexpected light. In Chapter 3 we saw how we can combine concepts, like 'introvert' and 'extrovert' with 'convergent' and 'divergent', to generate all sorts of unexpected, interesting ideas that free us from routine, predictable responses. Synthesising ideas in this way allows us to talk about 'divergent introverts', 'divergent extroverts', 'convergent introverts' and 'convergent extroverts'; classifications that can help us explain all sorts of behaviour, which we would otherwise find difficult to explain.

Example: Hotel guests. We saw how the researchers at Cornell University, examining the attitudes of hotel guests, broke them down into four research categories by combining four concepts: 'satisfied' and 'dissatisfied' and 'stayers' and 'switchers' to get 'satisfied stayers', 'dissatisfied stayers', 'dissatisfied switchers' and 'satisfied switchers'. Without doing this they might never have thought about the counter-intuitive categories ('dissatisfied stayers' and 'satisfied switchers'), which opens up all sorts of interesting ideas about those things that motivate us to come to one decision rather than another.

Equally important, this not only gives us fresh insights, different ways of looking at a problem, but a structure with manageable tasks and questions that organises the way we set about researching the problem. It opens up for us a layer of sub-problems and questions that will drive our thinking.

The way it works – three rules

Our problem is that we are burdened with too much baggage. We have all read the legendary accounts of scientists who tell us how they came to make their groundbreaking discoveries. It all seems a perfectly logical, even mechanical, process. But it misrepresents the practical problems involved in thinking of any kind.

Indeed, even among scientists, the suspicion is that such rationalisations of the scientific method reflect less what scientists actually *do* and more what they think they *should* be doing. Medawar argues that such talk is 'simply the posture(s) we choose to be seen in when the curtain goes up and the public sees us.'[1] It only seems to be logical in character, because 'it can be made to appear so when we look back upon a completed episode of thought.'[2] In fact, he argues, it is a much more imaginative and intuitive process than this account allows for.

Even so, this doesn't mean that we cannot understand how the process works so that we can learn to do it better. There are three principles that govern the way we manage concepts and the patterns of ideas they lend to our thinking. The first principle we know of already; the other two describe the way we synthesis and create new concepts.

1. Knowledge is expressed in the form of mental structures or patterns.
2. These patterns are in competition. Experience causes useful patterns to grow stronger, while less useful ones grow weaker.
3. Plausible new patterns are generated from the combination of old ones.

Together these principles explain how we generate new insights and arrive at solutions to our most difficult problems, including those significant moments in intellectual history when scientists made groundbreaking discoveries: Newton and the falling apple; Kekulé and the benzene ring; Einstein and special relativity.

As the first principle indicates, we organise our knowledge into stable patterns. Then, when we are presented with problems, we search among this stock of patterns – each one triggered off by a concept – to see if the evidence before us exhibits one of these patterns.

Example: Renaissance seminar.   In my Renaissance seminar, when the tutor used Hegelian concepts, he recognised in our discussion ideas that exhibited a pattern similar in important respects to those Hegel used, which might furnish us with fresh insights.

We do the same when we solve crossword puzzles or see a joke: we compare their underlying patterns of ideas. If this doesn't yield a solution, we synthesise our ideas as the second and third principles indicate. Having recognised the similarity between patterns, we combine or adapt them to explain the evidence before us or create a new concept out of old patterns.

A practical method

As this suggests, our minds are not naturally creative. We can only see what we have been prepared to see. Someone who is good at producing hunches works both ways: he depends as much on what he has to go on as he does his imagination. This is informed guesswork, rather than untethered creativity.

But this also means we can possess all the facts without seeing the pattern of interrelations that will eventually lead to a solution. They might just seem irrelevant from the perspective of our established patterns of ideas. So, the solution to the problem depends on our ability to see connections between things that are not obviously connected.

Example: Semmelweis and puerperal fever.   This was true of Semmelweis in 1847, when he set about trying to find the cause of puerperal, or childbed, fever at the General Hospital in Vienna. Deaths among women in labour had reached unprecedented levels and nobody had any idea how to cure or control the fever.

Conventional wisdom maintained that it was the result of two possible causes: external and internal. The external cause was the prevailing miasma that hung over the hospital. This explained the high death-rate in the hospital compared with those who had their labour at home. The internal cause was the accumulation of milk in the body instead of being discharged through the breast or uterus, resulting in milk peritonitis.

> But neither explanation fitted the facts. Women who were not pregnant also developed the fever. One of Semmelweis's patients, who came in to have a tumour removed from the neck of her womb, caught the fever and died. And in the doctors' division of the hospital, five times as many women died from it as in the midwives' division. It was impossible to see how a miasma settling over the whole hospital could have such a differentiated effect on the two divisions.

But where do you start, when you have no theory or alternative concepts to work with? Knowing the facts that Semmelweis did and without the benefits of hindsight, how would you get from the facts to a hypothesis that will explain them? What facts would you look for and what sort of pattern would you impose on them? Facts on their own don't suggest theories, so we have to process them, creating a pattern that will explain and solve the problem.

As we saw with causal thinking in Chapter 4, there are simple steps we can take to reveal the different patterns of interrelations between ideas. Some of these steps are similar to those we examined in causal thinking, although with conceptual thinking our focus is on revealing the patterns of logical relations between ideas rather than their causal relations.

Most of us use similar steps, although perhaps not in such a systematic way. Our thinking is guided by a set of assumptions and intuitions that are shorthand for this type of thinking. We condense these steps, relying more on instinct and experience. Unfortunately, experience can often be a poor guide, taking us down routine paths that may lead to poor decisions.

1 Lay out all the facts

First, we need to lay out a complete account of all the facts we know about the problem. Often we take it for granted that we are aware of everything, so we see no point in deliberately listing all that we know. As a result, we fail to think through all the possibilities. As we said in Chapter 1, we need to reprogram our thinking and allow ourselves to think naïvely. Some of the most stunning insights breaking a logjam to progress have come from researchers asking the most obvious questions about things that others regard as just common sense. Such questions seem unnecessary and trivial.

Example: Copernicus and Galileo. The most well known example is the question that Galileo, and Copernicus before him, posed about whether we are right to assume that it is the Sun that revolves around the Earth, rather than the Earth around the Sun. In the seventeenth century, to suggest the latter seemed plainly absurd. All the evidence suggested that the Earth was still and it was the Sun that moved.

In philosophy this sort of questioning has forced us to consider the sort of fundamental questions that have resulted in a significant re-shaping of our understanding of the world.

Example: Empiricism. Empiricists believe that our knowledge of the outside world depends exclusively on the evidence of our senses. John Locke assumed that this sense data was caused by physical objects; a commonsense assumption that seems obvious. But not to Bishop Berkeley, who questioned whether we can sensibly be said to have knowledge of such objects or any matter. All we can know is sense data, which are just ideas in the mind. Beyond these, we cannot be said to know of the existence of anything. We cannot know things like chairs and tables, but just colours, shapes, textures, smells and tastes. To conclude that these are physical objects, like chairs and tables, is to go further than the evidence of our senses: to infer things beyond empirical evidence.

But, if that seemed to be questioning the obvious, David Hume went even further and questioned whether we can even know the mind. Extending Berkeley's account to its logical conclusion, Hume argued that we know the mind only as we know matter: only as a bundle of perceptions. So the mind or 'self' is as unclear as matter. All we have is a succession of impressions, separate ideas, memories and feelings, which flash before us like the separate images on a reel of film. There is no bond between them. They are 'nothing but a bundle or collection of different perceptions, which succeed each other with an inconceivable rapidity, and are in a perpetual flux and movement'.[3] And with this Hume effectively destroyed the concept of mind as Berkeley had destroyed the concept of matter.

So, it's worth slowing yourself down and deliberately asking questions about things that may seem obvious and common sense. Once you've done this you will have in front of you a collection of facts and ideas, many of which will be interrelated in a complex pattern. Many of us already do this to some degree each time we are presented with a difficult problem or a complex decision to make, although perhaps not always as deliberately and as thoroughly as this.

> *Example: Ward sister or teacher.*   If you were a ward sister in a large hospital and you noticed a rise in the levels of infection on your ward, or a teacher who notices a fall in the academic performance of her students, your first step would be to assemble a complete and exhaustive account of all the ideas and facts that might be relevant. This would reveal the underlying structure, the complex pattern of interrelations tying them together, which might allow you to draw inferences and reach tentative conclusions.

1.1 Logical problem

To keep track of these interrelations and the inferences you might be able to draw, set it down in a clear structure: a matrix or similar structure that allows you to see at a glance the logical relationships between the ideas. The most convincing way of demonstrating the efficacy of doing this is to tackle a standard logical problem, the sort of thing you might find in the familiar recreational books of logical problems, in SAT or GRE papers, or in any of the general papers set at A level or Oxbridge entrance. Consider this one.

Simon, David, Clive and Justin are all professionals: one is a lawyer, one a dentist, one an accountant and one a teacher, although not necessarily respectively. So, what we want to know is what type of professional each of them is, given the following facts.

1. Both Justin and the accountant took courses taught by the teacher at the local college.
2. Clive has never heard of David.
3. The accountant, who got Simon out of serious financial trouble by reorganising his finances, is now going to sort out Clive's finances.
4. Clive and David were in the public gallery when the lawyer took on his first case in court.

Mapping out the structure of interrelations in this problem is best done using a matrix, something like the following.

	Teacher	Lawyer	Dentist	Accountant
Simon				
David				
Clive				
Justin				

From (1) we know that Justin is neither the accountant nor the teacher, so we can put crosses in the boxes opposite his name under the columns for these two professions. From (3) we can see that the accountant is neither Clive nor Simon, so again we can put crosses in the appropriate boxes. And from (4) it's clear that neither Clive nor David are the lawyer, so we can put crosses in those boxes too.

Having plotted these on our structure we can now draw inferences. By elimination David must be the accountant. We can therefore put Xs in the other columns alongside David's name. So now we know that according to (1) David has studied a course taught by the teacher, while (2) tells us that Clive does not know David. Consequently, Clive cannot be the teacher and thus, by elimination, he must be the dentist. This means we can now complete the dentist's column. As a result there are three crosses in Justin's boxes, so he must be the lawyer. And this leaves Simon as the teacher.

	Teacher	Lawyer	Dentist	Accountant
Simon	O	X	X	X
David	X	X	X	O
Clive	X	X	O	X
Justin	X	O	X	X

Although this is a simplified illustration, it shows how useful it is to map out the pattern of interrelations between all the facts. Drawing inferences from these is now a simple affair. Of course, this might still not bring you to a conclusion as it does in this case, but it will provide the clarity you need to frame solutions that are clear, precise and address the problem accurately.

If, however, you haven't been able to do this, you will need to consider convergences and divergences as we did when we mapped out the structure of causal relations in Chapter 4.

2 Convergences

As we saw there, one way of generating possible solutions is to search out all those facts and ideas that seem to reinforce each other. They may complement each other or one may be supplementary to another.

> *Example: Semmelweis and puerperal fever.* Semmelweis noticed that the different mortality levels in the two divisions (the doctors' and the midwives') seemed to be complemented by the fact that the women contracted the fever in the order they were examined by the doctors and by the fact that the midwives went nowhere near the dissecting room. The convergence of all three seemed to suggest the hypothesis that the doctors were infecting the patients with something they picked up in the dissecting room.

3 Divergences

The opposite strategy is often even more useful in narrowing down the possibilities.

> *Example: Semmelweis and puerperal fever.* Semmelweis reasoned that, as those women who were brought into the nurses' division were not subject to the same risks as those in the doctors' division, it couldn't be the miasma, as all the patients, irrespective of the division in which they were treated, were equally subject to that. So he concentrated on the differences between the two divisions to identify those factors that he thought might be the cause.
>
> Starting with the dissimilarities between the ways in which each division was run, he formed hypotheses based on each one and tested them one after the other: the different food that was served; the different positions in which the women gave birth; even the fact that the priest and his bellringer walked through the doctors' division, but not through the midwives'.

This rapid sequential framing and evaluation of hypotheses is not unlike the work of scientists as they do their early probing before they settle on a theory. Although much of his work was characterised by careful, patient collection of data, rather than being theory directed, Darwin still confessed that he could not resist forming a hypothesis on every subject.

4 Abstain from conscious effort

This will normally generate a number of competing solutions. Many of these will reflect the routine underlying patterns of ideas that we normally use to understand the situation. Some of them you will be able to eliminate because they are not consistent with the facts, while others on their own may only answer part of the problem.

At this point, with a number of competing solutions to choose from, it is time to put the problem to one side. When we have thought hard about a problem, but cannot find a solution, we have to learn to abstain from conscious effort, do something else, and let the subconscious take over the material, motivated as it is by the need to find some structured system to it all. We have to learn to move between the conscious and subconscious levels of our thinking.

What we need for the final synthesis:

1. The motivation to find a stable pattern.
2. Careful sustained work.
3. Incubation of our ideas.
4. The ability to move between the conscious and subconscious levels.

Writing about the creative process in her legendary book, *Becoming a Writer*, Dorothea Brande describes the subconscious as 'the great home of form'.[4] It is quicker to see types and patterns than our conscious intellect could ever be: 'Far behind the mind's surface, so deep that he (the writer) is seldom aware ... that any activity is going forward, his story is being fused and welded into an integrated work.'[5] Consequently, she argues, we must learn to trust this 'higher imagination'[6] to bring aid to our ordinary thinking. We need to come to terms with this 'enormous and powerful part of (our) nature which lies behind the threshold of immediate knowledge'.[7]

> **The subconscious:**
>
> 'the higher imagination'
> 'the great home of form'

Out of this process the final synthesis will occur and the insight appear almost effortlessly compared with the sustained work that preceded it. The lines of thought converge, the clues co-operate and we see the solution as one complete whole in which all the parts fit. Peter Medawar believes such insights share three characteristics:

1. the suddenness of their origin;
2. the wholeness of their conception;
3. and the absence of conscious premeditation.

And, as the Gestalt psychologist Wolfgang Köhler insists, there is no accident in this; it is not as if we have just stumbled on the solution by stabbing in the dark. When we say someone has an insight into a problem we mean he knows what the solution is, what he intends doing and how a solution can be achieved.

Although Einstein's sudden, brilliant insights might seem effortless and spontaneous, they were, in fact, born out of the sustained work that preceded them. We see this in his description of the way he worked: 'I think and think, for months, for years. Ninety-nine times the conclusion is false. The hundredth time I am right.'[8] After long hours of sustained thought, the solution would come when he was no longer thinking about it. He would be doing something else or just day-dreaming.

> *Example: Einstein.* One day in his early years at the patent office he was day-dreaming at his desk when he saw a builder on the rooftop opposite his window. A sudden inspiration came to him as he imagined the man falling off the roof. This he described as 'the happiest thought of my life'. He realised that the man would not feel his own weight, at least not until he hit the ground. It was the clue he needed to extend relativity to gravity. Max Born later described this as 'the greatest feat of human thinking about nature, the most amazing combination of philosophical penetration, physical intuition, and mathematical skill'.[9]

For others it comes in similar situations, when they are least expecting it. For Watson and Crick, as we saw earlier, part of the double helix solution to the structure of DNA came all at once on a train journey to Oxford. Watson describes how Crick was grabbed by an insight which suddenly appeared as if from nothing: 'Soon something appeared to make sense, and he began scribbling on the vacant back sheet of a manuscript he had been reading .... Quickly he began to draw more diagrams to show me how simple the problem was.'[10]

Conclusion

As with any new method some of this will seem familiar, close to what you already do, while other parts will seem strange. If it hasn't on its own revealed possible solutions to the problem, it will, nevertheless, have given you a pattern of ideas that comprehensively explains it. You are also more likely to have in front of you unusual ideas and surprising insights that you would not otherwise have seen.

Now we will look in Part 3 at different methods and techniques of working with this pattern of ideas, changing it and approaching it differently to design the solution to the problem. In the process we will learn to become more creative thinkers and more successful problem solvers.

Part 3
Creative Thinking

In Part 1 we generated our ideas about a problem. Then, in Part 2, through causal and conceptual thinking, we identified the stable pattern into which these ideas are organised. Now, it would seem, we are left with the simple task of pattern recognition to decide what to do. All we have to do is search through our own data banks to see if this pattern is reflected in our routine patterns of thought and behaviour, which we normally use to deal with this sort of problem. To make sense of the present, we compare it with a state of affairs in the past which exhibits a similar pattern of factors.

But in most cases it is not quite so straightforward. The knowledge and expertise of a practising professional or business person is not just made up of simple templates and rules: it is a dynamic understanding which is continually adapting to the context in which it is used. It is the result of adaptive interaction between these cognitive patterns, through which we learn to understand events and situations, and the environmental cues that trigger them into use.

Over the last 30 years, in a number of studies, cognitive psychologists have explored this aspect of professional practice, particularly the way professionals revise and adjust these patterns in the light of their experiences and reflective thought. They have found that this patterned knowledge is created out of a process of trial and reinforcement. Then it is refined through reflective thought, which performs the vital task of checking that it is still valid. This works as a safeguard against the repetition of routine responses that no longer work. Even so, evidence suggests that the original patterns used to interpret situations are often retained long after they have been discredited, as RBS's acquisition of ABN Amro illustrates so dramatically.

As we will see, this process of adaptation and reflection is a lot more complex than simple pattern recognition. Hoshmand and Polkinghorne describe it as 'a frame experiment in which the pattern used to understand a situation is altered to provide a better fit to the complexity of the situation'.[1]

But even this fails to reveal just how complex it is. Professionals identify the underlying pattern in any situation and search for an effective parallel. If this fails, they then work to adapt their pattern to find a solution. And all the while they are in the middle of a process of coming to a decision. Donald Schön describes this capacity to reflect-in-action as a type of double vision: that ability to keep alive in the middle of an action a range of different views about the situation without having to stop and think.[2]

The complexity of the process demonstrates just how vital it is to examine it in detail, so we can learn to do it better. Many of us do it well, but the evidence suggests that a surprising number do it poorly, with devastating effects on organisations, communities and individuals. Even those who get it spectacularly right, do so without ever understanding exactly what they're doing. And this has been a situation unchanged for centuries.

Example: Stonemasons and architects. The stonemasons and architects who built the huge, impressive gothic churches and cathedrals throughout Europe in the thirteenth, fourteenth and fifteenth centuries knew nothing of the forces and stresses of modern mechanics. They worked with structures and patterns of behaviour, standard operating procedures, handed down over hundreds of years from one generation to another. On the face of it they seemed the most conservative of workers, bound by traditional patterns of behaviour they dare not question, which constrained how they used their every skill.

Yet their boundless imagination produced these breathtaking buildings. They challenged what was thought to be possible by building ever higher, more daring, innovative structures. Abandoning their routine patterns of behaviour, they created flying buttresses, taking weight off the walls to open them up with large, beautiful stained-glass windows. The colour and light flooding through transformed the dark, forbidding interior and with it the vision of worshippers. As the great shards of light streaked across them, the geometry of each intersecting beam seemed to testify to the majesty and order of God's creation.

In the work of these medieval stonemasons and architects we can see all the problems faced by modern decision-makers. Like them, now that we have identified the stable pattern in our ideas about a situation, we must search for a parallel structure that will point towards a solution. If this is unsuccessful, we must work with our pattern, adapting it to find one that will meet the demands of change, rather than just repeat the lessons of the past.

In the following two chapters we will learn methods and techniques that will help us do this routinely. They will show you how you can design what might otherwise have seemed an inspired solution to the problem. And although it may seem surprising that such inspiration should find its source in such routine work, it's worth remembering that, in fact, every creative activity is grounded in the solid foundations of just this type of work. In the process we will learn to become more creative and innovative thinkers.

8
Problem Solving 1: Analogies

We have now revealed the pattern into which our ideas are organised. Having compared this with the routine patterns we have used in the past and found no match, we must either find other patterns that will offer us a solution or begin to work with this one to adapt it. In the next chapter, we will learn the different strategies we can use to adapt the pattern of our ideas. In this chapter, we will examine what we can do to discover alternative patterns that might give us a solution.

Good thinkers

Good thinkers can do two things when they approach a problem. First, they can detach their minds from routine patterns of thought and apply seemingly unrelated mental frameworks to the problem. In this way they liberate their minds from the narrow grooves in which they might otherwise be trapped, allowing them to scan a wide range of possible mental patterns.

Second, they can forget about themselves in their thinking. They realise they must forget about what they might wish will be the case in any situation, before they can see what the situation itself requires.

Good thinkers:
1. Detach their minds from routine patterns.
2. Forget about themselves.

Both of these transitions in our thinking can have a major impact on our lives and work, helping us become more innovative and original thinkers. They have resulted in some of the most significant moments in the development of thought, when thinkers actually see for the first time the solutions to problems that have evaded their grasp despite their most determined efforts. Freed from their own routine patterns of thought and from what they might wish to be the answer, they see solutions with the sort of sudden clarity that leaves them wondering why they hadn't seen it before.

Example: The Selfish Gene.   In *The Origin of Species* (1859) Darwin argued that species evolve through the competitive struggle for survival. Those best adapted to their environment survive to leave offspring, who pass on the same attributes to future generations. But one mystery puzzled Darwin and evolutionary biologists after him. Why is it that certain behavioural traits, like bravery and altruism, survive when these must reduce the chances of surviving long enough to have offspring? For example, birds give out warning cries to others even though this puts them at risk of being attacked themselves.

The answer came in 1964 when William Hamilton read an article by the geneticist J. B. S. Haldane, in which he joked that he would lay down his life for two brothers or sisters, four nephews or nieces, or eight first cousins, each one determined by the percentage of genes they share. While others may have dismissed this as just a joke, and where Hamilton himself might otherwise have argued along different lines or according to more generally accepted patterns of ideas, he took the joke seriously and pursued it. His solution to Darwin's puzzle was hailed as the greatest advance in evolutionary theory since *The Origin of Species*.

By restating evolution by natural selection at the genetic level, rather than the accustomed level of the individual, he was able to show that creatures sacrifice themselves to ensure that more copies of their kin's genes survive. Haldane's joke made sense: all siblings carry their parents' genes, so to sacrifice yourself for two siblings means that one set has been lost, while two sets have been saved, which from the level of genes is a far better outcome than all three being lost. The same argument in more diluted form applies to nephews, nieces and cousins. In 1976, in his famous book, *The Selfish Gene*, Richard Dawkins developed these ideas and brought them to a wider audience.[1]

Learning to become a good thinker

So, how can we learn to do these two things that good thinkers do?

1 Forgetting about ourselves

In an earlier chapter we said that good thinkers think about their thinking while they think. They question their own ideas and their own thinking as they think. They accept with humility that they may have got it wrong or only have part of the answer. They are also aware that the answer may come from the most unlikely sources. This means hanging a question over everything and suspending our judgement. For many of us this is unsettling; we find it difficult to admit uncertainty. But good thinking rarely occurs where there are answers that carry the weight of undisputed authority.

Unfortunately, the style of management in many organisations simply doesn't allow for good thinking, because managers are too aware of themselves and their role within the organisation as a source of certainty. Some wield undisputed authority, possessing all the characteristics of a leader of a New Age cult. There is often no communal context for decision-making; authority is placed entirely with the leader. From that point it's easy for those at the top to decide that all forms of argument or criticism amount to a form of personal betrayal or treason.

Paul Moore, the head of risk at HBOS, claims that when he warned Sir James Crosby of the risks that the company was taking, he was sacked. In classical Greek tragedy such hubris invites ruin and disaster: it was believed to offend the gods and lead to retribution. Perhaps worse still, it leads to blind spots, bad decisions and an organisation that is content to repeat its mistakes, as we saw in Chapter 1.

> *Example: Daimler-Benz and Chrysler.*   Juergen Schrempp, CEO of Daimler-Benz brought about the merger of Chrysler and Daimler-Benz, despite internal opposition. Ten years later they were virtually forced to give Chrysler away.

> *Example: Quaker and Snapple.*   The logic of Quaker's acquisition of Snapple was that it would repeat the success of their acquisition of Gatorade in 1983. But experienced managers, locked within their own routine thinking and without the countervailing influence of wider opinion, were led by the similarities between the two patterns of information to overlook the significant differences between the two.

In contrast, those who can forget about themselves and empathise with others see more and tend to make better decisions. Curious about the lives and experiences of others, they are more effective at trading places and conducting mental experiments in which they ask themselves what they would do or feel in similar situations. They hypothesise more, experience more things, albeit vicariously, and develop the capacity to create more structures through which to process and understand these things. As a result they develop wider sympathies and sounder judgement.

So the first thing we need to do is develop the habit of empathising with others, vicariously experiencing what others in a particular situation might feel, believe or prefer. Conducting this sort of mental experiment must become routine. In Chapter 3 we saw the importance of this in generating our ideas by thinking through a problem from different perspectives on different levels. Now, as we begin to adapt and work with the structures through which we routinely organise these ideas, it is even more important.

Good thinking:

1. Forgetting about ourselves – routinely empathise with others.
2. Detaching our minds from routine patterns – suspend judgement and ask 'What if' questions.

---

2 Detaching our minds from routine patterns

The easiest way of learning to detach ourselves from our routine patterns of thought is to cultivate the habit of asking 'conditionals': the type of question we all pose when we suspend our judgement and ask, 'What if I were to do X' or 'If Y occurred, what would be the results?' So, whenever you're presented with a categorical statement, start asking conditionals and search for the answers.

Example: Historians. Historians open up areas for investigation in just this way by asking counterfactual conditionals, where they ask what would have happened if something that did happen had not in fact happened. They might ask, 'What if the Napoleonic Wars had never happened? Would the industrial revolution have developed differently?' From this they might hypothesise, 'If the Napoleonic Wars had not occurred, then the British economy would not have been so dominated by heavy industry.'

Example: Scientists.   Scientists, too, in addition to counterfactuals, use subjunctive conditionals to set up experiments: the type of hypothesis that suggests 'If A should occur, then so would B.'

Finding 'What if' questions – analogies

As we said earlier, although breakthroughs in all forms of research might seem logical, even obvious, in hindsight, it is quite different the other way around from the viewpoint of the original thinkers. To them it seems full of confusion, doubt and uncertainty as they search for alternative patterns of ideas that will give them a different way of explaining things. Like them, we must also develop the art of recognising similarities between unrelated structures to generate 'What if' questions. If you find this difficult, there are deliberate steps you can take. The simplest and most used by good thinkers is to search for analogies.

Example: Darwin and variety in species.   After some years studying barnacles, Darwin realised he was wrong to assume stability in species was the norm and variety the exception. It was, in fact, the reverse: variety was the norm. But, now, how was he to explain this?

He found the answer in the analogy of industrial progress that he had seen developing in nineteenth-century Britain. It was clear that fierce competition in overcrowded markets favoured those who could use and adapt their skills to fill niches. The individuals who thrived in these circumstances were those that seized new opportunities and filled niches as they opened. When he looked at crowded markets he saw they were full of all manner of people with different skills, each working next to each other, but not in direct competition.

Nature, he realised, was no different. The same pressure of competition forced species to adapt to fill unoccupied niches. And the greater the functional diversity of species the more an area could support. Indeed, nature was even more efficient at this than industry. Natural selection increased the 'division of labour' among animals who were caught in competitive situations, resulting in the immense variation in species.[2]

As you can see from this, finding analogies involves searching for similarities between unrelated patterns that we gather from our everyday experience. As the word 'art' suggests, this is not a mechanical process; it calls for a selective imagination to identify previously unrelated patterns into which all the pieces fit. Finding them often produces the most surprising rewards. Insight can occur in response to a fact that means nothing to others.

To help you do this, ask yourself three simple questions:

Three simple questions:
1. Is there a parallel?
2. Does the pattern fit?
3. Would it solve the problem?

---

1 Is there a parallel?

The search for parallel structures is the search for analogies that have the same or a similar structure to our problem. It involves simple pattern recognition.

> *Example: Miss Marple.* Miss Marple, the main character in 12 of Agatha Christie's crime novels, often calls upon incidents and characters she has come across in St. Mary Mead, the English village in which she lives. Although they are quite unrelated to the problem she is working on, they usually yield a common pattern of behaviour and human motivation that can be used to explain and solve the problem.

But to do it well we have to prepare our minds thoroughly, immersing ourselves in the ideas. The analogies are there for all of us to see, if we can only prepare ourselves to see them. The problem is the mind is not naturally creative; it can only see what we have prepared it to see. But once you've immersed yourself in the ideas and prepared yourself to see them, the analogies will come. Then you will have to choose which is the most likely to work; which is the best fit.

2 Does the pattern fit?

To answer this question we have to concentrate on two things: the quantity and quality of the similarities. Obviously, if one structure is similar to another in many different ways we feel more confident in the conclusions we draw. But the quality of the similarities is important too: we have to ensure that the analogy establishes credible connections in our experience.

Concentrate on two things:
Quantity and **quality** of similarities

2.1 Quantity

When we search for such connections, we are identifying a sufficiently stable pattern in our previous experience which we think is reliable enough for us to conclude that given one event, the other will follow with high probability. The larger the number of As that have been Cs and the fewer As that have not been Cs, the likelier it is that all As will be Cs, and therefore that the next A will be a C.

2.2 Quality

In contrast, the quality of the connection might seem more difficult to pin down. What we are looking for is a credible connection. There may be many instances of one thing occurring with another, but is this just an accident, a coincidence, or is there likely to be a causal connection between the two?

As we will see in a later chapter, this points to the difference between a correlation and a causal connection. We might find a correlation between the sales of chewing gum and violent crime, but we are unlikely to see any real significance in this. But if we found a correlation between violent crime and the sales of violent films on DVD, we might begin to think there is good chance of a causal connection between the two.

> *Example: Accidental generalisations.* We might find that all the cars in our staff car park are Fords, but this doesn't mean we can conclude that therefore the next car to enter the car park will be a Ford. It is only an accidental generalisation. As the philosopher William Kneale famously argued, from the premise that all the men in the next room are playing poker, we cannot conclude that if the Archbishop of Canterbury were in the next room, then he would be playing poker too.

In other words, there must be something analogous between the two events. If I were to drop my pen and, just a fraction of a second later, we were both to look out of the window to see a car crash in the street below, it would not be convincing for me to argue that the first event caused the second, because we know of no law or uniformity in our experience in which the dropping of pens cause cars to crash.

However, if I were to argue that the light reflected off the falling pen, distracting the driver, who then lost control and crashed, it would still not be as convincing as it should be for a satisfactory explanation, but it is on its way. The reason is that we have had analogous experiences in our own lives when people have been distracted in what they are doing by loud noises or bright lights, and this has led them to make mistakes or have accidents. We have used such patterns of events before; they have a good track record, so we feel confident about using them again in this case.

3 Would it solve the problem?

Once we have established that the resemblance is more than superficial, we have to ask the third question: would it change our interpretation of the problem, suggesting an alternative way of approaching it – a 'What if' question? Often when this occurs – when the pattern fits the situation – something clicks; suddenly everything makes sense. It is one of those significant moments in the process of genuine thought.

Afterwards, it appears that the key to the problem was a hidden clue that we just didn't see or didn't take notice of because it seemed quite irrelevant. But, in fact, it wasn't irrelevant at all. It was just that we were using a different pattern to interpret the ideas. Change the pattern and it becomes relevant. The ability to do this can produce moments of genuine originality and real insight.

Effective analogies

To illustrate just how effective analogies can be in bringing real insight and enlightenment, consider the following example created by the American psychologists Mary Gick and Keith Holyoak, who set this problem for their students:

> *Example: Surgeons.*   Imagine you were a doctor faced with a patient who has an inoperable stomach tumour. You have at your disposal rays that can destroy human tissue when directed with sufficient intensity. At the lower intensity the rays are harmless to healthy tissue, but they do not affect the tumour either. How can you use these rays to destroy the tumour without destroying the surrounding healthy tissue?

Most students find the problem difficult to solve, but nine out of ten are able to do so after reading the following passage:

> A general wants to capture a fortress in the centre of a country. There are many roads radiating outward from the fortress. All have been mined so that while groups of men can pass over the roads safely, larger forces will detonate the mines. A full-scale direct attack is therefore impossible. The general's solution is to divide his army into small groups, send each group to the head of a different road and have them converge simultaneously on the fortress.[3]

Misleading analogies

However, vague associations are the source of almost limitless error and oversimplification. It is the stuff of superstitions, myths and rituals. Seeing a black cat, we are told, is lucky, presumably because someone, at sometime, saw a black cat and subsequently had good luck. To avoid this we have to test the key elements of the identity between the analogy and our problem.

Politicians are fond of using the most graphic analogy on which to hang their argument, even though with a little probing it is not difficult to see that it will bear very little weight.

> *Example: Political analogies.*   When they hold up a bag of purchases with one hand representing how little the pound or dollar will buy now, compared with the bag in the other hand representing what could be bought when they were in power, you know that a great deal is missing from the argument.

Why is each item more expensive? Is it the result of reductions in supply or increased production costs, rather than inflation which could be associated with the government? And does the comparison take into account the real value of a family's income and not just the money value, which could mean that, though the pound or dollar buys less, the average family still has the same or a better standard of living?

Conclusion

The ability to solve problems in this way – to see things differently by distinguishing the structure from the background and then comparing it with unrelated structures – can produce moments of genuine originality and real insight. Good thinkers can detach their minds from habitual routine patterns of thought and apply patterns which seem to have no relevance, except, of course, that they have a similar structure. At times you may think it absurd to connect two things that are so different. But, as the English philosopher A. N. Whitehead once said, almost all really new ideas have a certain aspect of foolishness when we first produce them.

9
Problem Solving 2: Adapting Structures

If we cannot find an analogy to give us an alternative way of approaching the problem, we must work with our structure to adapt it. Reformulating the problem in this way by shifting the factors that make up the situation is the defining characteristic of abstract thought. Over the years we've got used to describing the ability to think differently about a problem in this way as 'lateral thinking', although it's probably better described as 'non-linear thinking'. In other words, instead of working through our normal linear steps one by one, we take them in a different order.

Working with the structure

You can learn to do this quite simply by working through the following four strategies. Indeed, all creative work is grounded in the solid foundations of such routine work. Carefully working through them, we can place ourselves in the position of being able to think outside the norm and reveal what might otherwise have seemed an inspired way of approaching the problem.

Working with the structure:
1. Change the structure.
2. Approach it from a different direction.
3. Start from a different point.
4. Create a new structure.

Changing the structure involves reorganising the elements and their relationships. By contrast, the second and third strategies involve accepting the structure as it is, but looking at it differently. We either approach it from a different direction, looking at it from different points of view, or we start from a different point. The fourth strategy is perhaps the most radical. This involves creating a new structure, either by combining other structures, or by changing the basic concepts in terms of which the situation is described and interpreted.

Strategy 1: Change the structure

This is what we might describe as a bottom-up strategy in that, starting with the ideas we've gathered, we restructure them. It's the sort of processing we do when we tackle a crossword puzzle. We're given a clue which encourages us to think in one way, when the answer lies in changing this pattern of expectations. The fact that the solution comes through changing the structure, and not just one or two parts, explains why it always appears like a sudden insight with the answer revealed as a complete whole. In T. S. Kuhn's *The Structure of Scientific Revolutions*, he explains scientific progress using the same terms. The sudden shift between one incompatible paradigm and another comes in the form of a complete revolution; it is not a gradual process.

So the key to this strategy is learning to manipulate and change our normal patterns of expectations. The problem is that the brain allows information to self-organise into patterns, which we then become accustomed to using, so we need to learn simple methods to change the structure to see things from new and more effective perspectives. We can do this in three ways:

Changing the structure:
1. Split it up.
2. Rearrange it.
3. Reinterpret it.

---

1. Split it up

The simplest method is to split up the structure into two or more parts. In many cases this can reduce a bewilderingly difficult problem into two simple problems, whose solution is plain to see. Either we discover that each one can be solved by the application of a structure we have used before, or by a parallel structure, an analogy, which is the key to the solution. Failing that, once it's split up we can then use one of the other methods and rearrange or reinterpret the problems and come to a solution that way.

> *Example: Crossword puzzles.* The compilers of crossword puzzles often have this strategy in mind when they set their clues. To find the answer to the clue 'Savings book (7)' the compiler expects you to split it in two with both parts leading to the answer 'Reserve'. The same is true of the clue 'Frequently decimal (5)', which can be split into two and again both parts lead to the answer 'Often'.

> *Example: Quaker and Snapple.* In Chapter 1, we saw that Quaker's acquisition of Snapple was disastrous largely because executives overlooked the differences between the two patterns of information relating to Snapple and Gatorade. They were so convinced by the similarities between the two that they never questioned their conviction that they could repeat the success they achieved with the acquisition of Gatorade. They would have been more aware of the pitfalls if they had split the problem up, analysing separately, say, the similarities and dissimilarities of each product, or the contrasting markets for each product.

Similarities and dissimilarities

Splitting the problem up in this way would have revealed a number of smaller problems. Once they had thought about these and how they might solve them, they would have had a sounder grasp of the issues to take into account in deciding whether the acquisition made sense. They were already aware of the similarities, but their analysis of the dissimilarities would have revealed the following:

1. Gatorade had been a category leader on the rise, whereas Snapple was a category leader in trouble. They now faced new competitors who were taking a share of the market.
2. At Gatorade the management team stayed on after the acquisition, whereas at Snapple they moved on.
3. At Gatorade operations were in good order, whereas at Snapple the inventory and production were out of control.

Markets

The same could be said about analysing the significant differences between their respective markets. This, too, would have identified smaller problems. Once they had a solution for these, they would have had a clear idea of whether the acquisition made sense.

1. Snapple was an 'image' drink, whereas Gatorade was a 'fluid replacement product'.
2. Snapple's success was based on a unique form of marketing that had created a cult following. In contrast, Gatorade had been aggressively promoted in a more traditional fashion within a carefully defined segment of the market.
3. Snapple depended on entrepreneurial distributors, whereas Gatorade used a warehouse system.

In summary, Snapple used a more idiosyncratic promotional strategy that relied heavily on the company's knowledge of customers, channels and product promotion, whereas Gatorade was more traditional, which would fit easily into the promotional strategy employed for Quaker's other products.[1]

2 Rearrange it

Alternatively, with some problems the answer is found by rearranging the structure.

> *Example: Crossword puzzles.* Some crossword clues call for us to rearrange the letters. The clue 'Fibber and return rail fair (4)' is solved by taking the word 'rail' and reversing the order of the letters to make 'liar'.

With the sort of problems we face each day, rearranging the structure most often involves identifying a factor that can be moved or changed. The key to this method is seeing each factor as something that will change the situation.

> *Example: Semmelweis and puerperal fever.* Semmelweis adopted just this method when he changed, in turn, each thing in the

situation to see if they had any effect. Looking at the structure of the problem, he changed the position in which the women gave birth, their diet in the doctors' division, and the route of the priest and his bellringer to see if each one changed the situation.

Example: A teacher and study skills. If you were a teacher in charge of improving the academic skills of the sixth form of your school, the sort of question you would want an answer to is, why is it that so many students struggle to take notes, read texts and write essays, so they can meet what they believe are the demands of syllabuses and exams? The normal causal structure would suggest it is most likely because they are not given sufficient or effective instruction in how to do these things. But then, if you were to find that with most students this was not the case – that they did in fact get very good instruction, yet still manifested the same problems – you would have to identify a factor that could be moved or changed to reveal the most likely solution.

The normal structure suggests the following causal relationships: study skills instruction shapes the way we use our skills to meet our perception of the demands of syllabuses and exams.

study skills instruction → note taking, reading, essay writing skills → meet our perception of the demands of syllabuses and exams

Rearranging this by thinking about the influence of our perception of the demands of exams and syllabuses gives us an alternative explanation:

our perception of the demands of syllabuses and exams → study skills instruction → note taking, reading, essay writing skills

It may be that, despite all the instruction in study skills, the way teachers shape students' perception of the demands of syllabuses and modes of assessment, like essays and exams, results in students still taking notes, reading and writing in the same way, exhibiting exactly the same problems.

If teachers are encouraging students to believe that learning is largely about knowing things and exams test how many 'right' answers they can recall and trade for marks, despite taking study skills courses, they are likely to continue to read word-for-word and take verbatim, unstructured notes, fearing that if they leave anything out they might be missing a right answer. If this is the case, the solution lies not in planning more and better study skills courses, but in working with teachers to reshape students' perception of learning tasks, like exams and essays.

3 Reinterpret it

Failing that, we can reinterpret the structure, changing its meaning. The way we make sense of the structure can itself lead us in the wrong direction. So without even changing the structure we can sometimes find the solution by looking at it naïvely, without any preconceptions, as someone who has never seen it before.

Example: Five Graves To Cairo.   In the 1943 film *Five Graves To Cairo*, set in North Africa, the Allied forces are trying to figure out how it is that Rommel's forces can move with such speed without stretching their supply lines to breaking point. The answer seems to be that he must have large reserves of fuel stored in the desert somewhere; indeed, intelligence indicates that there are five of them. They stare at the map, but they cannot work out just where they might be.

Then, finally, they see it, and the answer is so simple. It has been hidden in full view. The insight finally dawns when they reinterpret the map by reading it in a different way. Across the map of North Africa the letters E, G, Y, P, T, are printed. Otherwise inconspicuous, as any similar entry would be on any map, they indicate precisely where the dumps are.

Example: Crossword puzzles.   Again, crossword compilers adopt the same strategy. One of the clues we referred to in a previous chapter is a good example. To find the answer to the clue 'H, I, J, K, L, M, N, O', we have to read the letters differently from the obvious way as a sequence of letters from the alphabet. Reinterpreting them gives us 'H_2O' and the solution 'water'.

Strategy 2: Approach it from a different direction

With some problems, without changing the structure, we can solve them by just approaching them from a different direction, from a different point of view. In Conan Doyle's story *The Problem of Thor Bridge*, Sherlock Holmes describes one aspect of his theory of detection when he says, 'When once your point of view is changed, the very thing which was so damning becomes a clue to the truth.'[2] The most common strategy we routinely use to approach a problem from a different direction is to reverse the order of things: to turn it upside down, inside out or back to front.

Approach it from a different direction:

1. Turn it upside down.
2. Inside out.
3. Back to front.

---

1 Turn it upside down

This may be a strategy we rarely use, although scientists and philosophers have used it to achieve their most spectacular and significant breakthroughs.

> *Example: Hume – the problem.* In his most famous work, *A Treatise of Human Nature*, the Scottish philosopher David Hume asked, how can we argue that one thing necessarily causes another, when we cannot see causes, only impressions of objects in the external world, or what we assume are objects? He insisted that all we see is one separate event following another, and if we see it often enough we assume out of habit or 'gentle custom', as a result of this 'constant conjunction' of the two events, that the first event must cause the second. Therefore, the necessary connection that we argue exists between a cause and an event is nothing more than the product of the mind.

After reading Hume's account of causation, the German philosopher Immanuel Kant awoke from his deep 'dogmatic slumber' to embark on his first significant work, *The Critique of Pure Reason*. Realising that

Hume was right, that necessity doesn't exist in the external world, but is merely a product of the internal realm of thought, Kant experienced what he describes as his 'Copernican Revolution'.

Example: Kant – the solution.   He solved the problem by turning Hume's argument upside down, reversing the relationship between our impressions and our intellect. As Copernicus removed the Earth from the centre of creation, so Kant removed the earthly experience of our senses, making it peripheral to the active processing of the mind. In other words, he argued that knowledge is not just the total of our sense impressions, but the product of the conceptual apparatus of the mind, which is itself not derived from experience.

In the same way, the German philosopher Karl Marx finds a solution to a problem that challenged his core beliefs by turning Hegel's argument upside down.

Example: Hegel – the problem.   Hegel maintained that history was the product of the 'Spirit', a rational force working through history; and the State was the latest and most complete manifestation of Spirit. In reason lies freedom, he argued, so for individuals to gain their freedom they must sacrifice everything to the State.

But Marx realised that in an age of mass production, sacrificing yourself to the State, which seemed to serve exclusively the interests of the ruling class, resulted in the progressive enslavement of individuals, reducing them to a meaningless factor of production in mechanised factories promoting the profits and wealth of the ruling class. Nevertheless, Marx had been a Young Hegelian for a number of years, so how was he to solve this problem?

Example: Marx – the solution.   He claimed to solve it by turning Hegel's argument upside down. He argued that it is not the Spirit, a rational force working through history, that determines man's freedom, but economic and material forces. In other words, it is not ideas and rational thought that determine the shape of material forces, but material forces in the form of social and economic factors, like production, that shape society, social relations, the individual and what he believes and values, indeed the whole extent of his freedom. Social and material forces are the basic causes of every fundamental change, whether in the world of things or in the life of thought. Change these and the objective social relations that develop out of them also change.

And, of course, out of this there emerged a philosophy every bit as revolutionary and influential as Hume's and Kant's. What's more, equally interesting, it's worth noting that not only do these break-throughs come about as a result of turning ideas upside down, but they are also excellent examples of good thinkers detaching themselves from their routine patterns of thought and forgetting about themselves and what they would most prefer to be the case.

2 Inside out

As for the second method of turning the problem inside out, this is more difficult to recognise, although it brings surprising results. The clearest examples are when we reverse our most intuitive assumptions, turning them inside out, to see what we find when we think the opposite.

> *Example: Hotel manager – the problem.*   If you are a hotel manager and you find that bookings are falling off, you will want to know why it is that guests are so dissatisfied with the services you offer. If you ask the direct question, you may just get the sort of infor-mation that reinforces the pattern of assumptions you already hold, which has failed to offer a solution.

So clearly you would need to change your strategy. One way is to reverse your most intuitive assumptions as the Cornell researchers did.

> *Example: Cornell researchers.*   They reversed their assumptions about hotel guests to design four research categories: satisfied stayers; dissatisfied stayers; dissatisfied switchers; and satisfied switchers. As we said in an earlier chapter, while it's obvious to think about

satisfied stayers and dissatisfied switchers, it's counter-intuitive to think there may be dissatisfied stayers and satisfied switchers.

When the government introduced the ban on smoking in public places, many owners of restaurants, pubs and bars were concerned about the effect it would have on their trade. But, as with the hotel manager, to ask the obvious questions will only produce predictable results, so it may be necessary to invent other questions and categories to get a comprehensive picture of the different types and shades of opinion.

Example: Smoking ban. It might be obvious to think of smokers who prefer unclear air and non-smokers who prefer clean air, but it would be counter-intuitive to think there may be smokers who prefer clean air and, even more, non-smokers who prefer unclean air. Nevertheless, inventing these categories alone may produce a wealth of useful and interesting evidence.

The asymmetries, the unusual conjunctions and contrasts, created by reversing the way we normally think about things are often the source of the most surprising insights.

3 Back to front

With the third strategy in which we turn the problem back to front, reversing the order of things, some of the best examples can be found in humour. In the 1950s comedy show, *The Goons*, a character says something like the following, 'Moriarty's suit was so cunningly tailored so as to leave the hands and face completely naked.' This is funny because it reverses the way we normally perceive a suit as covering the body, not as leaving some parts uncovered. There is an instant change in emotion following this sudden, unexpected change of perception.

As Sir Peter Medawar's example in Chapter 4 illustrates, it works by manipulating patterns of ideas and the expectations they raise. Our instant realisation that two patterns, united by the same word or phrase, are in fact asymmetrical gives rise to humour and creativity. Although it appears there is a structural similarity between them, we realise that in fact they raise quite different expectations.

When the word 'suit' is used this raises a certain pattern of expectations: we have in mind clothing consisting of a jacket, trousers, perhaps a waistcoat, all made out of the same material, covering the whole body. But then, when we approach it from a different direction, reversing the order of expectations, the comedian's punchline suddenly puts us into an unexpected pattern of expectations, the surprise and asymmetry of which generates humour.

> *Example: A mathematics teacher – the problem.* You might be a mathematics teacher and you want to improve your students' understanding of the way they reason in maths. At present they just do the calculations, but they aren't developing an understanding of the intellectual processes that they use to get the answer. You want them to realise that producing the right answer is not the most important aim. If they can develop their understanding of the processes involved, it will give them the confidence to be more creative.

So you have to find some way of getting them to reflect upon how they go about tackling problems. You could ask them to explain in class what they do, which would help, but you realise this would have little depth to it.

> *Example: A mathematics teacher – the solution.* You then think about getting them to write about how they reason in mathematics, but our normal pattern of expectations tells us that to write clearly we must first think clearly, so that doesn't seem to help. But then you wonder what would happen if we turned this relationship back to front: whether our normal expectations are wrong; that perhaps clear writing makes for clear thinking. Now you have an altogether different and interesting solution. You could get them to write journals, which they would then submit for marking along with other written explanations of how they solve the mathematical problems they are set.

You realise that by getting them to think through their ideas with greater clarity and care, writing could play a more important role not just in mathematics, but across the curriculum. By writing about how they come by their ideas and solve problems, students could begin to understand more about the processes of how they think in subjects, like mathematics and the sciences.

Example: Criminal psychologist – the problem. The American psychologist Stanton Samenow worked for many years with the criminally insane. As a classical Freudian therapist, his work was grounded in the belief that he could influence their behaviour, reforming many of them, so that they could lead normal lives. But, after years of work, he realised that he was not having the success he should expect.

Given this problem, what would you do? Samenow decided to turn the problem back to front. Hitherto he had assumed *he* was the one exerting the influence, but, he wondered, what if it's the other way around? He came to the conclusion that the inmates were not sick, but were just brilliant manipulators of the legal and psychiatric systems. Their mental life was a rich dreamscape of depredations and, rather than reform under classical therapy, they learned to fool their Freudian therapist, playing the psychiatric game by mouthing insights.

In his book *Inside the Criminal Mind* he argues that criminals cause crime – not bad neighbourhoods, inadequate parents, television, school, drugs or unemployment. They know the difference between good and evil, but just *prefer* evil. Criminals commit crimes because they like to. To them stealing and raping are exciting. Their entire way of life is predicated on the view that the world is there to suit them and if things don't go their way, they take matters into their own hands regardless of whether this harms others or breaks the law.

Example: Criminal psychologist – the solution. Having reversed the flow of influence, he changed his strategy. Under his new theory, the therapist begins by holding the criminal completely accountable for his offences. There are no excuses, no hard-luck stories. At the heart of the treatment is the premise that they are free to choose between good and evil. Gradually, the therapist teaches the criminal how to change his behaviour by learning how to deter criminal thinking. He learns how to make certain reasons more prominent than others: how to think of something else when he sees a woman and thinks of rape. In short, Samenow explains that it calls for criminals to acquire the sort of moral values that enables civilisations to survive.

Strategy 3: Start from a different point

In contrast to the last strategy, which involved a process of reversing things, this strategy works by starting at a point from which we haven't previously started. We focus our attention on different parts of the structure and start from there. The easiest way of doing this for most of us is to start with the key concepts around which our topic is organised.

As we've seen, at the heart of concepts are structures that organise our ideas. These are made up of organising principles. One or two of these are likely to dictate the way we generally use the concept. So, those we usually ignore give us different points to start from. They throw different light on the problem and present interesting angles from which to approach the problem.

> *Example: Company lawyer – the problem.* You may be a company lawyer advising a client. Up until now, you have considered the activity your client is involved in to be a case of bribery and, therefore, to be illegal. You have approached the problem using the concept of bribery to mean something that sidesteps the ethical norms of the market to gain a competitive advantage or extract unwarranted payments.

Unfortunately, your client insists that this practice has to continue in order for the company to maintain its position in the market. The company may be a removal firm, which has built up a deserved reputation over the years for handling delicate property or equipment, like computers. They have charged extra for this service, but now it seems this may be illegal, because it seems to be a payment extracted from the client under duress that unless it is made their property might be damaged.

> *Example: Company lawyer – the solution.* So you change the point from which you start, approaching the problem from the weaker notion of a bribe as a commission; a payment that is made as an incentive for working harder, more efficiently and for providing a better service. Now you can see that if your client adapts the nature of the payment slightly, he can avoid the charge that he is demanding a bribe. It can now be legitimately justified as a commission for using special techniques or materials or for investing in better training for his staff.

Example: Theatre promoter.   You might be the promoter of a new production of a well-known tragedy. But all the ideas you have come up with so far to promote it seem to be rather predictable. You want something that is new; that will give a fresh insight into the play. So you go back to the concept of 'tragedy' and analyse it carefully. Here you find an alternative interpretation of it as something that is self-defeating in that, without meaning to, we destroy the very thing we value most. Now you have a unique angle on the play and a fresh, innovative way of promoting it.

But if the key concepts of your topic don't offer you a way of starting from a different point, try something that might seem disarmingly simple: step back from your topic and approach it from a more general standpoint of someone who is not technically involved in your business or profession. Get used to asking questions that might seem too simple or obvious to ask.

Example: Einstein's naïve questions.   One reason for the stunning success of Einstein's four groundbreaking papers in 1905 was his habit of starting his work with naïve, simple, almost childlike questions. What would it be like to fly alongside a beam of light? If you flew at the same speed as the light beam, would it, for instance, appear to stand still? What happens to passengers in an elevator when it falls into emptiness?

When he was asked by a reporter why, as a man in his twenties, he should have been concerned by such childlike questions, he explained that he was a late developer. Unlike other people, he only got around to asking them as an adult. And, at his age, unlike a child, he wasn't prepared to be fobbed off with a simple, dismissive answer.

Strategy 4: Create a new structure

However, if none of these changes work, you may find the solution comes from creating a new structure. In contrast to the other strategies, this is a top-down strategy in which a new theory is put in place of the ruling one.

> **Creating a new structure:**
> 1. Combine structures.
> 2. Change the basic concepts.

1 Combine structures

We can create this new structure either by combining structures or by changing the basic concepts in terms of which the situation is described and interpreted.

> *Example: The crowd in history.* With the rise of totalitarian leaders in the 1930s and 1940s and their mesmeric influence on crowds, some historians began to wonder how significant the crowd and a leader's capacity to manipulate collective sentiment had been in previous periods with leaders, like Napoleon for instance. So they combined different structures by borrowing from social science aspects of the theory of totalitarianism. As a result they were able to open up new lines of investigation with surprising results.

So, ask yourself whether you can import a theory, or just another way of interpreting things, from elsewhere in your work, from another profession or even just from your everyday life. It is often possible to synthesise structures from different sources in this way to create new structures.

It's worth reminding yourself as you search for a solution that creative thinking often means disregarding our own cultural conventions, those that govern the way the business, organisation or the profession works. Within your profession there may be an accepted way of approaching your problem, but don't let this trap your thinking. It has been said that genius is the capacity for productive reaction against one's training.

> Creative thinking often means disregarding our own cultural conventions.

It starts with the realisation that there is no particular virtue in doing things the way they've always been done. Organisations that allow for this are likely to be the most successful, particularly if they have weak cultures and strong ethics. In other words, they allow for the creativity of employees by freeing them from unnecessary conventions as to how the organisation has always worked, while at the same time generating their trust that they can give of their creative best and be assured that they will be treated well by getting the rewards they deserve.

Study after study has shown that organisations work best when employees are asked to contribute and show initiative, even, or particularly, when they import unconventional ideas that challenge the way things are normally done. When they believe that managers and colleagues respect and understand them, and when they understand and appreciate the reasoning behind management decisions, they are more confident that their own contributions will be recognised. As a result, they are likely to be more motivated and engaged in their work.

- Can you import a theory or a different way of interpreting things?
- Don't get trapped by the accepted ways of approaching your problem.
- Does the organisation need to change to have a weak culture and strong ethics?
- Does it allow for the creativity of employees?
- Does it assure them that their ideas will be respected?

2 Change the basic concepts

Alternatively, think again about changing the basic concepts in which your problem is described. As we discovered in Chapter 5, a concept represents the structure through which we understand the situation. Each one is a system of learned responses which we automatically apply to organise data and make sense of our experience. Without concepts it would be impossible to understand it. In any situation we catalogue what we perceive using a ready-made set of concepts.

But concepts also influence our behaviour: they represent a response or a readiness to respond in a particular way. They codify certain higher-order responses in terms of which our more basic response patterns are organised. Not only do they relate what we have learnt in the past to the problems we face at present, but they influence and organise each other. In this way they form complex systems which can influence the course of our behaviour quite independently of our intentions.

Faced with an unusual situation, we attempt to place it in some familiar category and treat it accordingly. A word or phrase can then set off a train of thought which results in behaviour which is normal or conventional, but which might not lead to a solution of the problem. To solve it we must analyse and change the concept.

> *Example: Doctors, consultants, hospital administrators.* If part of your responsibility is to tackle the difficult problem of how to distribute limited medical resources to meet the needs of patients, you will at some point have had to analyse the concept of 'needs'. You may have begun by using it in an absolute sense as something necessary for basic survival. But you will have soon realised that it also has a relative sense meaning those things necessary for a certain quality of life, defined as a result of living in a particular society. It is this on which the solutions to many of the problems involved in the distribution of limited resources are likely to be based.

Conclusion

Creativity, like humour, arises from the asymmetry of the structures we carry around in our minds to understand the world and navigate our way through it. When we adapt and manipulate these structures, we see things differently; we have genuine insights. Using the methods we have described in this chapter will help you generate such insights more effectively, even routinely. At times the method may have seemed complex and fussy, but once you have set it down in a simple format and used it regularly, it will become almost second nature.

Part 4
Critical Thinking

Over recent years concerns about good thinking have largely focused on critical thinking, although, as we've seen, it involves much more than this. Teaching ourselves to think about our thinking while we think is a complex task, involving our thinking skills on different levels. We must learn to generate our own ideas and think conceptually, causally and creatively as well as critically.

Our reluctance to teach these skills in schools, colleges and universities, settling instead for teaching students *what* to think rather than *how* to think, is largely explained by the difficulty they present and the complex teaching skills they demand. It is so much easier to explain and describe facts and knowledge, which students are merely required to record accurately without any active involvement of their own thinking.

In contrast, improving our critical thinking involves the more complex task of developing our skills:

- to deal with all the problems that arise from the tension between logic and language;
- to criticise and discuss issues, playing devil's advocate by arguing for the side of an issue for which we have least sympathy;
- to reason deductively and inductively;
- and to evaluate evidence and draw reliable inferences from it.

It means replacing the simplified model of adversarial debate taught in so many schools and colleges with the more complex reasoning of a discussion, in which participants aim to reveal the truth and not just win the argument. It involves honestly confronting all the issues and not just those that support one side. It means carefully modulating our reasoning to reach an accurate and sensitive assessment of the evidence, irrespective of whether this reflects our views or not.

This more complete account of thinking was developed over 2400 years ago by Socrates, who railed against the barren simplifications of traditional debate and rhetoric. He developed a method of reasoning that stripped away all the misconceptions and confusion that obscured the truth. Carefully probing the pronouncements of authorities and the claims of his students, he began by taking nothing for granted, asking the simplest and most naïve questions. In this way he was able to reveal their confused use of words, the concealed implications of their arguments lying unnoticed in concepts they had taken for granted, the lack of adequate evidence to support their claims and the self-contradictory beliefs obscured by their confident rhetoric.

In the same way, using the same skills, we must scrutinise all the arguments we come across or create ourselves. For arguments to be convincing they depend on two things: that the premises or statements, which make up the argument, are *true*; and that the argument is *valid* – that the premises support the conclusion in the way it is claimed they do. Where truth is concerned with the substance of the argument, validity is concerned with its form, whether the conclusion can in fact be drawn from the premises.

With these two things in mind we need to be sure that there are no errors in our reasoning, that our use of language is consistent and clear, and that we have sufficient evidence to demonstrate the truth of our premises. As this makes clear, we need to think routinely about three things:

1. Arguments
    1.1 Are they valid?
    1.2 Do I draw conclusions that are consistent with my assumptions?
    1.3 Are there hidden assumptions in my arguments?
2. Evidence
    2.1 Do I have enough evidence to make my points?
    2.2 Do I describe the evidence accurately?
    2.3 Do I draw reliable and relevant inferences from it?
3. Language
    3.1 Is my meaning clear?
    3.2 Do I use words consistently?
    3.3 Does my language imply more than I acknowledge?

Even the best minds are filled with half-truths, superstitions, falsehoods and prejudices. We all make the same mistakes. We fail to apply the elementary tests of logic to determine whether one idea, which may or may not be true, does in fact lead to another. We rely on partial, untested evidence. And we use language in a misleading, inconsistent way without reflecting on its hidden implications. The key to solving all of these problems is to develop a deep suspicion about our own ideas and bring this centre stage in our writing and thinking.

In the next seven chapters we will learn to audit our arguments, evidence and language. We will learn simple methods and routines to check the components of our arguments and the connections between them; to make sure we have described our evidence accurately and drawn reliable inferences from it; and that we use language clearly and consistently, aware of all the implications of the concepts we use.

10
Thinking with Arguments 1: The Components

In Part 2 we found that the significance of our thinking lies not in the strength of our ideas, but in the quality of the connections we make between them. The distinguishing characteristic of intelligence is this ability to identify relevant connections and put together what ought to be conjoined. This is conceptual thinking. Then, once we have made these connections and created patterns of ideas, we work with them as we did in Part 3 to find solutions to problems. This is creative thinking.

Now we have to audit these new ideas to make sure that they are argued consistently. This is critical thinking. Although on its own it cannot generate one new idea, it can help us decide which are worth retaining. It will show us how to make the connections we want to, so we develop our ideas rationally and consistently. You may have generated the most revealing insights, synthesising ideas in new and fascinating ways, but unless you can make these connections in a consistent way, your ideas are likely to be valueless.

In this and the next chapter we will examine how we develop consistent arguments. First, we must check the components of our arguments: what types are we dealing with, are any missing and are we just taking some for granted? Then, in the next chapter, we will look at ways of checking the connections we make between them.

Two kinds of thinking

So, how do we learn to develop our ideas in arguments that move consistently from one point to another? First, we must distinguish between two kinds of thinking: deductive and inductive.

1 Deductive thinking

In a deductive argument we start with a general or major premise, usually referring to 'All' or 'Some' ('All bachelors are unmarried men'), and then by adding a minor premise, which refers to a specific case ('John is a bachelor'), we draw out the logical conclusion ('Therefore, John is an unmarried man'). As you can see in this simple example, the conclusion follows logically from the premises. Indeed, in a logical or 'valid' deductive argument, if the premises are true the conclusion must also be true, because the conclusion never states more than is contained in the premises – the assumptions that make up the argument.

> *Example: Valid argument.*   If my major premise is,
>
> All dogs are animals
>
> and I then add the minor premise that refers to just one dog,
>
> Aldous is a dog,
>
> then I can conclude consistently that
>
> Aldous is an animal.

1.1 Truth and validity

In this case we know that the major premise is true and, if the minor premise is also true, then the conclusion *must* be true, because the argument is valid: in other words the conclusion follows logically from the premises. Note the distinction here between truth and validity.

Validity	The form of the argument – its consistency.
Truth	The substance – whether the premises are true.

Validity is a way of ensuring that if we do have true premises then we also guarantee that our conclusion is true. When an argument is valid it is not possible for its premises to be true, while its conclusion is false.

Validity:
Validity guarantees that if the premises are true the conclusion will also be true.

2 Inductive thinking

In contrast, whereas a deductive argument never states more than is contained in the premises, an inductive argument always goes *beyond* its premises. In an inductive argument we start with singular observation statements that certain events, all similar in some important respect, have occurred, and then we derive a universal generalisation that applies to all events of this type, observed and unobserved, past, present and future. Even though we only possess a finite number of singular observation statements, we come to an infinite, universal conclusion on the basis of them. We have gone beyond what our observation statements will allow.

Inductive arguments go beyond their premises.

When Blaise Pascal, the seventeenth-century French philosopher and physicist, set about testing his law of atmospheric pressure, he had his brother-in-law Perier carry the barometer up the Puy-de-Dome several times before concluding that the height of the mercury decreases as the altitude increases. So, his justification for his law that barometers fall as the altitude increases was a series of singular observations statements something like the following:

1. The first time the barometer was taken up the mountain (that is, the altitude increased) it fell.
2. The second time the barometer was taken up the mountain it fell.
3. And so on until the nth time the barometer was taken up the mountain it fell.
4. Therefore, all barometers fall when their altitude increases.

To make this a valid argument, we would have to insert another assumption – the principle of induction – after the first three statements to the effect that:

All unobserved cases resemble observed cases.

With this in place, we can validly argue that 'All barometers fall when their altitude increases.' But unfortunately, as you can see, this assumption suffers from the same problem: it is a universal claim for which we can only have finite evidence. As the Scottish philosopher David Hume pointed out, it's a vicious circle: for the principle of induction to be true, we would need the principle of induction to be true.

So, it follows that all inductive arguments must be invalid; in that the premises they are made of can never justify the conclusions we derive from them. Even so, this is the best method we have for reaching general conclusions from empirical evidence. In Chapters 12, 13 and 14 we will examine what we need to do to avoid the most common problems when we use inductive arguments. In this and the next chapter, we will focus on deductive arguments.

In these simple structures, representing deductive and inductive reasoning, lie the immense power of human reason and the importance of logic as its auditor. With them, we made our earliest faltering steps to go beyond ourselves and our small world to an understanding of others and the world beyond. This powerful instrument has given us the ability to extend our understanding of singular, discrete things to make the sort of connections that have given us knowledge of the world and power over nature.

Checking the components – what sort of premises are there?

With deductive thinking, there are two simple things we must learn to check in our arguments:

1. the component parts – the premises that contain our ideas;
2. and the connections we make between them – our reasoning.

Facts and values

The first question we should ask is, what sort of premises are there? If we confuse one with another we're likely to make mistakes. Take the most obvious distinction between those that are factual and those that express value judgements. As we saw in Chapter 2, a statement of fact purports to represent the way things *are* and, therefore, can be assessed in terms of its truth or falsehood, whereas a statement of value is about how things *should* or *ought* to be and, therefore, cannot. One is descriptive, the other prescriptive. With many of the value judgements we make it is simply a matter of opinion: there is no objective criterion to which we can appeal to settle the issue.

Fact	Value
A statement about what *is* the case.	A statement about what *ought* or *should* be the case.
Descriptive	Prescriptive

The problem we have to guard against, therefore, is confusing the two and deducing a conclusion containing a value judgement from purely factual premises. In this way someone can sneak their own opinions in under our radar as if they are just statements of fact. You might find that someone argues:

> All major engineering projects result in increased taxes.
> The new power station is a major engineering project.
> Therefore, it should be stopped.

The major and minor premises are both statements of fact, whether or not they are true, but the conclusion is a value judgement. We said earlier that deductive arguments are valid, because they draw out conclusions that are already contained in the premises. The key principle to remember is:

Nothing can be drawn out by way of a conclusion that is not already contained in the premises.

This means that no value judgement can be deduced from any set of premises which do not themselves contain a value judgement. In the argument above, we could only have drawn out this conclusion if the major premise had been instead:

> All major engineering works should be stopped because they increase taxes.

Even though this seems obvious, it's easy to introduce a value judgement into an argument without even knowing it. As we saw in Chapter 2, some words, like 'honesty', 'heroism' and 'promise', are mixed, both fact and value. Using them in what appears to be a factual argument we can smuggle in a value judgement without realising it.

Are any missing?

Now that we're sure about the type of premises we're using, we must check that there are none missing.

Suppressed premises

Often, in our arguments we make assumptions without making clear that we're doing so: there are unstated premises which we have just suppressed. We're in a hurry or we simply assume the other person knows or agrees with the suppressed premise. Our arguments may be valid, but we won't know this until we have revealed the suppressed premise. See if you can identify the suppressed premise in the following argument:

1. Aldous is a dog.
2. Therefore he is very loyal.

Clearly, what would make this argument valid is the suppressed premise that:

All dogs are loyal.

That's not too difficult, but we often confront simple one-liners, like the following, which can need much more careful thought:

1. The customer can't expect much consideration from a multinational like XXX.
2. This year Dishglow washing up liquid outsold its three nearest competitors combined. It's clearly the best washing up liquid on the market.
3. The significant increase in church attendance in recent years shows that we are becoming a much more religious society.
4. If you don't believe him, who *can* you believe? After all, he is a member of the clergy.

Checklist

None of this is too difficult to understand. The most serious problem is organising ourselves to take account of these things routinely as we write and think about our ideas. It helps if you can ask yourself a limited number of short questions as you check your arguments.

The component parts:
1. Are my premises purely **factual**?
2. Are there **value judgements** that I haven't revealed?
3. Have I made clear all my premises? Does my argument rely on **suppressed premises**?

Conclusion

Most of our arguments in daily life are clouded with all sorts of irrelevancies, unexamined assumptions and verbose phrases. They are a long way from the clarity we need to check their consistency. So, to reveal the structure of the argument, we need to strip all this away and set it out as we have done in this chapter. At first this may seem difficult, but after you've done it a few times you will begin to sharpen your skills for picking out premises and discarding the rest. Then we can check each component to see what type they are, and whether any are missing or suppressed. Once we've done this, we can move on to check the connections between our ideas as we will see in the next chapter.

11
Thinking with Arguments 2: The Connections

Now that we know all the components are there, what type they are and that none are suppressed, we can move on to check the connections between them.

Qualifiers

As you connect your premises to the conclusion, check that the strength of your claims remains the same. If you've claimed in the premises that 'most' people agree about something, you cannot then go on to claim in the conclusion that 'all' people agree about it. Known as 'qualifiers', words, like 'some', 'most', 'all', and 'few', indicate the strength of the claim you are making. In the next chapter we will come across them again, when we look at how accurately we describe our evidence, but in this one we're concerned with the connection between our premises and our conclusion.

The problem is that we're not as attentive as we should be towards these important words. As a result we are more easily persuaded to believe things about which we should have doubts.

> *Example: A journalist or advertiser.* The less scrupulous journalist who has a point to make, or the advertiser whose only concern is to promote the sales of his product, deliberately omit qualifiers, like 'all', 'never' and 'sometimes', because if they appear in the copy they are likely to cause the reader to think more carefully about what's being said.

And, of course, we're likely to make the same mistakes ourselves. We might read in a report that a police spokesperson has claimed that older drivers are safer than younger ones. As a result we might argue that because Philip is older than Mark, he is a safer driver. But the spokesperson might have meant that it is only true 'as a general rule', whereas we have argued that it is 'always' true and, therefore, it must be true in the cases of Philip and Mark.

Such easy generalisations have a certain beguiling attraction for us. It's easy to slip into a categorical claim ('all', 'every', 'always', etc.) to avoid the effort of weighing up the evidence carefully and selecting just the right qualifier ('almost all', 'almost half', 'few', etc.) that reflects the right strength.

They also give us a sense of instant certainty, that we have suddenly uncovered something which makes things so much clearer. We can plan our lives and our thoughts with so much confidence as a result. In the hands of skilful writers such instant clarity can also be very witty. Much of the humour in the work of Oscar Wilde was of this type. In *Lady Windermere's Fan* he writes:

> If you pretend to be good, the world takes you very seriously. If you pretend to be bad, it doesn't. Such is the astounding stupidity of optimism.[1]

> It is absurd to divide people into good and bad. People are either charming or tedious.[2]

Their effectiveness depends upon us accepting that in 'every' case when people pretend to be good or bad this claim is true and, likewise, in 'all' cases people can be divided between charming and tedious and not between good and bad. These statements are witty precisely because they draw sharp, categorical distinctions, which get us to think about things from a perspective we wouldn't otherwise have entertained. In the following line from *The Picture of Dorian Gray*, even though we can doubt whether this is true of all philanthropic people, it gets us to think about a certain class of people in an entirely surprising and unexpected way:

> Philanthropic people lose all sense of humanity. It is their distinguishing characteristic.[3]

Of course, in Oscar Wilde's work we are not expected to take all of these claims seriously. In Arthur Conan Doyle's stories involving

Sherlock Holmes the intention is different, but it works in just the same way, in this case to demonstrate Holmes's legendary skills of deductive detection:

> 'Surely', answered Holmes, 'it is not hard to say that a man with that bearing, expression of authority, and sun-baked skin is a soldier, is more than a private, and is not long from India.'[4]

Once you analyse the argument you can see it takes the following form:

1. (All) Men who have this bearing, an expression of authority and sun-baked skin are soldiers higher than the rank of private and recently returned from India.
2. This man has this bearing, an expression of authority and sun-baked skin.
3. Therefore, he is a soldier higher than the rank of private and recently returned from India.

As you read the story the argument seems persuasive enough, but, when you bring to light the hidden qualifier 'All', the weakness of the major premise is revealed. It's not true that *all* men with this bearing, an expression of authority and a sun-baked skin are soldiers higher than the rank of private and recently returned from India. There may be any number of explanations for someone having these three characteristics.

What Holmes means, of course, is that 'many' men who have them are soldiers higher than the rank of private and recently returned from India and, therefore, this man is 'probably' one too. But this sucks all the certainty out of the argument, leaving it seriously weakened.

Qualifier – is it accurate and consistent between our premises and conclusion?

Distributing our terms

Omitting the qualifier gives rise to another very common problem. In many statements, like 'Businessmen treat their workers badly' or 'Journalists are not concerned with the truth', we've omitted the partial qualifier 'some'. But then, when we include it, the terms of the argument are not 'distributed' in a way which will allow us to draw a conclusion.

To distribute a term is to refer to every member of the class of things it represents. If we distributed the term 'businessmen' we might say,

All businessmen treat their workers badly

which means we can now argue that:

Malcolm is a businessman
Therefore Malcolm treats his workers badly.

But if, instead, we only have a partial qualifier, we are left with the argument:

Some businessmen treat their workers badly.
Malcolm is a businessman.
Therefore Malcolm treats his workers badly.

And this, as you can see, is not a valid deduction, because Malcolm may be one of those businessmen who treat their workers well. The best way to detect this mistake is to ask yourself, each time you make a generalisation, the simple question: 'Is this a universal claim?'

In fact, we learn the importance of distributing our terms at a very early age. Susan Stebbing in her famous book, *Thinking to Some Purpose*, gives us a very familiar example of it. A little girl, aged four, is reprimanded by her nurse for her table manners. 'Emily', the nurse says, 'nobody eats soup with a fork.' 'But', replied Emily, 'I do, and I am somebody.'[5]

Distributing our terms – is this a universal claim?

Processing our terms

If the problems with qualifiers and with distributing our terms are common enough, even more common are the problems that arise from badly processing our terms: that is, assuming they mean more or less than they actually do and, therefore, using them to assert in the conclusion more or less than the premises will allow. Take the following argument:

All children are innocent.
No grownups are children.
Therefore, no grownups are innocent.

While you might agree with the conclusion, the argument is invalid. The conclusion cannot be deduced from the two premises, because the major premise does not exclude other groups from the category 'innocent', like some grownups, who are ingenuous and unworldly. As you can see in the Venn diagram below, it doesn't follow from the argument 'All children (Cs) are innocent (Is)' that 'All the innocent (Is) are children (Cs)'.

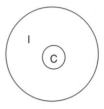

> **Processing our terms** – have I assumed they mean more or less than they do?

Illicit conversion

This is also a good example of illicit conversion. Conversion is the process of interchanging the subject ('All children', in this case) and the complement ('innocent') of a sentence. In many cases it is quite valid to do this, but not in this. We assume that as long as we can argue 'All As are Bs' we can also argue 'All Bs are As'.

The mistake is not in the premises themselves, but in the way we use them. We assume our premises allow us to do things that in fact we can't. You might assume, quite reasonably, that if a man drinks too much and becomes an alcoholic, he's likely to become destitute. He's likely to lose his job, his home and his family, and find himself living on the streets. But, from this it's a short step to arguing that if a man is destitute he must be an alcoholic.

The subject and the complement of certain propositions can be interchanged, but only if there is total exclusion between the two classes

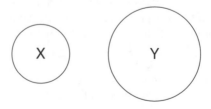

of things. If I say that no women are members of the football team, I can also say that no members of the football team are women.

The same is true when there is partial inclusion. If you can argue that 'Some patriots are pacifists', you can also argue that 'Some pacifists are patriots.'

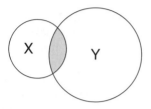

But where there's total inclusion we cannot reverse it. We can't argue that given all statisticians are mathematicians, then all mathematicians are statisticians. This would be a case of illicit conversion.

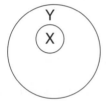

There are very few of us who haven't, on occasions, committed this error. In the middle of a discussion it's easy to assume that a universal statement about the subject equally makes a universal statement about the complement. A warning against this error is contained in the well-known proverb, 'All that glitters is not gold.'

Indeed, most forms of racism and discrimination begin with this mistake. Someone might hear or read about people being mugged in the street and every case appears to have been done by members of a certain ethnic group. So they come to the conclusion that all muggings are carried out by members of that group. Then they convert the generalisation, often without knowing it, and argue that all the members of that group are muggers. From arguing that all Xs are Ys, they conclude that all Ys are Xs.

So, there are two principles to remember:

1. Total exclusion is a convertible relation, whereas total inclusion is not.
2. Partial inclusion is convertible too.

> **Illicit conversion** – have I wrongly interchanged the subject and the complement?

Illicit obversion

Another common way of misusing premises is illicit obversion. Every proposition can be expressed in both a positive and negative way. The generalisation 'No golfers are non-competitive', is the same as saying 'All golfers are competitive'.

This form of the original proposition is known as the 'obverse' and the process of changing it is known as 'obversion'. However, in changing from the affirmative to the negative form it is easy to make a fairly common mistake and, as a result, to draw conclusions that are not justified. For example, from the generalisation that:

All golfers are competitive,

someone might conclude that:

All non-golfers are non-competitive.

Clearly this is invalid; it's an example of illicit obversion, as you can see from the Venn diagram below.

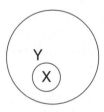

It doesn't necessarily follow that those who are excluded from the X class are also excluded from the Y class. The fact that someone is not a golfer doesn't mean they are non-competitive. There are many other sports, activities and occupations that call for people to be competitive if they are to be successful.

> **Illicit obversion** – have I wrongly assumed that not being one thing means you are not another?

Affirming the consequent and denying the antecedent

Finally, we come to just about the most common mistake we all make when we bring two ideas together to explain something. Without examining the following argument too closely, it might appear to be perfectly sensible and persuasive. As you can see, it is marked by the distinctive 'if/then' structure of a conditional or hypothetical proposition, but what's wrong with it?

> *Example: Management and employees.* If the employees of a business are involved in its management, then the business will flourish. But, since the employees in this business have no share in its management, it's not surprising that it hasn't flourished.

We might agree that people who are found to have taken performance enhancing drugs in sport (one idea) will be disqualified (another idea). So, we might argue:

> If an athlete is found to have taken performance enhancing drugs, then he will be disqualified.

The hypothetical proposition has two parts: the 'if' clause, known as the antecedent, and the 'then' clause, known as the consequent. In this case, if we were to use our hypothetical proposition as the major premise in an argument, we could argue:

1. If an athlete is found to have taken performance enhancing drugs, then he will be disqualified.
2. Stephen has been found to have taken performance enhancing drugs.
3. Therefore, he will be disqualified.

Affirming the antecedent

But there are two valid forms of this type of argument. The first, as you can see from this example, is to 'affirm the antecedent', in this case 'If an athlete is found to have taken performance enhancing drugs', which we affirmed in the second premise that 'Stephen has been found to have taken performance enhancing drugs.' Therefore, it was valid to conclude that '... he will be disqualified.'

Denying the consequent

The second valid form is to deny the consequent. Using our example again, the consequent of the hypothetical premise was '..., then he will be disqualified.' So, our argument will be valid if, in the second premise, we deny that Stephen was disqualified, and then conclude that therefore he has not been found to have taken performance enhancing drugs.

Two simple rules

There are, then, quite simple rules to obey. An argument is only valid if you affirm the antecedent or deny the consequent. Keep in mind the following simple table.

	Antecedent	Consequent
Valid	Affirm	Deny
Invalid	Deny	Affirm

As you can see, the fallacies we must avoid are to deny the antecedent and affirm the consequent.

Invalid forms:
1. to deny the antecedent.
2. to affirm the consequent.

Denying the antecedent

If we deny the antecedent, our argument takes the following invalid form:

1. If an athlete is found to have taken performance enhancing drugs, then he will be disqualified.
2. Stephen has not been found to have taken performance enhancing drugs.
3. Therefore, he will not be disqualified.

Clearly, this is invalid. Stephen may not have been found to have taken performance enhancing drugs, but this doesn't mean he will not be disqualified. He may have cheated in other ways.

Affirming the consequent

The other fallacy is to affirm the consequent, which produces equally inconclusive and invalid results:

1. If an athlete is found to have taken performance enhancing drugs, then he will be disqualified.
2. Stephen has been disqualified.
3. Therefore, he has been found to have taken performance enhancing drugs.

Again, Stephen could have been disqualified for many reasons; taking performance enhancing drugs is just one of them.

Necessary and sufficient conditions

One of the reasons many of us make these mistakes is that in the proposition 'If X, then Y', we confuse the claim that X is a sufficient condition for Y with the claim that it is the *only* sufficient and necessary condition. If something is 'sufficient' and 'necessary' for the occurrence of something else, no other alternative reasons need be sought. If we were wrongly to assume this, we would in effect confuse the hypothetical 'If X, then Y' with the proposition 'If, and only if, X, then Y.'

In Stephen's case we would in effect be arguing that 'If, and only if, an athlete is found to have taken performance enhancing drugs, then he will be disqualified.' This means that no other reason will count as justification for his disqualification. So, if he is disqualified, it can only be because he has taken banned drugs.

Hypothetical propositions – have I denied the antecedent or affirmed the consequent?

Example: Management and employees. This brings us back to the argument we started with. So, what was wrong with it? By now you will have realised that it commits the fallacy of denying the antecedent:

1. If the employees of a business are involved in its management, then the business will flourish.
2. The employees in this business have no share in its management.
3. Therefore it's not surprising that it hasn't flourished.

But, like Stephen's disqualification, although the employees have no share in the management of the business, this may be only one of a number of factors that have prevented it from flourishing. So, even if they had been involved, it might still not have flourished.

Still, you can see how tempting it is to accept the argument. What makes it superficially appealing is that we assume the involvement of the employees is both necessary and sufficient for the business to flourish. It is the only thing needed to ensure that the business flourishes. If this had been the case, then the argument would, indeed, have been valid. However, for this we would have had to argue instead, 'If, and only if, the employees of a business are involved in its management, then the business will flourish.'

Example: Sherlock Holmes. This mistake appears in a number of Arthur Conan Doyle's stories about Sherlock Holmes, who frequently takes great pains to convince the impressionable Doctor Watson and the hapless Inspector Lestrade that his success in detection is entirely due to his famed deductive method. In *The Boscombe Valley Mystery* Conan Doyle explains:

> It was about ten minutes before we regained our cab ... Holmes still carrying with him the stone which he had picked up in the wood.
> 'This may interest you, Lestrade,' he remarked, holding it out. 'The murder was done with it.'
> 'I see no marks.'
> 'There are none.'
> 'How do you know, then?'
> 'The grass was growing under it. It had only lain there a few days. There was no sign of a place whence it had been taken. It corresponds with the injuries.'[6]

The reasoning appears to have been as follows:

If the murder weapon was a heavy object, then we will find it with grass growing beneath it.
This stone was found with grass growing beneath it.
Therefore, this stone is the murder weapon.

Holmes assumed there was only one reason why the stone was lying there, recently discarded, with grass growing beneath it: the murderer had thrown it away as he escaped from the scene. In other words, he assumed:

> If, and only if, it was the murder weapon, then it would be found with grass growing beneath it.

But, although this is a *necessary* reason for thinking the stone is the murder weapon, it is not a *sufficient* reason: we can think of a number of other reasons which would explain its discovery just as well. A boy returning from school might have picked it up to see how far he could throw it, or it may have been dropped by a gardener who was collecting stones to build a wall or a rockery in his garden.

Checklist

In this chapter we've examined the way we connect our ideas by developing the relations between the component parts of our arguments. In the checklist below you'll see the most common problems listed so you can identify them easily whenever they appear in your own work or in the work of others. Like the other checklists, after you've used them a few times you will have prepared yourself to spot them routinely each time they appear without having to rely on the checklists. Even so, it helps to keep each of them near your work, just to refresh your awareness from time to time.

The connections:

Qualifiers: is the strength of my conclusion equal to the strength of my premises?

Distributing our terms: are the terms of my argument distributed in a way that will allow me to draw a conclusion? Is my generalisation a universal or a partial claim?

Processing our terms: do they mean more or less than they actually do? Do I conclude more or less than my premises will allow?

Conversion: do I draw conclusions that are not justified by interchanging the subject and the complement of a sentence when I shouldn't?

Obversion: do I draw conclusions that are not justified by making a mistake changing from the affirmative to the negative form?

Hypothetical propositions: have I denied the antecedent, or affirmed the consequent?

Conclusion

We began the last chapter by arguing that the distinguishing characteristic of intelligence is not what you know, but what you do with it: the ability to identify relevant connections and put together what ought to be conjoined. Neither logic nor critical thinking can help us in this: between them they cannot help us generate a single new idea. But they can help us decide which are worth retaining. In the next two chapters we will learn what's worth retaining as we use evidence in our inductive arguments and the problems we must avoid.

12
Thinking with Evidence 1: Describing It

The French writer André Malraux insists: 'It is not emotion that destroys a work of art, but the desire to demonstrate something.'[1] In the same way, it is not emotion that destroys good thinking, but the urge to establish a conclusion in harmony with it regardless of the evidence.

Inductive thinking

Now that we know how to avoid the problems in developing our arguments deductively, we can turn our attention to our inductive thinking. Here our concern is to draw sound conclusions from our evidence by making sure of two things: that our descriptions of the evidence we're using are accurate and then that we draw the right inferences from them.

Unfortunately, all too often, well-constructed arguments are rendered ineffective by the way we describe our evidence. Unless we're careful, it's easy to exaggerate or underestimate it, or generalise on the basis of untypical examples, or on insufficient or weighted evidence.

Generalising is the first step in any intellectual enquiry. Without it our understanding of the world would be limited to particular isolated facts. We would lose the security that comes from knowing that the world works with predictable regularity according to certain universal laws. But at times, particularly when our thinking is affected by strong emotions or when we have firm convictions about something, we do this badly and invalidate the conclusions we come to.

Untypical examples and insufficient or weighted evidence

Generalising on the basis of untypical examples or on insufficient or weighted evidence is, perhaps, the most common problem. It occurs frequently, as a result of three fairly common errors: we generalise from single or isolated instances, from selected instances, or just rely on unexamined assumptions or prejudices about what we think something should be like. We can easily avoid these errors by just asking ourselves three simple questions:

Three questions:

1. Is my generalisation based on a sufficient number of observed instances?
2. Do these instances represent a fair sample?
   2.1 Are they typical?
   2.2 Are there special conditions prevailing?
   2.3 Are there any exceptions?
3. What is the probability of such a generalisation being true? Does this make it reasonable to believe it *is* true?

Probability

Even when we've met the first two questions, we then have to consider how probable it is that such a generalisation could be true. We might claim that 'All heavier-than-air objects fall to the ground when unsupported', but we only have finite evidence for what is an infinite, universal claim. Every observed instance supports this, but we can never claim to have observed 'all' instances of it. A universal claim covers not just those instances in the past and present, but, of course, those in the future too.

So our claim must rest on our confidence that we have observed sufficient cases and that such a law being true seems highly probable. In subjects like history, anthropology, social sciences and in some natural sciences, where experiments cannot be done to demonstrate the reliability of such generalisations, we must take extra care to ensure this confidence is well-placed. The appearance of comets, supernovas and the decline and fall of civilisations are, after all, relatively rare events. But the same applies, probably even more so, in our business and professional lives, where we cannot conduct anything like a reliable experiment when it involves people's lives.

Exaggerating or underestimating evidence

As for exaggerating or underestimating our evidence in our descriptions of it, the most common mistake is to claim more than the evidence will allow.

1 All/some

Consciously or unconsciously we don't make enough effort to match the strength of our words to the strength of the evidence. We might claim something is 'always' the case when in fact it is only 'usually' so. We might argue, 'The bad weather always comes from the West', when in fact the most we can claim is that it 'usually' comes from the West. Qualifiers like 'usually', 'almost', 'seldom', 'hardly ever' are replaced by simple absolutes, like 'all', 'always', 'never' and 'none', even though there is rarely sufficient evidence to support such claims.

- Matching our words to the strength of the evidence
- Using simple absolutes carefully

1.1 Analytic propositions

In some circumstances and with some types of claim, of course, we are quite justified in using such simple absolutes, but their use is more restricted than we generally acknowledge. Either they're statements describing a particular known group of things: 'All of my friends are graduates', or 'All of the coins in my pocket were minted in 1974'; or they're trivially true, that is true by definition, by virtue of the meaning of their constituent parts.

For example, we would be quite justified in claiming that 'All bachelors are unmarried men', or 'All cats are animals', or 'All bicycles have two wheels', because this is what we mean by these terms. These sentences are true by virtue of what we agree to put into them in the first place. The fact that we agree the word 'bachelor' shall mean 'male' and 'unmarried' makes the statement true. In the same way when we unwrap the meaning of other words, like 'cat' or 'bicycle', we find that their meaning too links two or more characteristics in 'all' cases.

1.2 Empirical propositions

But aside from these analytic truths, we are faced with propositions that go beyond the meaning of their terms. In some of these, as we've just seen in the cases above, it is safe to use simple absolutes when our claim is about a particular known group of things, like our friends or the coins in our pockets. We can generalise that 'All the people in this room are male', or 'All the members of the party voted for Mr X', because the evidence for these claims is easy to verify.

However, most of the claims we make are not like this: they cannot be verified either by demonstrable fact or by analysis of the meaning of their constituent parts. They're claims like 'Nobody believes it's right to kill dolphins', 'Everybody agrees that terrorists should receive capital punishment', or 'At no time over the last seventy years has anybody seriously doubted the value of the automobile.'

Challenging each of these in the way we've suggested above, it's clear that there are exceptions. You need find only one person who believes dolphins should be killed, or that terrorists should be sentenced to life imprisonment, or that the automobile has damaged the quality of our lives, to have disproved them.

1.3 Choosing the right qualifier

Once we've avoided exaggerating our evidence through simple absolutes, we then have to choose carefully from the range of well-qualified words and phrases available to us.

> *Examples.* If we claim that 'usually bad weather comes from the West', we need to ask ourselves whether the evidence only supports the claim that 'some of the time' it does. If we argue 'very few people believe the public should not know that convicted paedophiles are living among them', does the evidence really support this or is the proportion just less than 50 per cent? If we use adjectives like 'probably' or 'likely', is the balance more like 50/50?

1.4 'Some' statements lose significance

There are very obvious reasons why we would much prefer to use the simple absolute 'all' in a statement. In the previous chapter we saw that, because categorical ('all') statements distribute their terms, we can draw conclusions from our premises. Equally important, once we use the word 'some', unless we establish how great this proportion is, the statement has at least lost a lot of its significance, if it hasn't actually become meaningless. 'All' statements are easily disproved: all we have to do is find one counter-example. So if a statement passes this test, it carries some significance. But 'some' statements are almost impossible to disprove and, therefore, carry little significance.

> *Example: Businessmen.* If we argue that 'Some businessmen treat their workers badly', there is little point in arguing about it. All we have to do is find two businessmen that treat their workers badly to have proved the statement to be true. But then it says very little, unless we can establish precisely how great the proportion is.

2 'Typical', 'normal', 'average'

2.1 Typical

As this suggests, the way to avoid these problems is to present the evidence on which the claim is based and describe it carefully, with as much precision as it allows. One way the media attempts to inject this sort of precision into its claims is to use adjectives, like 'typical', 'normal' and 'average', but, before you use them yourself, make sure what you mean by the 'typical homeowner', the 'normal family' or the 'average worker'.

> *Example: Journalists.* Journalists are fond of summing up whole cultures in an imaginary individual. They talk about the 'British worker', the 'American taxpayer' and the 'Australian farmer', as if they represent simple homogeneous groups whose values, aspirations, interests and needs are instantly known to us all.

But what are they typical of and how many don't conform to this stereotype? We may know someone is British and he or she works, but we may not know any more than that. So to use this to identify a certain sample of evidence, we must carefully qualify it.

> *Example: Pollsters.* The compilers of modern opinion polls go to the most elaborate lengths to create a representative sample of respondents to test current opinion. They ensure it not only covers all the main categories in sufficient numbers (incomes, educational qualifications, occupations, geographical spread, etc.), but that the appropriate weight is given to each category.

2.2. Averages

Even the more precise 'average' creates almost as much confusion. We have to be clear what we have in mind: mean, median or mode? In most cases we seem to imply the mean average (usually 'arithmetical mean', not 'simple mean'), calculated by adding up all the figures in a series and then dividing the total by the number of figures. In contrast, the median is the middle number in the series, while the mode is the most common figure among them.

> *Example: A teacher and exam results.* So, if you were a teacher and your students produced the following set of exam results, which would be the most useful average?

92%, 87, 86, 85, 84, 84, 82, 81, 81, 81, 81, 79, 76, 72, 70, 70, 70, 68, 65, 62, 59, 55, 53, 47, 43, 38, 26, 20, 14.

Mean: 65.9%
Median: 70%
Mode: 81

The mean average may be misleading, because it doesn't give us informa tion as to how the results are distributed. They may be clustered around the centre, or evenly distributed from the lowest mark to the highest, or an unrepresentative few at the top may pull up the mean average or a few at the bottom pull it down. If we were to use this to calculate the average income of inhabitants of many industrialised countries, we're liable to get a very false impression, because wealth is unevenly distributed.

Mean average	No information about the distribution

For this the mode average is more useful. When the range of distri- bution is considerable it represents the group better, because, as it identifies the item that occurs most frequently, it indicates the largest sub-group in the whole series. For this reason it is often regarded as the 'typical' representative of the series. In our everyday speech the aver- age usually means mode: the thing you are most likely to run into; the 'mode' or 'model person'. It's not affected by being pulled up or down by the extremes on one side or the other, like the mean average.

3 Statistics

One way of avoiding these problems should be to use the precision of statistics. But we all know how misleading these can be. As the Scottish poet Andrew Lang once said, at times they are used as a drunken man uses a lamppost – for support rather than illumination. Any of three common errors can be the cause of this: hidden qualifications, the lack of uniformity between different sets of statistics used for comparison, and confusion between absolute and comparative figures.

Statistics – three common errors:

1. Hidden qualifications.
2. Lack of uniformity between different sets.
3. Absolute vs. comparative figures.

3.1 Hidden qualifications

Perhaps the most common error, which can make an argument compelling when it least deserves to be, is the failure to reveal hidden qualifications.

> *Example: Crime statistics.* It may be reported that the annual crime statistics show an alarming increase in certain crimes, but it may not be pointed out that these are 'reported' crimes, which are likely to be inflated by factors outside the criminal justice system.

The improved availability of telephones may make it easier to report crimes that might otherwise have gone unreported. Insurance companies might change their policies, insisting that they will only pay out on loss or damage from certain crimes if the claim is accompanied by an official police report. The reported rates of some crimes, like rape and child abuse, go up when investigators adopt procedures which are more sensitive to the feelings of the victims. Others, like vandalism, seem to be understated because most people realise that the clear up rate is extremely low, so, they reason, there's not much point in reporting them.

> *Example: Breakfast cereal.* In a recent advertising campaign the makers of a popular breakfast cereal made the claim that 'Research shows that when they eat a cereal like ours kids are 9 per cent more alert.' To assess the reliability of this claim we need to know at least two things: the number of children involved in the study and any hidden assumption. In particular we need to know whether this just means that if children eat a breakfast *at all*, of any sort, then they will not be falling asleep at their desks. Having eaten something, their energy levels will be maintained so they can concentrate and perform better.

3.2 Lack of uniformity

We also need to know what was meant by 'alert' and how it was measured. As we argue for the broader issues, it's easy to take certain things for granted, believing that we all share the same assumptions about those things we're measuring. We might assume we all mean the same thing when we use words like 'stress' and 'depression', or that our perception of a problem matches everybody else's.

> *Example: Stress and breast cancer.*   Recently it was reported in the *British Medical Journal* that an 18-year study involving over 6500 women found that those with high levels of stress were 40 per cent less likely to develop breast cancer than those who described their stress as low. But another study, this one over 24 years, published in 2003, found that women who endured high levels of stress ran twice the risk.

Comparing the two studies, there seems no uniformity between what each describes as stress. It means different things to different people. It is also difficult to disentangle stress from other factors that may have a significant influence, like lifestyle, diet and family history of the disease. Even more, in the first study it may be that those who were better at reporting their stress levels were also better at noting other things that might lead to cancer and thus do something to lesson the danger. To evaluate both of these findings we must be able to compare them on the same basis.

3.3 Absolute and comparative figures

Our third problem, it would seem, is the most obvious and easy to avoid. But still, it's surprising how often we read reports in which simple totals are given to indicate trends over a certain period.

> *Example: Crime figures.*   Official figures might show what appears to be an alarming annual increase in crime, but unless we are also told how fast it has been growing in previous years and how fast the country's population is increasing, we have no way of knowing how significant this is. A more reliable indicator is the number of crimes per 100,000 people.

Figures like these showing ratios are safer indications of trends, although even these can be manipulated to suit the purposes of an advocate, who needs statistics, like the drunken man, for support rather than illumination.

Testing descriptions of evidence

So far we have examined the types of mistakes we're prone to make in describing our evidence, which could serious weaken our arguments. To avoid them the checklist at the end of this chapter will help you assess your work in a routine way so that you have a better chance of identifying them when they occur.

But still, once you've made your argument, it helps to have a technique composed of simple steps that you can work your way through routinely to test the descriptions of your evidence. What follows is just such a technique. It is made up of four-steps that will help you generate the sort of questions you need to ask, so you can decide whether a claim stands up, needs to be qualified, or should be abandoned altogether. You can follow each step on the structure below. If you run off a copy of this, it will help you incorporate it into your normal way of working.

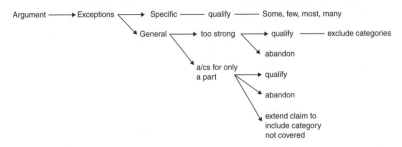

Testing descriptions

Step 1: Are there exceptions?

Even though you might have no obvious reason for doubting the argument, play devil's advocate: ask yourself, are there exceptions to it?

> *Example: A politician's argument about criminals.* A politician might argue that 'All criminals come from socially deprived backgrounds'. If we were to think of an exception to this we could argue that we've all read in the newspapers about convicted criminals, who, on the contrary, have come from quite privileged backgrounds.

Step 2: If there are exceptions, are they general or specific?

2.1 Specific exceptions

Next, if you can think of exceptions, decide whether they are general or specific.

> *Example: A politician's argument about criminals.*   If they are specific, then, while the politician can still retain her claim, you've found sufficient grounds to qualify it in order to take account of the special cases you've uncovered. If the exceptions were just limited to one or two individuals from privileged backgrounds, she would have to qualify the original claim.

2.2 General exceptions

However, if you have found a general category of exceptions, then you will have to move onto steps 3 and 4.

> *Example: A politician's argument about criminals.*   Say you've discovered that most white-collar and computer crime is, in fact, committed by criminals with university degrees. In this case the objection cannot be dealt with so easily: you will have to ask the following questions.

Step 3: Is the claim too strong?

If you've found a general category of exceptions, you must first ask yourself, does this make the original claim too strong, more than the evidence can support? If it does, the politician cannot maintain her claim: she must either rein it in, qualifying it in general terms, or abandon it altogether.

> *Example: A politician's argument about criminals.*   In our case the evidence can't support the claim, so, if she wants to maintain it, she must qualify it by excluding all white collar and computer crime. However, this might weaken and restrict it so much that it might be wiser to abandon it altogether, particularly when it leads you to suspect that you could probably find other groups, too, if you looked hard enough.

Step 4: Does it account for only part of the case?

Alternatively, if it can't be qualified, and there is sufficient merit in the argument to warrant not abandoning it, then the only thing she can do is extend the claim to cover the general category of cases that is currently excluded. However, if this is possible, it is quite likely to lead to conclusions she either didn't see in the first place, or wouldn't agree with on the basis of her argument so far.

> *Example: A politician's argument about criminals.* You might, for example, agree with the claim the politician has made, although question the notion that it is the 'socially' deprived who are the source of crime. You might argue that there are others responsible for crimes, who are deprived in different ways. They may never have been socially deprived, but they may not have had a stable father-figure in their lives: there may have been a family break-down, or they may have been moved from one boarding school to another without ever being able to establish long-lasting paternal relations.
>
> So, in this case the claim may be worth holding on to, but only in the extended form to cover this new category of deprivation. However, this may lead the politician either to conclusions she didn't foresee, or in a direction which doesn't serve the main purpose of her argument, which may have been to establish the claim that all crime can be identified with a particular social class.

Whichever is the outcome, whether you step off at steps 2, 3 or 4, you will have discovered for yourself that you have well thought out reasons for criticising the argument, and, if the argument is your own, you have uncovered ways of saving and improving it.

Checklist

In this chapter we have seen a number of common problems we all experience when we process our evidence into descriptions and generalisations.

Some, like generalising on the basis of insufficient or untypical samples, are often the result of our urge to establish a conclusion in harmony with strong emotions or prior commitments regardless of the evidence. We see at an early stage what we need to be true for our arguments to be convincing and this shapes our description of the evidence.

Others result from our failure to ask the right questions about descriptions. We uncritically accept terms, like 'typical', 'normal' and 'average', or statistics that on the surface seem convincing, but in reality are misleading.

The most common problems are listed in the checklist below.

Evidence – descriptions and generalisations:

1. Are my generalisations based on a sufficient number?
2. Are they a fair sample?
3. Is there a reasonable probability that they are true?
4. Have I used simple absolutes, like 'all', where other qualifiers, like 'some', would be more accurate?
5. Have I presented my evidence with enough precision?
6. Is it clear what I mean by 'typical', 'normal' and 'average'?
7. Have I chosen the right average to use: mean, median or mode?
8. Have I checked in the statistics I've used that,
    8.1 there are no hidden qualifications;
    8.2 there is uniformity between the comparisons I make;
    8.3 I have not confused absolute and comparative figures?

Conclusion

Many of our worst errors in describing evidence arise from the problem André Malraux identified at the start of this chapter. Our thinking can be hijacked by strong emotions and prior convictions that leave us unable to give accurate descriptions of the evidence. If we can avoid this and arrive at accurate descriptions, we place ourselves on firm foundations. Now we must learn to draw the right inferences from them. In the next two chapters we will see the sort of mistakes we can make and how to avoid them.

13
Thinking with Evidence 2: Drawing Relevant Inferences

With our evidence now accurately described we can safely begin to draw inferences from it. Of course, there are all sorts of inferences we can draw about all manner of things. Some are worthwhile, some not. The question is, how do we decide which are worthwhile?

Using analogies

The most natural thing to do is search for a close analogy. We assume that, because things resemble each other in some respects, they will continue to resemble each other in a further respect and this gives us our inference. So the key to understanding the implications of our evidence lies in the way we understand something familiar that is similar. Indeed, we learn to reason by such analogies long before we learn to reason using abstract concepts.

> *Example: Parables.* From an early age we're impressed by the power of parables to convey a moral message. They depend for their effectiveness upon our ability to see that one story or situation is similar in important respects to another.

By using what we know we can already rely on, analogies give us an invaluable way of extending our knowledge. The work of scientists illustrates this perfectly. Fruitful analogies have provided models and pictures out of which to construct scientific theories.

Example: Newton's theory of light.   The original molecular theory of matter pictured molecules, atoms and electrons as extremely small solid bodies moving about in space, behaving like billiard balls. This created a tangible bridge to everyday experience: we can touch billiard balls and observe them in motion. Given this analogy, Sir Isaac Newton argued in *Optiks* that light was composed of different sized molecules, each refracting at different angles as it passes through the denser medium of a glass prism to produce the spectrum of colours that make up white light.

Example: Darwin and natural selection.   Darwin, too, used the everyday analogy of the way botanists and the breeders of dogs, horses and pigeons bred from those they carefully selected to get the characteristics they wanted. He then wondered whether a similar thing had taken place on a much larger scale in nature.

Not only do analogies create an effective bridge with what we know, so that we can extend our knowledge, most are also remarkably persuasive, helping us clarify, simplify and make more vivid a complex idea. In this lies not just their power, but their capacity to mislead too. Not all analogies are so reliable: not all things alike in some way are alike in others.

Example: Business management and Darwinian theory.   Some business people use the analogy between competitive markets and Darwin's theory of the competitive struggle for survival in nature to justify their methods of doing business. Cut-throat economic competition, they argue, is the natural state of affairs and the rise to the top of the strongest is an inevitable law of nature. They describe their working lives as a jungle, in which they are continually engaged in a struggle with others for survival. Everything, they argue, is justified as long as it promotes survival.

But Darwin's theory of natural evolution is driven by blind forces that select from random mutations those characteristics that improve the chances of survival. Business, on the other hand, is driven by conscious intentions and nothing guarantees that this will result in the best run businesses surviving, while the worst lose out: it is just as likely that bad management will drive out good.

Analogies can only be a guide. Although we use them to *suggest* a conclusion, they are incapable of *establishing* one. We still need to test them against the evidence to find the causal connection. We can only safely argue from the possession of one set of characteristics to another when there is a causal connection between them and not just a vivid similarity.

Analogies can only *suggest*, not *establish*, a conclusion.

Therefore, if you use an analogy to draw your inferences, check the following three key points: the nature of the connection between the analogy and the explanation; the number of similarities involved; and the reliability of the relation between the analogy and the conclusion derived from it.

Analogies – check:

1. Connection:
   1.1 Causal connection.
   1.2 When does it break down?

2. Numbers:
   2.1 The number of samples used.
   2.2 The number and variety of characteristics thought to be similar.

3. Relation to the conclusion:
   3.1 Is it the right strength?
   3.2 How significant are the differences and similarities?

---

1 Connection

The first thing to check is whether the analogy establishes a causal connection and is not just a vivid way of presenting an idea. In Chapter 8 we found that, if I were to argue that the car crashed because I had dropped my pen, this wouldn't be convincing because there is simply nothing analogous between these two events: we know of no law or uniformity in our experience in which the dropping of pens causes cars to crash. For the analogy to work, there must be a credible causal connection. It could only have some chance of working if I could argue that light flashing off my falling pen somehow distracted the driver, because we do know of uniformities in our experience in which people have accidents when they are distracted.

But the second thing we need to ask is when does the analogy break down? They all have a tendency to at some point. A good thinker is always looking for the point at which this breakdown occurs.

Example: Newton's theory of light.   As we saw earlier, Newton used the analogy of billiard balls to explain the behaviour of light as molecules or particles. Although useful, it reached a point when it became clear that light behaves in ways the analogy cannot help us explain. Along with other electromagnetic radiation, it behaves like a wave motion when being propagated and like particles when interacting with matter. So, a conflicting theory appeared, modelled on a different analogy of light as waves travelling through an elastic medium.

2 Numbers

Up to a point, the number of samples we can find between which the analogy is thought to hold, the more confidence we are likely to have in it. The same is true of the number and variety of characteristics shared by the analogy and the actual situation. But problems arise when we ignore differences and push similarities beyond what is reasonable – the 'fallacy of false analogy'.

Example: The economy.   In the 1980s, in an effort to persuade us that cuts in government expenditure were unavoidable, some governments seized upon what seemed like a useful analogy, telling us that 'The economy is like a household budget', and we were simply spending beyond our means and getting into debt. But, despite their similarities, there were significant differences between the two. For one thing, what you spend in a household budget doesn't usually generate more income and jobs in the household, whereas in the national economy such investment not only can improve productivity, but can have significant multiplier effects, lifting economic activity, increasing revenue from direct and indirect taxes, and reducing welfare costs by taking more people into jobs.

3 Relation to the conclusion

Lastly, we have to be sure that the conclusion drawn from the analogy is of the right strength and takes into account all the significant similarities and differences between the analogy and the situation it helps to explain.

> *Example: Life on other planets.*   You might argue that there must be life on other planets in our solar system, after all, they are similar to Earth in so many ways: they revolve around the sun, their sole source of light; all are subject to gravitation; some revolve around their axis, giving them day and night like the Earth; and some have moons. With all these similarities, by analogy, it is reasonable to assume they must be inhabited too.
>
> But these are not the most relevant conditions we would look for in a planet that could sustain life. Among others, we would want to see a plentiful supply of water and for this we need the so-called 'Goldilocks zone': an orbit that is not too far from the sun, where water freezes, and not too close, where it boils, but just right. And, of course, we need a breathable atmosphere.

As we can see from this, once we have noted all the similarities and differences we must decide how significant they are and whether we've overlooked other conditions, which need to be considered to make the analogy safe. Usually, the greater the number of differences, the weaker is the conclusion.

> *Example: A newspaper report.*   A newspaper account of a speaker at a conference reported, 'He told the Conference last week that football hooliganism was exacerbated by press coverage. This was rather like blaming the Meteorological Office for bad weather.' It may indeed be true that in many cases newspaper reports had no influence on the activities of football hooligans at all, but the analogy the report uses differs in such significant and obvious ways as to make the argument untenable. As you can see, the key difference which weakens the argument is that the weather cannot be influenced in its behaviour as football hooligans can by reading press reports of them and their behaviour.

Questions:

1. Is the conclusion of the right strength?
2. Does is take into account all the similarities and differences?
3. How significant are these?
4. Have I overlooked conditions I need to take account of?

Creating causal connections

Once we're sure about the relevance of the analogy and how much weight we can place on it, we can begin to draw inferences. As we saw in Part 2, these can be either conceptual or causal. The conceptual inferences derive from the internal logic of a concept that links two or more ideas together. Checking the validity of these involves analysing how we use language, as we will see in Chapter 15. For now, our concern is for the causal connections we create to explain why a certain event or pattern of events occurred. These are often weakened by two common errors: drawing inferences that are irrelevant and unreliable.

Drawing irrelevant inferences

Our eagerness to defend a point of view to which we're committed often results in irrelevant inferences and arguments that we press into service to support our case. The technical name for this fallacy is *ignoratio elenchi* (ignoring the issue): we appear to strengthen our argument by proving another that is irrelevant to the issue. Instead of keeping to the point, we shift attention to a different question on which we feel a lot more confident. Of the number of forms this can take, the following are worth looking out for and avoiding:

Irrelevant inferences:

1. The person (*ad hominem* – to the man).
2. Popularity (*ad populum* – to the people).
3. Authority (*ad verecundiam*—to awe or reverence).
4. Fear (*ad baculum* – to fear).
5. The greater evil.
6. The counter-accusation (*tu quoque* – you're another).
7. The compromise.

---

1 The person

Often this takes the form of appeals to prejudices and emotions. In the argument *ad hominem* (to the man), the argument is sidestepped by discrediting the person who proposed it. Presenting supposedly damaging evidence against someone's motives, character or private life diverts attention from the argument to a subject which is more likely to stir prejudices.

> *Example: Political journalists.* Journalists may dig up material on the private life of politicians to criticise their effectiveness as political leaders. They may be condemned by innuendo or by associating with the wrong people.

> *Example: Female professionals.* The expertise of female politicians, executives and professionals has often been devalued by reports that refer to them using adjectives that turn the focus away from their ideas to their physical characteristics.

2 Popularity

The argument *ad populum* (to the people) is similar in that it deals with a difficult argument by appealing to the sentiments of popular opinion. It sidesteps or supports the argument by appealing to mass emotion, assuming that whatever the crowd thinks must be right. Rhetorical questions are a common way of making such appeals: 'Surely you agree that Mr X should be elected to the post?' They are designed to appeal to our like-minded attitudes and opinions.

They have built into them the expected answer. When they're successful they compel agreement on the grounds that failure to agree would place us on the other side of a vast body of opinion that thinks otherwise. So, whenever you begin a sentence with words like 'surely', 'plainly', 'clearly', which often introduce such appeals, ask yourself if you're really developing the argument, or just appealing to the like-mindedness of the reader.

3 Authority

The argument *ad verecundiam* (to awe or reverence) is a similar method of diverting attention, but this makes an appeal not to popular opinion, but to a prestigious or authoritative name or figure, a revered authority, even conventional propriety.

Of course, there's nothing wrong with appealing to legitimate authorities. The problem begins when we appeal to an authority that is not really an authority, or is not a relevant authority in the field that the argument is about. We should beware of giving or taking advice from someone who is being paid to give it, and we should remind ourselves that competence in one field doesn't necessarily transfer to another. Get into the habit of asking yourself these simple questions about the so-called authority:

Assessing authorities:
1. Does he know what he's talking about?
2. Are her views based on careful study or extensive experience?
3. Does her position offer her greater authority than others?
4. Has he shown himself to be a better observer and a shrewder judge than the rest of us?
5. What are his motives? Is he promoting his own self-interest?

Even when we're citing relevant authorities we need to ask who they are and do they have sufficient experience and a good reputation in this area.

4 Fear

This diversionary tactic works, of course, by reassuring people that they can trust your opinion because a well-known authority shares it too. But the opposite tactic works just as well. Rather than reassure someone that your argument can be trusted, you raise fears in them that your opponent's arguments cannot. This is known as the argument *ad baculum* (to fear): you deal with an opposing argument by evoking fear in others.

Example: The government and the opposition. A government that looks as if it is going to lose an election tells the electorate that the opposition has no experience of government and voters will experience all sorts of disasters if they are voted into power.

Example: Far right parties and immigration. Far right parties attempt to defeat the arguments for a relaxation of immigration rules by telling voters that their national culture will be diluted or 'swamped' by a huge influx of immigrants, leaving fewer jobs and homes for the rest.

5 The greater evil

A similar diversionary strategy is to discourage action against some admitted evil by citing an even greater evil, about which the original argument is not proposing to do anything. The fear of an even greater evil diverts attention away from the original evil, even though there is no good reason for not tackling both.

> *Example: A doctor and the risks of smoking.*   As a doctor you might argue that we should tackle the number of people dying from smoking related illnesses by raising the price of cigarettes to levels that would force people to give up. But then the opposition, whose interests would be badly affected by such a policy, might argue that more people die in road accidents, so if we are interested in saving lives, we should be tackling this instead.

The extreme flexibility of this makes it a very popular strategy. You can always find an even greater evil to something. But still, if Y is a greater evil than X, this is no reason for not tackling X; and, at the same time, it is a sound reason for working energetically to tackle Y.

6 The counter-accusation

A similar irrelevant diversion is the argument *tu quoque* (you're another), which occurs when someone replies to a charge made against them by making the same or similar charge against that person. A candidate running for office might respond to the accusation made by his opponent that the money for his campaign was obtained illegally, by launching a counter-accusation claiming that the money his opponent has obtained for *his* campaign was obtained illegally. Such an argument is described as fallacious because no relevant reason is given in answer to the initial charge.

7 The compromise

Finally, beware of the argument which is presented as a compromise between two undesirable extremes, so that anyone who refuses to accept it comes across as unreasonable. This exerts strong pressure on you to agree with the argument. And yet, almost any argument can be presented as a compromise between two others, so this alone doesn't mean there is good reason to accept it. The truth is just as likely to lie on one of the extremes as in the middle. Using this device, attention is diverted away from the strength or weakness of your argument and trained, instead, on its appearance as the most 'reasonable' compromise.

Checklist

Drawing relevant inferences:

Analogies – check:

1. Connection.
2. Numbers.
3. Relation to the conclusion.

Irrelevant inferences

1. The person (*ad hominem* – to the man).
2. Popularity (*ad populum* – to the people).
3. Authority (*ad verecundiam*—to awe or reverence).
4. Fear (*ad baculum* – to fear).
5. The greater evil.
6. The counter-accusation (*tu quoque* – you're another).
7. The compromise.

Conclusion

We began this chapter by pointing out how natural it is to use analogies for the basis of the inferences we draw. We learn the power of them from an early age listening to parables. But as naturally as we learn the tools and techniques of good thinking, we also learn bad habits. We use unreliable analogies, stretch them too far and draw irrelevant inferences from them. In the next chapter we will examine the bad habits that result in unreliable inferences and what we can do to avoid them.

14
Thinking with Evidence 3: Drawing Reliable Inferences

Now that we're sure our inferences are relevant, we can turn our attention to their reliability. As we draw inferences from our evidence, we must make sure the causal connections we make are sound – that they are neither oversimplified, nor invalid.

Oversimplifying

As we've seen, for much of our existence humans have survived by reacting to situations and problems in certain programmed ways that experience has shown to be effective for survival. By their nature they involve simple, routine reaction patterns, rather than the complex patterns of ideas that develop out of deep and sustained thought.

The danger, of course, is that when we are faced with complex problems that call for analytical and strategic thinking, we're likely to oversimplify the issues. Making decisions by limiting the number of issues we must consider is almost certain to produce the worst results. Yet we're all inclined to do this in a number of familiar ways.

Oversimplifying causal connections:

1. Stereotypes.
2. The straw man.
3. Special pleading.
4. Fallacy of false dilemma.

---

1 Stereotypes

Perhaps the most common way is to use a stereotype. In some circumstances, of course, these are justified, particularly if we're targeting an advertising campaign or managing police resources effectively to target a certain type of crime. Those that aren't are most often racial and social. It's easier to find a causal connection between two things if we restrict the factors involved to someone's membership of a particular group, about which we've made a few glib assumptions to help us understand the diversity of it. But such connections are very rarely reliable.

2 The straw man

Equally familiar is the fallacy of the straw man, committed when we oversimplify our description of a situation or a proposition, either deliberately or accidentally, so that we can dismiss it as false.

> *Example: A filmmaker and violent movies.*   After years of research, forensic psychologists have concluded that violence seen on movies, videos, computer games and television can make aggressive people more prone to violent crime. This suggests that governments should control the levels of violence that are seen, particularly by children. Responding to this prospect one filmmaker argued:
>
> > Does that mean that we mustn't have any villains in any film ever again? We must only have nice people doing nice things, because these already perverted and violent people, who should be in prison anyway, will identify with the villain? So we should only have films about flower-arranging?

The straw men in this argument are all too easy to find. It is clearly an oversimplification of the researchers' argument to say that they claim the only way we can control violence is by not having 'any' villains in 'any' film 'ever' again and that in future we can only have 'nice people doing nice things'. What's more, villains come in many different forms, not all are violent: some are burglars, some petty thieves, some are involved in fraud and so on. So to argue that no films should feature villains is not a consistent inference to draw from the researchers' arguments.

Similarly, the filmmaker draws the inference that the group the researchers describe as 'aggressive' are 'perverted and violent people'. In fact the group is much larger than this, including those who have had the misfortune to grow up within families where they witnessed violence, or were the victims of it, and learnt aggression as the only way of coping. And finally, just because a government might want to control the amount of violence, doesn't mean that we're right to infer that all movies thereafter must restrict themselves to flower-arranging.

To guard against this, ask yourself if you have accepted without analysis or justification any preconceptions. You might find the defence of these is now distorting your selection and interpretation of evidence.

3 Special pleading

The fallacy of special pleading is similar and just as easy to fall into when we are so convinced of our side of the argument that we're tempted to present just the evidence that supports our view, ignoring all that contradicts it. Alternatively, we can find ourselves doing this when we use an argument in one context, but refuse to use it in another where it would lead to an opposite conclusion.

Special pleading:
1. To present just the evidence that supports our view, ignoring all that contradicts it.
2. To use an argument in one context, but refuse to use it in another, where it leads to an opposite conclusion.

In practice, be aware of doing this particularly when you use generalisations in your arguments. This can take two forms:

1. We argue from a **specially qualified** case to a **generalised conclusion** that ignores the qualifications. In this way we can avoid having to consider all the characteristics of a particular case.

> *Example: Tattoo artists.* Officials in the health department of a large city in the USA decided to close down all tattoo parlours, because they believed that tattooing may be transmitting serum hepatitis directly into the bloodstream through dirty needles and dyes. They claimed to have traced over the previous three years 32 cases of hepatitis, including one death, which they believed were due to tattooing.
>
> In their defence one tattoo artist argued, 'I think tattoos do the city good. How many guys have the FBI caught from tattoos? How many people have we helped by covering up scars?'

2. The converse: we argue from the **unqualified statement** to a statement about a **special case**. In this form the fallacy consists in arguing that the circumstances are relevantly different when in fact they are not at all.

> *Example: Trickle down economics.* In the 1980s the supporters of the theory of 'Trickle down economics' – those in government, CEOs and heads of industry – criticised the high wage demands of workers on the grounds that they were over the rate of inflation, while they awarded themselves increases many times higher. Justification was sought by arguing that they were a special case, although, in fact, there appeared to be no relevant differences. They argued that as they spent their increased incomes, this would trickle down into the economy and generate jobs, even though workers could argue the same and in even greater numbers.

Special pleading – generalisations:

---

1. Qualified   ⟶   unqualified.

2. Unqualified ⟶   qualified.

3.1 Rationalisation

As you can see in these two examples, when we have a strong desire to believe something we set about assembling reasons and rational arguments for supposing the belief to be true. It is not the belief that follows from the reasons, but the reasons from the belief. And, of course, as we search around for the reasons we need to support our belief, we are selective in those we are prepared to use, omitting unfavourable, though relevant, points, which threaten our beliefs, even distorting the facts to make our arguments seem stronger.

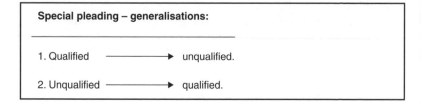

Desires ⟶ Belief ⟶ Reasons ⟶ Truth

3.2 Remedies

As you come across the different forms of special pleading in your own and other people's work, do one of three things. First, **compare** what is said by the same person at different times. Second, try to evaluate the **credentials** of those who make the claim – does it come from an interested party? And, third, for those arguments that omit relevant points and gloss over the omission using general, unspecific language with wide implications, get into the habit of asking those who make the claims to **specify** what they mean – ask them who, what, why and how?

> *Example: Breakfast cereal.*   In the case of the advertisement for the breakfast cereal that we referred to earlier, we need to know:
>
> 1. **Who** did the research?
> 2. **What** numbers were involved?
> 3. **Why** should the same effect not be found with a breakfast of any type?
> 4. **How** was the children's alertness measured?

Remedies:

1. Compare what is said by the same person at different times.
2. Credentials – does it come from an interested party?
3. Omitting relevant points – specify! Who? What? Why? How?

---

4 Fallacy of false dilemma

In the 'all-or-nothing' fallacy, or the fallacy of false dilemma, we assume that the problem we're dealing with has an either/or solution; that there are just two alternatives, when in fact there may be several. In political, religious and moral controversies, attempts are often made to convince us that there are only black and white choices available, although most of the decisions we make are not of this type.

Some of the most intractable international conflicts have only been resolved by a patient process, in which these simple alternatives have been rejected in favour of carefully negotiating step by step towards a solution that takes into account all sides of a very complex situation. So, when you find yourself presenting a case in these terms, ask yourself whether there are in fact more than these choices available.

Invalid causal connections

Equally serious are the inferences we draw from our evidence which create invalid causal connections. Like oversimplifying, they can seriously weaken our arguments by striking at the key elements of our solution to a problem. There are five ways in which we commonly do this.

Invalid causal connections:
1. The *post hoc* fallacy.
2. Cause/correlation.
3. Multiple causes.
4. Underlying causes.
5. The fallacy of false cause (*non-sequitur*).

---

1 The *post hoc* fallacy

Probably one of the most tempting is the *post hoc* fallacy (in fact, the *post hoc ergo propter hoc* fallacy – 'After this, therefore because of this'). This is the mistake of assuming that just because an event follows another, it must be caused by it. When we see two things regularly occur together, one after the other, we're inclined to associate them as cause and effect. In fact, so common is this mistake that, like analogies, it's the source of many of our most enduring superstitions. No doubt someone noticed often enough that walking under a ladder was followed by bad luck, so the superstition got started that the former was responsible for the latter.

> *Example: Economic depression and sunspots.* The economist W. Stanley Jevons noticed that in timing and duration the cyclic nature of economic depressions and the appearance of sunspots resembled each other with the former following the latter. From here it was a relatively short step to argue that the sunspot cycle was the cause of economic depressions.

2 Cause/correlation

A similar mistake occurs when we confuse a cause with a correlation.

> *Example: Crime.* In our attempt to explain the rise in violence in Western societies we might find that 80 per cent of all those convicted of violent offences regularly watch violent programmes on TV. Such a correlation is very persuasive, but is it any more than

this? Is it just a correlation or is it also the cause? We might find that 80 per cent of those convicted also chew gum, but we're less likely to believe that this is the cause.

So, prior to identifying such regularities, we must have something analogous between the two events, something that allows us to conclude that one might be the cause of the other. We know of no causal link between violence and chewing gum, so we probably wouldn't have looked for any correlation between the two, but we do have an idea how there might exist a causal link between violent programmes and violent behaviour.

3 Multiple causes

As this suggests, situations are often more complex than we imagine. It's a warning that for most events there are almost certainly many interrelated causes and not just one: the causes of the outbreak of the Second World War; the reasons why many students struggle with their study skills; or why house-martins are arriving three weeks earlier that they were ten years ago. A single cause is confirmed only if it *alone* can produce the effect, which is, in fact, much rarer than we like to believe.

Example: A doctor's diagnosis.   A doctor will ask a battery of questions to get at the causes of someone's heart attack. They will be carefully devised to search out evidence of the long-term causes (diet, lifestyle and genetic history), medium-term causes (controls over diet and cholesterol) and short-term causes (recent levels of stress, overwork and poor sleep patterns).

To assume that there is only one cause often oversimplifies the explanation, which frequently leads to the *post hoc* fallacy.

4 Underlying causes

Nevertheless, in some circumstances, where there appear to be multiple factors operating, there may either be an underlying cause explaining them all, or they may not be causally related at all. Take the first case: you may come across a situation where you find two conditions side by side, say, poverty and gambling. The obvious causal explanation is to argue that gambling causes poverty, but the person involved may be in a poorly paid, boring job, so he turns to gambling to inject a sense of excitement into his life. So gambling has not caused his poverty: they are, in fact, both the effect of the underlying problem of his poorly paid, boring job.

5 Fallacy of false cause

Alternatively, two or more factors may not be causally related at all: the fallacy of false cause (*non-sequitur* – 'does not follow'). Strictly speaking, we commit this fallacy when we draw a conclusion that doesn't follow logically from the premises. More loosely, it is basing a conclusion on insufficient, incorrect or irrelevant reasons.

> *Example: Stress and breast cancer.*   In the study which found that women with high levels of stress were 40 per cent less likely to develop breast cancer than those who described their stress as low, it could be that both stress and breast cancer are linked non-causally. It might be that the women who are better at reporting stress are also better at monitoring their health and responding promptly to lessen the danger of other unstated factors.

Checklist

> **Drawing reliable inferences:**
>
> **Oversimplifying causal connections**
>
> 1. Stereotypes.
> 2. The straw man.
> 3. Special pleading.
> 4. Fallacy of false dilemma.
>
> **Invalid causal connections**
>
> 1. The *post hoc* fallacy.
> 2. Cause/correlation.
> 3. Multiple causes.
> 4. Underlying causes.
> 5. The fallacy of false cause (*non-sequitur*).

Conclusion

Many of the problems we have examined in this chapter will no doubt be familiar. We have all used the most attention-grabbing stereotypes to advance our arguments, even though they simplify the problem. And there are few of us who can argue that we have never resorted to special pleading to present the evidence for our case in the strongest possible light. Others, like the *post hoc* fallacy and mistaking a correlation of factors for a cause, are mistakes that often slip beneath our radar unnoticed.

Now we must turn our attention to the inferences we draw when we use concepts and the problems that our use of language pose for the logic of our arguments.

15
Thinking with Language 1: Clarity

Writing is a form of thinking – the most difficult form. The effort of giving our ideas form in words and sentences is indispensable to clear thinking. It crystallises our ideas, giving them the sort of clarity and consistency they might not otherwise have had.

The underlying problem is the tension between the language we use and the logic of our arguments. We use language for many different purposes: to express our feelings, to influence the ideas, attitudes and actions of others, to establish social relations, and to communicate the conventions of the society and culture in which we live. Even as a vehicle for what seems the simplest of tasks, to communicate ideas and knowledge, it needs the flexibility to label not just concrete objects, but abstract qualities: different classes, distinctions, similarities, relations and combinations.

But such flexibility, the capacity of words to hold many shades of meaning, even different meanings altogether, is at odds with the logical consistency we need for clear thinking, which calls for sharp, clear and constant meanings. In this and the next chapter we will learn how to settle this conflict and meet the needs of both clarity and consistency in our thinking.

Clarity

The clarity of our ideas owes much to the way we use them. As we communicate with others we give them clearer shape and form. But many of us in our professional lives are inducted into ways of expressing our ideas that lead to obscurity, rather than clarity. We seem to assume that a simple style is a sign of a simple mind, whereas in fact it is the result of harder thinking and harder work.

Without this it can be like reading a foreign language. We have to translate it into simpler, more concrete language that makes contact with our own everyday experience. Indeed, in this lies the heart of the problem. In much of what we read there appears to be a determination to keep such vulgar sensibilities as our personal feelings at bay and to insulate what is said from the concrete details of everyday life. But without this, without creating a bridge to our normal lives, it is difficult, often impossible, to understand what's being said.

The answer lies in ridding our work of passive verbs, long generalised nouns and unnecessary jargon, and learning to write unpretentious prose that carries our ideas clearly, grounding them in the concrete reality of our lives. No matter how complex the subject, it can be expressed simply: there is no subject that cannot be made accessible in good, clear English. If you doubt this, just read any passage from Einstein's *Relativity: The Special and the General Theory*, or Bertrand Russell's *The Problems of Philosophy*. Each of them explains the most esoteric and difficult subjects, yet in a simple, elegant language that makes the most complex idea accessible to all.

1. A simple style is the result of harder thinking.
2. Passages that are insulated from concrete details of everyday life will be difficult to understand.
3. There is no subject so complex that it cannot be expressed simply.

Clear, unpretentious prose:

1. Short words.
2. Active verbs.
3. Concrete details of ordinary speech.

---

1 Jargon

There is no better way of exposing the gaps in our thinking than writing our ideas down. It's the most effective way of revealing what we don't know or understand, and where our thinking has broken down. The most common and effective way of concealing this is to resort to jargon and abstractions. Some professions have a poor reputation for this. Too busy to think seriously, people sidestep the effort and use jargon instead. Inevitably such poor thinking results in poor writing and readers are lost wondering what precisely it all means.

But still, a large part of professional life involves learning the language of our profession. So, how are we to distinguish between using jargon and a legitimate concept, which we can use with absolute clarity and precision?

Concept

A simple way of answering this is to say that a legitimate concept can always be analysed with clarity and precision into its parts, each of which can be expressed in language grounded in our everyday lives.

Jargon

Jargon is the language of specialists who have convinced themselves that their ideas cannot be expressed in any other way. A word that is merely jargon makes people feel like insiders, but, in fact, is quite meaningless.

1.1 Jargon Immunises ideas from criticism and evaluation

At times our use of jargon can seem like deliberate obfuscation in the hope that this will pass for depth and meaning.

> *Example: University teachers of English.*   In her account of her time studying English at a top US university, Helena Echlin describes the long sentences, received with awe and thoughtful silence, which sounded like English, but lacked all meaning:
>
>> The ode must traverse the problem of solipsism before it can approach participating in the unity which is no longer accessible.[1]
>
> As she says, 'How can one "traverse" a problem, or "participate" in a unity?' Indeed, how can you participate in something which is no longer accessible? Words are adorned with suffixes for no other reason than to make them seem more obscure and arcane: 'inert' becomes 'inertial', 'relation' becomes 'relationality' and 'technology' is substituted for 'method' as in the sentence,
>
>> Let's talk about the technology for the production of interiority.

Such obfuscation immunises the sense of what's being said from all evaluation and criticism. As Echlin says, 'Where there is no paraphrasable meaning, dissent is impossible, because there is no threshold for attack.'

But as writers we have an obligation to make sure our readers are comfortable with the words we use, not use them to impress them or make them feel excluded. We are not the gatekeepers to an exclusive club, in which only an esoteric language is spoken.

1.2 Cleaning up our language

We all have an obligation to clean up our language wherever we can to make it simple, elegant and accessible to all. One way of doing this is to reduce what you want to say to a logical sequence of clearly thought-out sentences. In this way you will reveal the gaps in your knowledge and reasoning. Where you don't understand something, except in terms of a sequence of jargon, break the jargon down into concrete words that ground your ideas in everyday reality. Rather than describe an educational initiative as a

communication facilitation skills development intervention,

a description in which no human activity has been allowed to intrude, translate it using concrete language of everyday reality, so that it reads a

programme to help people communicate better.

- Reduce what you want to say to a logical sequence of clearly thought-out sentences.
- Break the jargon down into concrete words that ground your ideas in everyday reality

2 Abstractions

Nevertheless, we use words in many different ways and not all of them have their meaning fixed by tying them to concrete things, so that we all know what we're referring to. From numerous, largely different, situations we take a common set of characteristics to form an abstract general concept. Having described a number of individuals as 'honest', we may then go on to another level of abstraction to talk about 'honesty'.

As the process continues there are different levels of abstraction. When we describe an object as white we ignore all its other attributes, but then, when we use the concept of whiteness, we take one further step into abstraction, omitting consideration of concrete objects altogether.

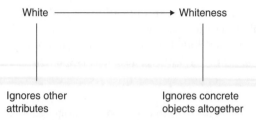

Ignores other attributes	Ignores concrete objects altogether

2.1 We use them as if they are real in themselves

These are powerful tools for thinking. They give us the means of creating significant relations between ideas that can generate the most
revealing insights, advancing our understanding of ourselves and the
world around us. But at times we trade in abstractions as if they are real
things in themselves and, because there is no object to which we can
relate them, we allow ourselves to give them the meaning we want
them to have. It's tempting to believe that because we see them in a
dictionary there are concrete referents by virtue of which they can be
defined. But in many cases there are no such referents; they are just
high-level abstractions.

> With no concrete referents we give them the meaning we want
> them to have.

2.2 We assume other people share the same meaning

And from there it's easy to take the next step and assume that when
we use them other people share the same meaning, even though the
referents of a word (if there are any) may be different from one person
to another and for one person in different situations. To talk of 'liberty'
or 'equality' is to know how having either will affect our lives in actual
terms in the society in which we live.

> **The two steps:**
> 1. We give them the meaning we want them to have.
> 2. We assume other people share the same meaning.

These two simple steps can result in meaningless, though very persuasive,
nonsense, like Helena Echlin's example: 'The ode must traverse the
problem of solipsism before it can approach participating in the unity
which is no longer accessible.'

Example: A physics teacher and postmodernism. In 1996, Alan Sokal, a physics teacher at New York University, was so outraged at the nonsense that some postmodernist thinkers were publishing about objectivity in science that he wrote a hoax paper which parodied the worst of these arguments. Despite the fact that his paper made no sense and was just built around quotes from these writers, his paper was published unchanged by a peer reviewed journal. He considered his biggest challenge was to write sufficiently incomprehensibly: 'I had to revise and revise to achieve the desired level of unclarity',[2] he explained.

In other cases, such nonsense is created with no intention of it having any objective meaning or cash value at all. Instead, the abstractions have just subjective value in their capacity to evoke certain emotional reactions. Political propaganda, speeches and editorials can be full of abstractions with not a concrete word in sight. Their aim is to evoke a certain type of response. The following passage is taken from the first issue of *The Freeman* a magazine for American conservatives:

In terms of current labels, *The Freeman* will be at once radical, liberal, conservative and reactionary. It will be radical because it will go to the root of questions. It will be liberal because it will stand for the maximum of individual liberty, for tolerance of all honest diversity of opinion, and for faith in the efficacy of solving our internal problems by discussion and reason rather than suppression and force. It will be conservative because it believes in conserving the great constructive achievements of the past. And it will be reactionary if that means reacting against ignorant and reckless efforts to destroy precisely what is most precious in our great economic, political and cultural heritage in the name of alleged 'progress'.[3]

There are no concrete words in this passage: no pronouns that indicate a particular person, no names, numbers or dates. With passages like this, that are full of abstract, general, metaphorical language, there is nothing to argue with. All that you read will prompt unanswered philosophical questions. If the author fails to address these, you are left with the conclusion that it all depends what he means by 'honest', 'constructive', 'ignorant' and all the rest.

2.3 *Our writing becomes heavy and difficult to understand*

What's more, passages with only abstract concepts in them – no people, no human agency – are heavy and ponderous. They are drained of all their vigour. Nouns denoting abstract concepts, like 'liberty', 'justice' and 'humanity', mean little until applied to concrete cases set in a particular cultural context. Good, clear, vigorous writing is specific and concrete. It is vivid, grounded in details we recognise from our own experience. In this way it makes contact with the humanity of the reader. Given a familiar picture they instantly recognise, readers know the meaning we want to convey.

- Good, clear, vigorous writing is specific and concrete.
- It makes contact through a familiar picture we all recognise.

What can we do?

Nevertheless, the answer is not to refuse to use abstractions or be suspicious of any argument that does. Isolated concrete facts are meaningless on their own without abstractions, generalisations and theories to make sense of them.

So, as you write, keep to the following three guidelines:

1 Balance.   Get the balance right between abstractions and the concrete details of everyday life that grounds them in our experience.

2 Distance.   Become more conscious as you use them of the distance they are from their concrete referents and the implications this may have for the reliability of the way you use them. Most abstractions have a fascinating appeal, legitimising arguments that we would otherwise question. Therefore, we must know their cash value. What difference would they make to our lives? How can we come to understand the way they work in our experience?

3 Move back and forth.   Get into the habit of moving back and forth between the abstractions and the things they represent. In this way you can assess whether you can use them reliably in all different contexts or whether there are limitations on their use which you should acknowledge.

It's easy to deceive ourselves into thinking that because we're familiar with a word and frequently use it, we're also familiar with the idea it represents and its implications. It's also easy to believe we're thinking when we're only stringing together words that have a warm familiarity. If, in fact, these words stand for nothing, then the passage makes no sense.

> **Routine questions:**
> 1. What is the cash value of what I'm saying?
> 2. What do these words stand for?
> 3. What is their objective meaning?
> 4. What difference would they make to our lives?
> 5. How can we come to understand the way they work in our experience?

Analyse abstractions and translate them into everyday language. We have to ask what difference they make to our lives: how will our readers come to understand the way they work in their experience. Above all, be constantly vigilant against the tendency to view abstractions as something in their own right.

> **Using abstractions:**
> 1. Get the balance right.
> 2. Be aware of the distance between them and their concrete referents.
> 3. Move back and forth between abstractions and the things they represent.

3 Loaded language

The underlying tension between language and the logic of our arguments is also revealed in our struggle to control our ideas to ensure we develop them in the direction we want them to go. Instead of us controlling our language, it is often language that controls us. Our thinking gets directed and structured without us being critically aware of it. Many of the words we use routinely are 'loaded': they carry more than what they mean descriptively. There is an emotional content or a value judgement, which manipulates our responses without us being conscious of it. In this way a writer can encourage us to accept her argument without us looking at it too closely.

> *Example: Spin.* A commentator, who wants to put a positive spin on someone refusing to budge on what he believes, might describe him as someone 'standing up for his principles', whereas another, who is not so sympathetic, might describe him as 'obstinate' or 'stubborn', perhaps even a 'hardliner'.

> *Example: Management and trade unions.*   In the 1980s the Glasgow University media group studied the way loaded language of this kind was used by the media to describe industrial disputes in the United Kingdom. They found that whereas management was invariably depicted as 'offering and pleading', workers 'demanded and threatened'. While the trade unions 'bullied', 'blackmailed' and 'intimidated', the government and employers were depicted as acting reasonably and responsibly.

What can we do?

To avoid this happening in your own writing, use the following four strategies:

1 Separate the ideas from the language.   Strip away emotionally charged language and unsubstantiated or irrelevant assumptions smuggled in without you realising it. If you then find that the situation is not as you normally describe it, ask yourself whether this is because the language you normally use has accustomed you to believe this, or if there is a substantive issue that has guided your judgement, which means there is good reason to think this way.

2 Reverse the description.   See if your attitudes change when you use the same language to describe the other side. If you find that such an account jars with what you believe to be the situation, then again ask yourself if it is the language that is leading you to believe this or if there is, indeed, a substantive issue that has influenced you.

> *Example: Management and trade unions.*   In this case one prominent left-wing politician reversed the language to show how manipulative this was. It resulted in a startlingly different account of the news in which workers 'offered to work for 15 per cent and pleaded with their management not to cut their living standards. Management demanded they worked for 2 per cent or 5 per cent and threatened to sack them if they did not accept that'.[4]

3 Translate.   Take the passage you suspect might be loaded and translate it into neutral terms so you can see whether the argument is then so convincing.

4 An adjective audit. Count the adjectives in the passage and then see whether any convey unsubstantiated attitudes, rather than a line of thought. Can you do without the adjective? Does it affect the meaning of the passage? Adjectives are easy to attach, but they are dangerous if they have no basis in fact and express an attitude almost unnoticed. They slip beneath the rational radar more easily than just about any other word. Try to tune your radar for them as you read a newspaper or listen to the news.

5 Three-step technique. If you're not sure whether a word does convey substance and genuinely develops a line of thought, use the 'Three-step technique' we learnt in Chapter 6 and analyse the word. Ask yourself, 'But what do I mean by X?' This will unfailingly get to the bottom of things. It may take you a little longer, but you will be left in no doubt as to what is happening when you use this word.

Loaded language – 5 strategies:
1. Separate the ideas from the language.
2. Reverse the description.
3. Translate into neutral terms.
4. Do an adjective audit.
5. Analyse the word.

---

4 Begging the question

But loaded language is only one way in which we lose control over the direction of our ideas as a result of being unclear about the implications of our words. The other way is through begging the question, which occurs when we accept as an assumption what we are arguing for as a conclusion. We manipulate ourselves and our readers without knowing, by smuggling into the premises the conclusion about to be deduced. Strictly speaking, this is what we know as arguing in a circle or, more familiarly, the fallacy of the vicious circle. We use a premise to prove a conclusion and then use the conclusion to prove the premise.

Begging the question	To accept as an assumption what we're arguing for as a conclusion.

Example: Business people.   A politician might make the following argument:

Ensuring that every business person has unrestricted freedom to pursue their individual interests must always be a good thing for the country, because it is in the interests of the community that each individual should enjoy complete liberty to maximise their own income.

But, as you can see, 'a good thing for the country' means 'in the interests of the community'; they are synonymous. The conclusion clearly repeats the reason or premise. So the very issue that is in dispute is begged. The argument, therefore, is only trivially true, as all examples of these arguments are. They are tautologies: the politician has so arranged things that her argument is true by definition and by no reference to anything outside it. And, of course, it's easy to persuade someone of anything if you're free to monopolise words and give them your own meaning. At best such an argument is useless: A in and of itself does not give us grounds for saying A is true.

Nevertheless, even though in this form it seems obvious, begging the question infects our thinking in various ways, so be alert to the following forms:

Begging the question:
1. Common notions.
2. Moral words.
3. Verbal propositions.
4. Vague definitions.

4.1 *Common notions*

We hear these so often that they tend to go unchallenged: sentences that begin 'Everyone knows that ...', 'It's common knowledge that ...', 'It's all too clear that ' or 'It's obvious that ...'. So, challenge them and ask what evidence there is for what they claim.

4.2 *Moral words*

Even more subtle are moral words, like 'goodwill', 'honesty', 'generosity', 'promise' and 'murder'. Their meaning embraces not just a description of the facts, but a value judgement too.

Example: Honesty. When we say of someone that they are very honest, we are not just making a simple statement of the facts, but also passing judgement on their behaviour. The word 'honest' means not just someone who has a strong sense of justice and treats others fairly, but also that it is a good thing to be honest and bad to be dishonest.

So to argue that 'Generosity is a good thing' or 'Murder is wrong' begs the question, because the conclusions are already contained in the words themselves – they are tautologies. Generosity is good and murder is wrong by definition, so the statement says nothing substantive; it does nothing but unwrap part of the definition of the word.

4.3 Verbal propositions

An interesting variant of this is the 'verbal proposition'.

Example: Social workers and teachers. If you are a social worker you might be challenged by someone who asserts, 'You must admit that too much help for single parents is a bad thing', or if you are a teacher someone might insist, 'You can't deny that giving students too much freedom in the classroom is not a good thing.' And you cannot avoid agreeing, not because giving help to single parents or freedom to students is in principle a bad thing, but simply because of the meaning of the phrase 'too much'.

This is just a verbal proposition, not a factual one: 'too much' means 'a quantity so great that it is a bad thing'. We are presented with a mere tautology, nothing more significant than 'X is X', which is trivially true and cannot be used to prove a fact. Too much of anything is a bad thing, so the real point at issue is what do we mean by too much freedom or too much help, and this gets us back to questions of fact.

4.4 Vague definitions

As you can see, some of the most common ways in which we beg the question develop out of the role of definitions in the argument, particularly when these are used in a vague way. If someone uses a vague definition, it is likely to contain all they need to develop their argument. Then, when they are challenged by an example that doesn't fit and they're pushed towards a precise meaning, they try to save their case by insisting that the example isn't a 'real' sportsperson, musician or whatever the argument is about. But, of course, when you stretch the meaning so far in this way to defend a certain point of view, the word ceases to do any real work and you end up making no point at all.

So, beware of people who ground their arguments in what they describe as 'the real sense of the word'. Such a distinction implying 'real' or 'unreal' senses is probably meaningless, or else an obvious attempt to beg the question in favour of some sense of the word that best suits their own argument. The same can be said of all those epithets that perform a similar function, words like 'true', 'sound', 'good', 'bad' and 'honest' as in the claim that 'All good musicians play many instruments.' Put them to the sword and ask, 'But what do you mean by X?': 'What do you mean by "good" musicians?'

Checklist

Clarity:
1. Jargon
2. Abstractions
2.1 Balance.
2.2 Distance.
2.3 Move back and forth.
3. Loaded language
3.1 Separate the ideas from language.
3.2 Reverse the description.
3.3 Translate.
3.4 An adjective check.
3.5 Three-step technique.
4. Begging the question
4.1 Common notions.
4.2 Moral words.
4.3 Verbal propositions.
4.4 Vague definitions.

Conclusion

We might think language is just the vehicle for our ideas, but, as we've seen, it is not without its own influence on those ideas. As perception shapes what we see, language can shape what we think. An idea converted into words takes on a different form than we intended. An argument put down on paper goes in a different direction than we expected. Wittgenstein argued that the role of the philosopher was to protect the truth against language.

Now that we've learnt how to do this by pinning down our meaning clearly, we must maintain it consistently throughout our arguments. In the next chapter we will learn how to recognise and deal with the problems this raises.

16
Thinking with Language 2: Consistency

As we develop our arguments, the way we move from one premise to another must be logically consistent. At times, even though we have taken great care to make sure of this, our efforts can be undermined by the flexibility of our language. And the more familiar we are with the terms we're using the less likely it is that we'll see the mistake.

Flexibility

Nevertheless, with some terms, insisting that we define them precisely can be an unreasonable demand. It might not reflect the complexity of the situation.

1 Opposites

With relatively simple classes of things, for which there are opposites, like 'mortal' and 'immortal', there is no problem. There's no common ground, just contradictories, so it's easy to define each one. But, for things to be opposites, they must comply with two logical laws: the Law of Contradiction and the Law of the Excluded Middle.

The Law of Contradiction simply says that A is not not-A; that something cannot be in the same sense A and not-A. The Law of the Excluded Middle says either A or not-A; that there is no middle ground – the two terms are mutually exclusive. The combined effect of these is that something has to be A or not-A and both of these are mutually exclusive.

| The Law of Contradiction | A is not not-A. |
| The Law of the Excluded Middle | Either A or not-A. |

2 Contraries

But there are many things that don't exclude their opposite. Instead, they include it as their most extreme form. These are 'contraries'. They represent the two extremes of a continuous series of changes. So, where the statement, 'This is white', has only one opposite – 'This is black' – it has many contraries including 'This is not white', 'This is coloured', 'This is grey', 'This is dirty' as well as, 'This is black.'

It's not difficult to think of many examples of things like this:

young and old
sane and insane
intelligent and unintelligent
religious and irreligious
civilised and uncivilised
good and bad

There is a real difference between each term, but we struggle to say with any certainty when a thing or person stops being one and becomes the other. There is no sharp dividing line, just a series of imperceptible degrees of change. If we call something white and another thing black, we have created a continuum of imperceptible changes, which stretch from white to black moving through many shades of white, grey and black. As a result, we are left wondering at what point white becomes grey and grey becomes black.

When we do need exact distinctions, as we do when we set speed limits, they are usually arbitrary. Drivers travelling at 30 mph probably cause just as much harm when they collide as those travelling at 31 mph. But still we set the speed limit at 30 mph in a built-up area, making one a legal speed and the other illegal.

3 Two common errors

Failure to recognise the difference between opposites and contraries is the source of two fairly common errors:

1. We demand a sharp distinction where none exist – we distinguish between the two extremes of a continuum as if all we have are opposites with a sharp dividing line.
2. We deny that there are differences between two things because they are at either end of a continuum and we cannot find a point where one ends and the other starts.

3.1 Demanding a sharp distinction where none exists

Someone might insist that you define precisely what is and what is not covered by a term you are using. In the process, they succeed in forcing you to accept a precise definition where none exists. In effect, they have forced you to apply the Law of Contradiction and the Law of the Excluded Middle in cases where only contraries are in question.

For example, you might be discussing an issue that raises the contraries 'sane' and 'insane'. Those who hold a different view to yours might mistake them for opposites and insist that you must be clear about the definition of the terms you are using, so you can identify the point where one becomes the other. Knowing how important it is for you to define your terms, you can easily be encouraged to search for a clear dividing line and use them as opposites, when in fact it is quite reasonable for you to hold your ground and treat them as contraries.

It is quite legitimate to resist the pressure to create clear and sharp definitions that are too precise to fit the facts they are intended to describe. It doesn't help our thinking to mark off something sharply, which is not sharply marked off in fact. All that we're likely to achieve by doing so is to substitute clear-cut abstractions for untidy facts. As a result, although we might have created arguments whose validity is plain to see, in the process we will have lost contact with those matters of fact about which we want to think effectively.

> Resist the pressure to substitute clear-cut abstractions for untidy facts.

Nevertheless, it's often assumed, misleadingly, that unless we are using precisely definable terms we cannot be arguing logically. But thinking logically is not simply confined to thinking about clear cut abstractions. We use all sorts of terms, some clear, others less clear, and all levels of probability in our premises, which must reflect accurately the substantive nature of what we are arguing about. For our arguments to be true, our terms and our premises must accurately reflect the strength and nature of the evidence.

Logical argument is not about the clarity of our terms, but about the way we connect our ideas and move from our premises to our conclusion. It means not making mistakes in our reasoning, not in what reasoning is about. We think logically when we reject contradictory statements and when we draw from our premises only that which they entail.

Resist the assumption that unless you have precisely defined terms you can't be arguing logically.

3.2 Denying there are differences between contraries

This brings us to the second error. In different circumstances those who are opposed to your views might insist that because you cannot find a precise point on a continuum at which one thing ends and another starts, there cannot be any difference between them. As we've seen, this is to confuse contraries with opposites. The fact that there might not be any perceptible difference in the accident rate when we drive at 30 mph as opposed to 31, and between 31 and 32, and so on right up to 70 mph, does not mean that there is no difference between driving at 30 and 70.

In *Thinking to Some Purpose*[1] Susan Stebbing asks the question, when is a man bald? Is it when he has no hair at all, or when he has just one hair, or perhaps 10 hairs, or as much as 100? If you were to say he is bald when he has 99 hairs, but not bald when he has 100, you have established a clear distinction. But we can go on adding one hair at a time making no perceptible difference until we've gone from a man with no hair to one with a full head of hair. Yet clearly, although there is no sharp dividing line, there is still a difference between the two.

Flexibility:
1. Opposites.
2. Contraries.
3. Two common errors:
   3.1 Demanding a sharp distinction where none exists.
   3.2 Denying there are differences between contraries.

Consistency

However, even though we may have to insist on arbitrary distinctions where there is only a continuum of imperceptible change, once we have done this we must stick to these distinctions and use our terms consistently. Often the most difficult errors to identify are the result of such inconsistency. The most common mistakes are the fallacies of equivocation and the fallacies of division and composition.

> **Consistency:**
> 1. The fallacy of equivocation.
> 2. The fallacies of division and composition.

1 The fallacy of equivocation

As we've seen, many of the words and expressions we commonly use have indefinite or changing meanings. When we use them in two or more different ways in the same argument, we commit the fallacy of equivocation, if that argument depends on the words maintaining constant meaning throughout. The argument itself may be valid, but we have no guarantee of its truth if the terms change their meaning in the course of it.

> *Example: Australian commercial.* An Australian advertisement promoting concern for the environment has the presenter surrounded by people planting trees. He is clutching a handful of soil, which he allows to fall gradually through his fingers, while he tells us that those who fought for this (holding up the soil), their land, in the two world wars would be deeply disappointed by our generation, if we fail to protect it.

Those who wrote the commercial clearly sought to play on our inattention in not seeing that there is a difference between the 'Land' that we fought for, and the 'land' as in soil. By 'Land' we mean our culture, values and heritage, indeed our whole way of life, which might be threatened by an invader. This is quite different from the soil in which we plant crops. Clearly, the persuasiveness of the argument rests on the equivocation of the concept 'land', which means different things at different stages in the argument.

> *Example: Advertising campaign.* A company might decide to promote its product by arguing that all citizens have a patriotic duty to protect their country from attack from other countries. This you agree with, but then they go on to argue that, therefore, you have a patriotic duty to buy home-manufactured products like theirs, because the country is under attack from foreign imports. Clearly, the persuasiveness of the argument rests on the equivocation of the concept 'attack', which means different things at different stages in the argument.

What can we do?

The remedy, of course, is to ask whether the definition of the term at one point of the argument is the same as in the other and, if it isn't, replacing the doubtful words with others. In the Australian advertisement, the word 'land' with a small 'l' should be replaced with 'soil', but then this would rob the advertisement of its persuasiveness. So, ask yourself the following questions:

Questions:
1. Does the persuasiveness of my argument depend on similar equivocation?
2. Have I been consistent in the way I've used words at different stages in my argument?

---

2 The fallacies of division and composition

Another equally common form of equivocation is found in the two fallacies of division and composition.

2.1 The fallacy of division

The fallacy of division is committed when someone argues that something, which is true only for the whole, is also true of its parts taken separately.

Example: Harvard and lawyers. You might argue that Harvard University produces the best lawyers in the country. So, John Smith, who recently got his degree from the University, must be an excellent lawyer. But although the lawyers of the best universities are generally excellent, to infer that any particular graduate is excellent merely because he attended one of these universities is not guaranteed to be a safe inference.

This fallacy can be found at the root of most forms of racism, in which someone is judged not on their own personal qualities, but by virtue of belonging to a certain ethnic group which is judged to possess certain characteristics. Still, in other situations we can argue quite validly that what is true of the whole is also true of the parts. I can argue that my computer is brand new, so all the parts are brand new.

The fallacies of division and composition:			
Division	whole	$\longrightarrow$	parts
Composition	parts	$\longrightarrow$	whole

2.2 The fallacy of composition

In contrast, as you would expect, the fallacy of composition is the converse of this: it is assumed that what is true of the part is also true of the whole.

> *Example: Football team.* You might argue that because your favourite football team is made up of the best players in the game it must be the best in the country. But the fact that you might have the best players in your team does not ensure that you will have the best team. It will certainly help, but there are other important factors, like how well the players harmonise as a team and learn to work together, complementing each other's style, so that each player is able to play to his or her strengths and get the best out of themselves.

Checklist

Consistency:
1. **Flexibility**
   1.1 Opposites.
   1.2 Contraries.
2. **Consistency**
   2.1 The Fallacy of Equivocation.
   2.2 The Fallacies of Division and Composition.

Conclusion

As we have worked through each part of this book, it won't have escaped your attention that we have in effect been describing a method composed of distinct stages. In the first part we generate our ideas on a problem, then we structure them and then work with these structures to design a solution. Finally, once we have our solution, we evaluate it critically to make sure there are no errors in our thinking. Developing the skills involved in each stage and routinely using the techniques and methods described will help us design more effective solutions and improve our decision-making.

Among the many areas in which all organisations and professionals must improve their problem solving and decision-making are ethical problems. Indeed, the way we relate to our employees, suppliers and customers, and our clients, students and patients, pose the most serious challenges to our thinking. Yet, despite their difficulty, these, too, can be solved using the same skills and techniques. In the next four chapters we will examine our moral thinking and work through different cases and problems to demonstrate the effectiveness of this method.

Part 5
Moral Thinking – A Case Study

Just about anyone today it seems can be called a professional. A window cleaner is a 'fenestration hygiene executive' with as much right to the epithet as a doctor or a lawyer. In some sports, competitors who feign an injury to get an undeserved penalty are sometimes described as acting like a true professional, as if their actions are, somehow, a fine example of the highest standards of their profession. So what exactly do we mean when we say someone is a professional or is acting professionally?

The concept of a professional grew from the idea that, unlike others, a professional is someone who 'professed' or promised to meet certain moral standards in their work. So, besides having particular expert knowledge, professionals are committed to a distinctive ideal of service, which imposes ethical obligations on them, to which other members of the community are not subject. It means they cannot just pursue their own self-interest without regard to the wider implications.

Of course, in some, notably the 'caring professions', moral thinking is centre stage. But then, the closer you look at *every* profession the clearer it is that none are free of the moral responsibility to take more into account than their own self-interest. And these are likely to pose the most difficult problems we face in our professional lives.

> *Example: Journalist.* As a journalist, should you break a confidence when somebody has said something to you strictly off the record, which could be the key to a major story? Should you reveal a source, when it might save someone's life?

> *Example: Engineer or architect.*   If you're an engineer or an archi-
> tect, how do you strike the balance between profits and public
> safety? And what moral responsibilities do you have for taking
> into account in your designs the concerns of the community
> about the environment? The code of ethics of the Institution of
> Engineers in Australia makes clear that,
>
> > The responsibility of engineers for the welfare, health and
> > safety of the community shall at all times come before their
> > responsibility to the profession, to sectional or private interests,
> > or to other engineers.[1]

No matter what your profession, your organisation or how you inter-
act with the public, you will have to find solutions to these difficult
ethical problems. But then, what about the business world? Here things
often seem quite different. There are many business people who are
reluctant to believe they have responsibilities for anything more than
the bottom line: their profits and shareholders. In the business world
the conflict between this distinctive ideal of service and self-interest is
clearly exposed. Indeed, the list of ethical issues it raises can at times
seem endless:

bribes, commissions and gifts;
whistleblowing;
misleading and deceptive marketing;
gender discrimination and sexual harassment;
privacy;
offensive advertising;
environmental protection, including climate change;
affirmative actions and preferential treatment;
and many more.

But, at the same time, the argument that there should be no ethical
limits, that anything goes, seems to ignore the reality that it is in the
interests of all organisations, including businesses, to attend to ethics.
The evidence appears to suggest that high-ethics organisations are simply
better at what they do.

Mark Pastin argues that the most effective companies are those that
have weak cultures and strong ethics. The culture of a company is the

historically created rules and conventions that explicitly or implicitly act as a guide to the way things should be done. Pastin explains that cultures are often irrational and always conservative: they judge the future by the past. But for a company to respond creatively to change it must be able to learn, to question what seems unquestionable. As Pastin says,

> unquestionables must be questioned for an organisation to be quick on its feet, strategic, and just plain smart. Because cultures are rooted in tradition, they reflect what *has* worked, not what *will* work ...[2] For a culture to persist and serve those who work and play in it, the culture must *learn*. It must allow challenges to its basic principles in a setting that tolerates some change without threatening to undo the culture. [3]

There is a lesson in this, he insists: 'If you want to change the culture of your organisation, start discussing ethics.'[4] The most successful companies get ethics right, particularly in an age where their major assets are intellectual: the skills, imagination and creativity of their employees. Without these the organisation cannot learn and make the changes it needs to be successful.

But the problem that all organisations face is that they struggle to keep these assets without discussing ethics. Charles Handy warns that, as the value of these assets increase through experience and training, they become more attractive targets in the employment market to be prized away by competitors. As employees are now their most important assets, companies can no longer control their assets as they used to: they control themselves. Those who possess and control the means of production are no longer the capitalists, but the workers, and nothing can prevent them taking their skills elsewhere.[5]

So the problem faced by modern organisations is how to strengthen the loyalty of their employees so they don't take their skills elsewhere. The answer is to become more ethical employers. The more workers feel they can trust management to treat them well, to make sure they receive the credit and rewards they deserve for their hard work and creativity, the more they are likely to be loyal to the organisation and contribute without reservation to its progress. Otherwise, if they suspect the organisation is not treating them fairly, they are more likely to pursue their own agenda, getting as much out of the organisation as possible to reflect what they believe to be the value of their contribution, while looking around for better opportunities elsewhere.

Trust is the key to high productivity and to employees' willingness to make the changes necessary if the company is to do well. The business consultant Robert Levering argues that when employees say they have a great workplace, they mean three things: 'you trust the people you work for, have pride in what you do, and enjoy the people you work with.'[6] But in turn, trust depends upon whether employees believe the employer respects them, whether they think the employer is fair and credible.

So, business, like any profession, depends for its success on getting ethics right, and not just in its dealings with employees, but with customers and suppliers too. Business scandals and recessions tend to clarify our thinking about these issues. The Enron and WorldCom scandals made us more aware of the consequences for workers, consumers and the wider community of unrestrained pursuit of self-interest, after the 'Greed is good' ethics of the 1980s. Now, the worldwide recession, triggered by loosely regulated financial markets and the generous bonuses that drew bankers into ever more risky business, may have left us more willing to surrender our belief that self-regulating markets and the primal drive to maximise our self-interest are superior to good thinking.

17
Moral Thinking 1: Generating Ideas

It is not uncommon to believe that morality is all about individual opinion; that there is nothing objective or absolute about it to which we can appeal to arbitrate between conflicting views. It's just a matter of individual opinion, a matter of taste. We are all just committed to our own particular values.

However, these and similar views disguise the fact that moral thinking is no different from any other form of thinking: that we can simply do it badly and make mistakes. If you look at it closely, you will see many of the weaknesses we identified in Part 4. We tend to be dogmatic, to see moral stereotypes everywhere, to appeal to authorities whenever we are without a reasoned justification for our view, and we are often quick to pass judgement. So, it is as important to learn to think morally as it is to learn to think logically or mathematically.

In what follows you will see that moral thinking is not a matter of entrenching our own principles and values, but about the nature of moral reasoning and the skills we need to develop in order to do it better – the same skills we have seen in previous chapters. As in any form of reasoning, we can use these skills well or badly. We can learn to do it better and avoid the mistakes we usually make. So, we need to understand the process and develop our skills.

Generating moral facts

First, we must generate all the facts, using the same strategy we learnt in Chapter 3. There we examined problems from the different perspectives of all those involved and on different levels. The key to this is to remember we are not concerned with general moral issues – whether bribery can ever be condoned in business or whether those suffering from self-inflicted illnesses, like smoking, should be placed further down the queue for hospital treatment – nor are we concerned with moral principles that tell us we can never condone lying or breaking promises. Our concern is simply to gather the facts about just this situation as seen from the perspective of all those involved. It's a bottom-up strategy. In this situation, how would you be affected? What would be your preferences, interests and needs?

> What are the preferences, interests and needs from the perspectives of all those involved?

Two rules

You will find it helpful to keep two simple rules in mind. First, postpone all criticism. As you record your ideas you may already see that they conflict with others you have recorded from a different perspective. For the moment ignore this. Your concern is to compile as complete a picture as possible. Even though, later, you may have to compromise on some things, perhaps dropping them altogether, you must list all those things you think are important.

The second rule is related to the first: quantity is important. As you explore the situation from the perspective of each person, remind yourself there is no upper limit to the number of issues you list. Your aim is to compile an exhaustive account of all the issues from each person's perspective without criticising, evaluating and excluding any.

> **Two rules:**
> 1. Postpone all criticism.
> 2. Quantity is important – there is no upper limit to the issues you list.

Perspectives

As we saw in Chapter 3, generating ideas in this way involves approaching the problem from different perspectives, each explored on different levels. The first step, then, is to list all those people who affect and are affected by the particular situation – all the stakeholders.

> **Perspectives:** All the stakeholders: those who affect or are affected by the situation.

List the different perspectives of those involved in the following problem.

> *Example: Assistant manager of a chain store.* I was working for a discount chain store that was expanding very rapidly. I was the assistant manager for a new store that was opening in the suburbs of Richmond, Virginia. There is an awful lot of work to be done in opening a new store; you have to order the merchandise, and when it comes in you have to check it off against the right orders, put it in the right racks and on the right shelves, add the right price tags, and generally keep things organised despite the chaos of last-minute construction and cleaning. I was helped by five really good people, who had been convinced to move from other stores in the chain because this was billed as a 'training program' for management. We worked long hours. We got the job done. One week after the store opened, I was told to find a reason to fire three of them because 'we only have room for two trainees'. When I objected I was told, 'Hey, there's no problem. They can go back to the jobs they came from.'[1]

As you can see, if we assume that the assistant manager's boss represents the company and its shareholders, the perspectives involved are:

Assistant manager
The three trainees to be fired
The two trainees to be retained
The assistant manager's boss

Now that we've listed them, we need to take each one in turn and put ourselves in their position and ask how we would be affected in terms of our preferences, interests and needs.

Levels

This will give us the different levels in terms of the different types of normative issue that we think is involved. Some of these reflect our concerns about justice – a sense of fairness; others are about what we believe we have a right to; others are about values we think ought to be respected; then there are the virtues we think it is important to promote; and, finally, there are the harmful consequences we believe we should avoid or the good consequences that we should bring about.

Levels	Different types of normative issue:
	1. justice
	2. rights
	3. values
	4. virtues
	5. consequences.

Trigger questions – the ideas generator

In the ideas generator below, the list of trigger questions for each normative issue will help you work your way through each of them. But these are not exhaustive lists. Like all trigger questions, you will think of more, while you adapt those on the list to reflect the sort of concerns you regularly confront. As we discovered in Chapter 3, most creative thinkers are constantly refining and adapting their routine trigger questions, adding new ones they might hear elsewhere. So, as you think of different ones, add them for future occasions.

As this suggests, many of these questions will not be relevant to every problem you have to tackle. They are designed to get you to think about the problem on different levels, so you can trigger off ideas you might not otherwise have considered. Nevertheless, once you have exhausted your thoughts check through the structure to see if you have overlooked anything.

Additional questions

On the structure you will see that there are two additional questions: one on non-interference and the other on special obligations. It's important to ask yourself at the outset what would happen if you were just to do nothing. Would you find this acceptable? In some situations it might be better not to interfere and let those involved work the problem out for themselves.

As for special obligations, in some professions our relationships with others are structured by certain obligations that are unique to that profession. Doctors must respect the privacy of patients. Journalists must respect the anonymity of their sources or opinion expressed off the record. Lawyers' conversations with their clients are privileged.

More broadly, in business employees are reminded that the customer is always right and a company has particular obligations to its shareholders. It will also have obligations to the local community in which its operations are based. It will know that it must respect the local environment, so that it doesn't pollute the atmosphere or local streams and rivers, or make traffic congestion impossibly heavy in local towns and villages. It will also be aware that it has a responsibility for the impact it has on the local economy.

In the example above of the assistant manager in the chain store, we would take each of the four perspectives in turn and work through the questions listed under the five types of normative issue. Taking just the assistant manager and the three trainees who are to be fired, this is what we might produce.

Example: The assistant manager.	
Justice	I should not be treated unfairly in this way.
Rights	I have been denied the right to know it was the intention of the company to fire these three from the start.
Values	My freedom of choice is being restricted.
	I am being manipulated.
	No respect is being shown to me as an individual.
Virtues	This is likely to weaken my sense of personal responsibility.
	It fails to reward me for my hard work.
	I am likely to be less willing to put myself out for the company in the future.
Consequences	Direct: This will diminish my sense of job fulfilment.
	Direct: It will weaken my sense of self-esteem.

The ideas generator – normative issues

Non-interference: What would happen if I just did nothing, if I let the problem sort itself out? Is this acceptable?

Justice	Rights	Values	Virtues	Consequences	
				Direct	Indirect
1. Have I been treated unfairly compared with others?	1. Does the proposed action reduce the choices I can make in the future?	1. What would be the effects on the wider social, economic and cultural values in society?	1. Will this make us less self-reliant?	1. Are those directly affected likely to be happier as a result?	1. What are the likely consequences for those not directly affected?
2. Do I have fewer opportunities than others in similar positions?	2. Has my privacy been invaded?	2. Is the value I place on my own well-being threatened?	2. Does it promote more or less personal responsibility?	2. Is their well-being threatened?	2. Do the disadvantaged benefit?
3. Is there a fair distribution of the costs and benefits?	3. Am I being denied my right to know?	3. Does the proposed action go against market values or democratic principles?	3. Does it reward people for their hardwork?	3. Will they suffer more? If so, in what way?	3. How are those, like doctors and nurses, who have to carry out the decision, affected by it?
4. Am I being punished for something I didn't do?	4. Am I being denied my freedom of expression?	4. Is it likely to result in too much government interference?	4. Is it likely to promote a spirit of co-operation and community?	4. Is it more likely that their chances of fulfilment will be diminished?	4. How does it affect the family and friends?

5. Have I been given a fair hearing?	5. Is my safety or my life being jeopardised?	5. Is the individual's choice being restricted?	5. Will it promote more sensitivity and compassion for others?	5. How will it affect their sense of self-esteem?	5. Are there substantial benefits or costs to the community?
6. Am I being given fair compensation for the harm done to me?	6. Is my right to a clean environment being threatened?	6. Are we being manipulated rather than being appealed to on the basis of reason?	6. Does it reward honesty and straight dealing?		6. What will be the wider effects on society?
7. Is any group unfairly penalised?	7. Am I or my family being denied education or affordable healthcare?	7. Does the situation reflect a poor respect for others?	7. Is it likely to foster respect for others?		
	8. Is the public's right to safety being threatened?	8. Does it threaten important traditions?	8. Will it increase or decrease the willingness of others to contribute to society and social welfare?		
	9. Have I had any of my rights ignored?				

Special obligations: Are there any special obligations owed to those directly and indirectly affected: managers, workers, customers, clients, patients, students, suppliers, distributors, shareholders and the community?

Example: The three trainees to be fired.	
Justice	I should not be treated unfairly compared with others.
Rights	I have a right to know the real reason for my dismissal.
Values	The proposed action goes against the value we place on equal opportunity.
	I am being manipulated to suit the needs of the company.
	No respect is being shown for me as an individual.
Virtues	It doesn't reward me for my hard work.
	It is likely to weaken management's willingness to show sensitivity and compassion in the future.
	It will tend to promote dishonesty and a lack of straight dealing with employees.
	It will weaken the willingness of other employees to co-operate and contribute to the company's well-being.
Consequences	Direct: I will be less happy and fulfilled as a result.
	Direct: My sense of self-esteem will be badly damaged.

Empathy and imagination

The ideas generator helps us cope with that sense of confusion when we first embark on such a new and open-ended task. Thinking about a problem from different perspectives beyond our own and on different levels is not something we do easily. As we have seen in previous chapters, our routine patterns of thought and behaviour can leave us blinkered to these other perspectives. We are so used to thinking in one particular way that we find it difficult to change our perspectives and approach a problem as others would approach it.

But to be successful all professionals have to develop the habit of empathising with others, vicariously experiencing what others in a particular situation might feel, believe or prefer. Conducting this sort of mental experiment must become routine. Take the following example and place yourself in the position of the social worker, who is, in turn, empathising with a potential client who presents her with a problem that most of us will have never experienced.

> *Example: Suzanne and the social worker.*   The Beeton Community Health Authority has been running a series of workshops on building self-esteem and confidence. One of the issues raised in the group discussion is domestic violence. Following the meeting a young woman, Suzanne, comes to see you, the social worker.
>
> Suzanne is in a wheelchair. She tells you that she enjoyed the meeting, but would like to talk to you about the person who helps with her attendant care. She feels extremely uncomfortable with this person and says she sometimes feels afraid. She says she feels that she cannot complain, because she is already lucky to have someone coming to her house at all. She understands there is a waiting list for attendant care and many of her friends are unable to get any support hours at all. She is worried that if she complains she might lose the small amount of assistance she has.
>
> She tells you that since she has been able to access attendant care she has been able to live on her own and has now begun a college training course. She is concerned that if she loses her attendant care, she may have to return home to live with her parents. They have been extremely protective of her and she says she thinks it will reinforce their view that she cannot live independently.[2]

In this case the perspectives we need to explore are significantly different:

Suzanne
The Community service
The attendant
The social worker
Suzanne's parents

Each one presents its own unique challenges. In Suzanne's case we would probably argue that

she should be free from harm and the fear of harm;
she should be able to have her independence and build up her self-esteem and confidence;
she should have the same opportunities to educate herself as others;

she should have the opportunity to have her concerns listened to by
   those in authority;
she should not be intimidated into not complaining.

As you can see, each one is phrased in terms of what we think 'should'
or 'shouldn't' happen to us in these circumstances. But not all the issues
are of this form. From the Community service perspective we are likely
to argue that

they have a responsibility to deal with these fears in a thorough and
   sensitive manner;
they have a responsibility to ensure clients are not harmed;
they should investigate the problems impartially without seeking
   retribution or to protect staff if they have acted badly.

The complete picture from the perspective of each stakeholder might
look like the list of normative issues in the table below. Of course, you
may see more, or just different, issues than I have.

Stakeholder	Normative issues
Attendant	1. Her views should be heard before any decision is made.
	2. She should know what is being said about her.
	3. She should not lose her job or chances of promotion if the allegations are unproved.
	4. She should be sensitive to the feelings of others.
You (the social worker)	1. Should take up Suzanne's concerns with management as confidentially as possible.
	2. Should offer to talk with parents with an objective assessment of her ability to cope independently.
Parents	1. Should provide Suzanne support.
	2. Should respect her independence.
Suzanne	1. Should be free from harm and the fear of it.
	2. Should be able to have her independence and build up her self-esteem and confidence.
	3. Should have equal opportunity for education.
	4. Should have the opportunity to have her concerns heard.
	5. Should not be intimidated into not complaining.
Community service	1. Have a responsibility to deal with these fears in a thorough and sensitive manner.
	2. And to ensure clients are not harmed.
	3. Should investigate the problems impartially without a desire for retribution or to protect staff if they've acted badly.

Universalism

Empathising in this way is also essential in meeting one of the defining characteristics of moral thinking. When we come to our moral judgements, we must make sure they are universalisable. As in logical thinking, our moral thinking must comply with the rules of consistency: we must be able to universalise our behaviour and the moral judgements we reach. I must be able to approve of an action or decision irrespective of the part I play, whether I am the perpetrator or the subject of it and whether I gain or lose as a consequence.

This means, as we have found, that we must be able to put ourselves in the position of those affected by our decisions; vicariously experience what they are experiencing with their preferences, interests and needs; and approve of the same thing being done to us. This is the Golden Rule, so familiar to us all regardless of our beliefs or culture: 'Do unto others as you would have them do unto you.'

The eighteenth-century German philosopher Immanuel Kant famously encapsulated this in his 'categorical imperative':

> Act only on that maxim through which you can at the same time will that it should become a universal law.[3]

In other words, I must want all people (including myself) finding themselves in similar circumstances to act in accordance with the same rule. Every action should be judged in the light of how it would appear if it were to be a universal code of behaviour. It should not be based on subjective feelings or inclinations but conform to a law given by reason – a universal law, the categorical imperative. To think morally is to think objectively, beyond our own interests and feelings.

We must put ourselves in the position of those affected by our decision and approve of the same thing being done to us.

In our professional lives, it is quite common to be confronted by problems that raise just these issues. The following might be typical:

Example: Finance director. You are a finance director of a small company, which was founded just a year ago. The owner is someone who makes quick intuitive decisions, relying on his own judgement alone. This seems to have worked because the company has attracted experienced staff and is doing well. Now, one of the sales people has pulled off a big order and the owner wants to make a generous incentive payment to encourage others. But you see the problem with this in that it sets a precedent, which cannot be repeated every time someone gets a big order, and it puts a strain on relations with others, like the head of production, who works just as hard, but gets no similar reward. You clearly want to encourage people, but not without these and similar problems.

Does and don'ts

Unfortunately we have very few good models of moral thinking to draw upon, so it is easy to fall into certain routine habits of thought, which side-step the need to generate our own ideas freely in this way. So, in addition to the 'does' – 'Postpone all criticism' and 'Quantity is important' – we must identify the 'don'ts' that would otherwise sabotage our attempts to generate our ideas.

Does	Don'ts
1. Postpone all criticism.	1. Relativism.
2. Quantity is important.	2. Appeals to authority.
	3. Stereotypes.
	4. Rationalisation.

As you can see, the key to this stage of moral thinking is the quantity of ideas we can produce to create a complete picture of the situation. For this reason the two simple rules we began with are important. But for the same reason we should strive to avoid two other things which are different sides of the same coin: relativism and appeals to authority.

1 Relativism

One way of side-stepping the demands made upon us by the sort of open-ended thinking involved in generating ideas is just to argue that all values are relative: they are the products of different social and cultural influences and, therefore, as all values are equally valid, there is no way of arbitrating between them.

But in terms of our normative values, this merely explains how we *come by* them; it doesn't address the question of whether we are using our moral thinking skills well: whether we are arguing consistently, universalising our moral judgements, and generating ideas freely from different perspectives on different levels, using our capacity to empathise. In other words, it doesn't excuse us from the responsibility of evaluating our thinking and trying to use our skills better.

2 Appeals to authority

The other method of side-stepping is to argue the opposite, that there is only one set of answers to moral problems and these can be found by deferring to one authority. The problem here is that the grounds for such putative authorities are seldom clear.

> *Example: Socrates and Euthyphro.* In *Euthyphro,* one of Plato's dialogues, Socrates asks Euthyphro whether actions are right because God commands them, or whether God commands them because they are right. If Euthyphro chooses the former, any action God commands must be right regardless of what we might think of it, and for all we know God might be capricious and arbitrary, wielding his infinite power not for justice and mercy, but to satisfy his own desires and thirst for vengeance. We must comply with his commands blindly, even though it might involve actions that horrify us.
>
> So, it seems the answer to Socrates's question lies in the second part of the dilemma. What God commands may indeed be right, but we need to determine it independently of God: we need an independent criterion by which we can judge the commands of God. In effect we must have a criterion even higher than God, against which his and our moral judgements can both be evaluated. But now we have left behind our appeal to authority in favour of making our own judgements.

As this illustrates, by appealing to authorities we are not just side-stepping our need to generate our ideas, but moral thinking entirely. We merely act as *though* we are moral. We are no longer using and developing our moral skills, instead, like children, without any judgement of our own we simply apply the rules given us by a superior authority.

If we blindly comply with the commands of authorities, we are merely acting as *though* we are moral.

2.1 Moral rules and authorities conflict

As we will see, moral decision-making is a complex business. It is not simply a process of recognising what type of situation we face and then applying the appropriate rule we have acquired from elsewhere. Rules often conflict with other rules, so we are still left with the task of thinking morally to decide why we should choose one rather than another. Like Euthyphro, this means we must step outside of the appeal to authority to find reasons not dependent on it. As the Euthyphro argument shows, authorities cannot be self-supporting; we still need good reasons for complying with their rules.

2.2 In practical terms

In practice, the implementation of the dictates of authorities can be even more confusing. Real situations requiring a moral decision are almost always too complex and too specific for simple rules to be the answer. Moreover, we have to decide which ones to apply and how to apply them.

Example: Leviticus.   You might believe that homosexual intercourse is wrong because Leviticus says it is, but then it also condemns wearing garments that mix linen and wool (Chapter 9, verse 19), cutting beards and hair (19,27), eating pork, ham and anything that swims in water without fins or scales (11,7), harvesting right up to the corners of fields (19,9), and tattoos and other marks on your body (19,28).[4]

3 Stereotypes

However, even when we've realised that authorities are not the answer, there is still the temptation to allow stereotypes to control our thinking. Just as convenient as authorities, they, too, relieve us of the demands of generating ideas by freeing us of the obligation to relate to other people as people. Instead, they substitute caricatures that trigger routine responses.

Example: Loggers and the green movement. If someone objects to the cutting down of woodlands, they might be dismissed as mere 'tree-worshippers', who put the environment before jobs and the communities that depend on the logging industry. The other side might then resort to their own stereotypes, describing the loggers as 'mindless vandals' out to line their own pockets at any expense.

This relieves us of the obligation to universalise our judgements by putting ourselves in the other person's position and asking how we would feel if we were in their shoes. Once we acknowledge that some-one else has an inner life as we do, which we can only understand by empathising with them, we move past the stereotypes with all their labels and prejudices.

Like the appeal to authorities, stereotypes deny the moral complexity of situations. Indeed, some of the most potent stereotypes work by dimin-ishing a person or a whole group to mere things.

Example: 'Hands' and 'Pieces'. In the industrial revolution work-ers lost their personality and became mere 'hands', while in the concentration camps inmates became 'pieces'. Franz Stangl, the Kommandant of the Treblinka extermination camp, admitted that this depersonalisation was the way he coped with the situation. He only allowed himself to see the many thousands of Jews exter-minated each day as mere numbers.[5]

4 Rationalisation

Finally, beware of one more problem, which, like stereotypes, we came across in an earlier chapter. Confronted by a complex problem we are all tempted to abandon the challenge of generating our ideas altogether and accept our own preconceived opinion about the situation. We then set about rationalising our point of view by searching for ideas and evidence that will sustain it.

To generate our ideas freely it's essential to cleanse the mind of all such preconceptions that might hijack thought and send it down rou-tine pathways. What might seem like premature clarity is, in fact, worse than confusion. It is rarely possible to say exactly what we think about a complex problem without careful and extensive probing. We need to give ourselves the freedom to explore the issues and accept that there is more to the picture than we immediately see.

The ideas generator is an effective way of dealing with the sense of confusion that might otherwise drive you to the safety of such familiar routine habits of thought. At the outset, it seems anything and everything counts and you don't know where you are. But the ideas generator gives you an efficient method of making ordered progress: once you have worked through each section asking yourself the trigger questions, you will have covered all the important approaches to the problem.

As a result you should be able to develop the confidence to suspend your judgement and live with doubt, until you have gathered all the ideas and a clear understanding of the issues involved. To think freely in this way and generate our ideas we need structure and organisation. The ideas generator gives us just that.

Checklist

Generating ideas:
1. Perspectives – all those who affect or are affected.
2. Levels – normative issues:
   2.1 justice
   2.2 rights
   2.3 values
   2.4 virtues
   2.5 consequences.
3. Trigger questions – the ideas generator.

Conclusion

Throughout this chapter our concern has been to train our mind's eye to see what needs to be seen, but is so often missed or just filtered out. It starts with the humility to admit that there is so much about the problem that we don't understand. From that point, using our trigger questions, we can begin to generate our ideas from the perspectives of all those involved on different levels without criticising or editing them. Now that we have assembled all our ideas we can process them into structures.

18
Moral Thinking 2: Structuring Ideas

Now that we have generated our ideas we must process them into structures by identifying the general categories or classifications of which they are specific examples. In Part 2 we found that we can structure our ideas in this way, using different methods depending on the nature of the problem and the ideas we generate.

Some problems can be solved through causal thinking, in which we tie our ideas together by identifying the universal causal explanations into which they fit. Then we work with this structure, changing and adapting it to design a solution.

Others can be solved through conceptual thinking by analysing the concepts we use into their constituent ideas. In Chapters 5 and 6 we learnt that concepts are universal classifications that tie their constituent ideas together in logical relations. This internal structure gives us a way of structuring the ideas we have generated. We can then design a solution in the same way by working with this structure, using one or more of the strategies we examined in Chapter 9.

Synthesis – from the specific to the general

Both of these methods involve thinking that goes from the general to the specific: the abstract to the concrete. The alternative strategy moves in the opposite direction: it synthesises our ideas by moving from the specific to the general. In Chapter 7 we learnt that this is the way we come to understand complex situations, either by creating new concepts out of ideas we have generated or by synthesising them under an existing concept.

Some of the ethical problems we confront can be solved by analysing the concepts we use to describe them, but by far the greater proportion involve synthesising our ideas under existing concepts. This gives us the structure into which they are organised, so that we can then work with this in the same way, changing and adapting it to design a solution.

Normative issues to normative principles

When we generate our ideas about ethical problems we do so in the form of the normative issues we saw in the last chapter. Each of these reflects our commitment to certain underlying normative principles.

> Each normative issue we generate reflects our commitment to certain underlying normative principles.

Example: Suzanne and the social worker. In Suzanne's case we found that she should be free from harm and the fear of harm. Underlying this normative issue is our general commitment to a normative principle: the right to safety. We believe that we all have a universal right, no matter who we are, to be free of harm and any threat of harm.

We also found that she should have the same opportunities to educate herself as others. Underlying this normative issue is our commitment to the normative principles of justice; in this case that we should all have equal opportunities.

Normative issue	Normative principle
Free from harm/fear of harm ⟶	Right to safety
Opportunity to educate herself ⟶	Justice: equal opportunity

Taking each stakeholder in turn we can convert each normative issue into their underlying normative principles. In the table below you can see all of the stakeholders involved in Suzanne's case, their normative issues and their corresponding normative principles. In some cases there is more than one principle that matches up with the normative issue, indeed, there are often two or three.

Stakeholder	Normative issues	Normative principles
Attendant	1. Her views should be heard before any decision is made.	Justice – procedural
	2. Should know what is being said about her.	Right to know
	3. Should not lose her job or chances of promotion if the allegations are unproved.	Justice – opportunity Justice – procedural
	4. Should be sensitive to the feelings of others.	Respect for the dignity of the individual Universalism
You (Social worker)	1. Should take up Suzanne's concerns with management as confidentially as possible.	Right to privacy
	2. Should offer to talk with parents with an objective assessment of her ability to cope independently.	Virtues – Compassion Virtues – Friendship
Parents	1. Should provide Suzanne support.	Virtues – support w/out being overbearing
	2. Should respect her independence.	Virtues – Self-reliance Virtues – Independence Respect for dignity of ind Autonomy
Suzanne	1. Should be free from harm and the fear of it.	Right to safety Values – security
	2. Should be able to have her independence and build up her self-esteem and confidence.	Virtues – independence Virtues – self-reliance
	3. Should have equal opportunity for education.	Justice – opportunity Values – education
	4. Should have the opportunity to have her concerns heard.	Justice – procedural Values – democratic
	5. Should not be intimidated into not complaining.	Justice – procedural Values – Cognitive: limits to manipulation
Community Service	1. Have responsibility to deal with these fears in thorough and sensitive manner.	Virtues – sensitivity
	2. Have responsibility to ensure clients are not harmed.	Right to safety Values – security
	3. Should investigate the problems impartially without a desire for retribution or to protect staff if they've acted badly.	Justice – procedural Values – democratic accountability

The converter

Of course, it helps to have by your side a list of the sort of normative principles that your normative issues point to. Although the converter below cannot lay claim to being a comprehensive list of normative principles, it does make it easier for you to convert each issue into their appropriate principles and compile a list of those involved. Like the ideas generator, it is divided into columns for each of the different types of normative principle: justice, rights, virtues, values and consequences. In the same way that you add questions to your list of trigger questions on the ideas generator, as you come across other principles that you think should be on the converter, add them to the lists.

However, before we look at each of the normative principles, we must consider three non-overridable principles: that is, principles on which we cannot compromise, because to do so would mean we are no longer coming to a moral solution.

1 Non-overridable principles

There is a logic to moral thinking as there is to all types of thinking. This means we make mistakes each time we break these internal logical rules. We do this just as easily and frequently in moral thinking as we do in logical, mathematical or scientific thinking.

Like each of these, moral thinking has certain necessary features. When a scientist presents a scientific explanation she knows it must be empirical, testable and universal in its claims. Likewise in moral thinking: our judgements must be universal; they must respect the dignity of each individual, treating them as ends and not as mere means; and they must preserve each individual's autonomy, so that they are free to make their own choices and not coerced into behaving in the way we want them to.

Non-overridable principles:

1. Universalism.
2. Respect for the dignity of the individual.
3. Autonomy.

If we were to ignore these principles, we would simply no longer be arguing morally: we would, perhaps, be making a political or legal argument, or perhaps arguing prudentially that this is the best way of achieving something that we want to achieve because it is in our interests. In the same way, if a scientist were to present a theory that was not empirical

The converter – normative principles

Non-overridable	Overridable				
	Justice	Rights	Values	Virtues	Consequences
1. Respect for the dignity of the individual 1.1 Is the intrinsic worth of anyone involved ignored? 1.2 Are they treated as mere means rather than as ends in themselves?	1. Opportunity – equality of opportunity – social equality	1. Individual: Right to know to privacy to free speech to safety/ security to own property to life	1. Personal well-being: education health security employment	1. Medieval: 1.1 Seven cardinal virtues: Faith, hope, charity, prudence, temperance, justice, fortitude 1.2 Seven deadly sins: Pride, wrath, envy, lust, gluttony, avarice, sloth	1. What is the balance of costs and benefits from each proposed action?
2. Universalism 2.1 Can we insist that in similar situations all individuals and organisations act in the same way? 2.2 Can we impose the same decision on ourselves independently of the role we occupy – whether we win or lose? 2.3 Are we treating others as we would have them treat us?	2. Distributive – justice provides a fair distribution of benefits and burdens	2. Public: Rights of future generations Right to a clean environment to education to affordable health care to public safety	2. Social-political: free market system democratic values the environment	2. Modern: Independence self-reliance responsibility self-discipline hard work prudence, fortitude friendship compassion benevolence sensitivity generosity charity, honesty loyalty, trust	2. How deep and wide are the effects on those directly and indirectly affected?

(Continued)

The converter – normative principles

Non-overridable	Overridable				
	Justice	Rights	Values	Virtues	Consequences
3. Autonomy Have those involved been denied the freedom to make up their own minds and choose for themselves?	3. Retributive – justice provides punishment as it is deserved 4. Procedural – provides a fair chance of due process 5. Compensatory – provides fair compensation for harm done	3. General principles: principle of harm of honesty of fidelity of confidentiality of lawfulness	3. Economic: free enterprise competition limited government intervention freedom of choice consumer sovereignty 4. Cognitive: information limits to manipulation appeals to reason 5. Culture/aesthetic: environment respect for others respect for traditions controls over public environment	3. Care in relationships: patience nurturing trust trustworthiness support without being over-bearing	3. What is the size of the number affected? 4. Do some people benefit at the cost of others? 5. Are these short or long term effects?

or testable, she would be open to the charge of doing, not science, but pseudo-science or she might be going beyond science to present, say, a metaphysical argument. As we design a solution to a moral problem, therefore, we cannot ignore any of these three principles.

1.1 *Universalism*

In the last chapter we argued for the importance of universalism: that in any moral judgement we must want all people finding themselves in similar circumstances to act in accordance with the same judgement. We are not just saying that this is what *I* should do in this situation, but that *all people* similar to me and in a similar situation should behave likewise. It means that we must be prepared to prescribe our moral judgements independently of the role we occupy and independently of whether we gain or lose by their application.

Consequently, we must ask ourselves, 'Would I like to be treated like this?' In this the two key concerns for us all are:

1. That we should be treated as having intrinsic value in ourselves and not just extrinsic value to serve someone else's ends;
2. And that we should have the freedom to make our own informed choices.

1.2 *Respect for the dignity of the individual*

The first of these underscores the importance we attach to the dignity of the individual as an end in him- or herself and not as a mere means of promoting someone else's ends.

If, as universalism dictates, we must treat others as we would expect to be treated ourselves, and as we place the highest intrinsic value on ourselves, we must place the same intrinsic value on others. In other words, in the same way that we would resist being treating as a mere means for someone to achieve some other end of their own choosing, we must likewise avoid treating others as a mere means to achieve our own ends.

> *Example: Surgeons and lawyers.*   We would be justified in questioning the judgement of a surgeon who pursues ground-breaking surgery, because it will promote his career, when it presents unacceptable risks to his patient. We would also be right to question the decision of a lawyer who pursues a high-profile strategy in a case, because it will elevate her profile, when the client would be better advised to follow some other strategy.

When we treat someone as a mere means we are elevating some other end to more importance than the person herself: we are sacrificing that person, refusing to recognise that she has her own preferences, interests and needs. To come to this sort of judgement is to act prudentially, not morally, in that we refuse to consider others as we strive to bring about another goal we consider to be more important.

A 'mere' means

Nevertheless, this is not to say we can never treat individuals as means, it is just that we cannot treat them as *mere* means, that is, to treat them without dignity, without any intrinsic worth in themselves.

> *Example: A ticket clerk.* In our haste to catch a train we might swear at, and even abuse, a ticket machine for failing to produce our ticket in time to catch the train. Subsequently, we might feel embarrassed at our behaviour and disappointed at our inability to control our rage, but our actions would carry no moral dimension, that is unless someone of a tender age had seen our poor behaviour and we were afraid of setting a bad example.
>
> But, if we were to replace the ticket machine with a ticket clerk, the implications and significance of our actions would be altogether different. If we were to abuse a ticket clerk for her failure to produce a ticket fast enough, we would be abusing not just a mere machine, a 'mere' means, but an individual with her own preferences, interests and needs, who deserves to be treated with respect.

The ticket clerk is still a means of our getting a ticket, but she is not a 'mere' means. Reflecting on our actions afterwards we would certainly be aware of a moral dimension, which was missing in our abuse of the machine.

1.3 Autonomy

In turn, this has an obvious bearing on a person's autonomy. When we consider ourselves as ends and not mere means we are endorsing our autonomous status as the fashioners of our own ends. We are not just mere means to achieve someone else's ends, without a choice of our own.

And, equally significant, our decisions are not just driven by our desires – what we *want* to do – but by what we think we *ought* to do: not by prudential reasons about what will most effectively satisfy our desires, but by moral reasons. If we were driven by our desires, we would no longer be ends in ourselves and we would no longer have a choice: it would not be us that determine what we should do, but our desires and appetites.

> *Example: Drug addicts and smokers.* Many drug addicts and smokers believe they *ought* to give up their addiction, but they *desire* the drug. They are driven by what they *want*, not by what they believe they *ought* to want.

The actions and lives of individuals must be determined by the dictates of their own reason, by their own self-imposed judgements. Therefore, in our professional lives the decisions we make must maximise the freedom of choice of those stakeholders involved by taking into account as many of their concerns as possible.

As you can see, if I ignore any of these principles, I have made a moral mistake as clearly as I make similar mistakes in mathematical, logical and scientific thinking when I ignore their internal rules.

2 Overridable principles

While these principles are non-overridable, the rest are not. We have to choose in any situation which are the most important in order to reach the best moral solution to the problem. None can trump any other, although in any situation some will be more important than others.

2.1 Virtues

Each set of principles is self-explanatory, except, perhaps, 'virtues' and 'values'. When we consider the importance of virtues, we are asking ourselves questions about character: are we acting as a good person ought to act; living up to the best of what we are? Our concern is with the sort of persons we are, or are becoming, by taking the sort of decision we plan to take. In any situation we have to ask whether our decision is likely to promote the sort of virtues we think people should have. So we need to be clear which virtues ought to take precedence in any situation and how we can show these virtues ourselves or bring them forth in others.

> *Example: A dentist and an estate agent.*   A dentist who recommends that a patient undergoes unnecessary dental work and an estate agent who convinces people to buy a property when he knows it is not in their interests, both need to ask themselves if they want to be someone who uses their professional expertise to exploit others.

I have listed those virtues considered to be the most important by different groups and at different times. The medieval Christian world saw the seven deadly sins and the seven cardinal virtues as the standard by which to judge individuals. As a result of the nineteenth century and the rise of the Protestant Work Ethic other virtues gained prominence, like self-reliance, self-discipline, hard work and prudence.

In our own time, with the rise of the Welfare State and a better understanding of the causes of poverty, more caring virtues, like patience and nurturing, have become more important. As we look at moral problems through the perspective of each stakeholder, we have to recognise the importance that others might place on virtues we might not see as important ourselves.

2.2 Values

As for values I have examined five areas in which we all seem to believe there are important values at stake, which we need to take account of in the decisions we make. Where we place importance is likely to depend upon the culture in which we live and work.

You may place overwhelming emphasis on limited government regulation, the importance of the free market system, free enterprise, competition and liberal democratic values. Alternatively, you may believe that government intervention is important to ensure adequate protection for those who might be the subject of prejudice and discrimination, to guarantee universal access to good education and health services, and to protect the environment. But no matter what your values, the challenge is the same as it is with virtues: to see through the perspective of each stakeholder the possibility of holding different sets of values.

Structuring – tracing their interrelations

Once we have identified all the normative principles involved we can then trace their interrelations, their underlying structure. You will see that each principle has a certain value, a certain relative importance compared with other principles. There is a hierarchy among them and it is this that gives us the structure to the particular problem.

> *Example: The right to life and the right to privacy.* We consider that our right to life is more important than, say, our right to privacy, no doubt because we reason that the former is a precondition for the latter: without life we have no rights at all. So, depending on the circumstances, we are likely to argue that a lawyer's privileged communication with her client should be revealed if this information is necessary to save his life.

By revealing the structure of the problem in this way we identify the most important, the decisive, normative principles in this problem, while we isolate those that are peripheral to it, which can be dealt with separately. We can then see more clearly ways of resolving conflicts, where they exist, between these decisive normative principles. Once this is done, we can prioritise the remaining principles according to their importance and create the structure we need to solve the problem. With this, we can move on to step three and design a solution by changing and adapting it as we did in Chapter 9.

So the stages we have to work through to reveal the structure of the problem are the following:

1. Identify the relevant normative principles.
2. Identify the decisive normative principles/
   Isolate and deal with those that are peripheral.
3. Where it is possible, resolve problems and conflicts between the remaining decisive principles.
4. Prioritise the remaining principles, revealing the underlying hierarchical structure.

Stage 2: Identify the decisive normative principles/Isolate and deal with those that are peripheral

There will always be some principles that are not central to the problem and can be dealt with separately, or can be put to one side, while you deal with the main problem. So put yourself in the position of each stakeholder and ask yourself, 'What do I really want sorting out here?' You will find that some are less important than others and can be put aside to tackle the really important issues. With this done, out of the 20 to 30 you may have listed, you will be left with, say, 8 to 10 that are decisive normative principles. We must focus on these to solve the problem.

Example: Suzanne and the social worker. Having talked to Suzanne you might find that what really matters to her is securing for herself the opportunity for training and education, which will bring greater independence, self-esteem and confidence. Although she places importance on procedural justice and the opportunity to have her concerns heard and dealt with, she might be willing to set these aside, if she could only secure her main objective of greater independence and the self-esteem that will come from this.

If this is not the case and she wants procedural justice and to be free from the fear of harm, then we might be left with the following:

Stakeholder	Decisive normative principles
Attendant	Justice – procedural
	Respect for the dignity of the individual.
Parents	Virtues – support w/out being overbearing
	Virtues – self-reliance
	Autonomy
Suzanne	Right to safety
	Virtues – independence and self-esteem
	Justice – equal opportunity
Community service	Right to safety
	Justice – procedural

Stage 3: Resolving problems and conflicts between them

Once you've done this you will be left with the decisive normative principles, between which there are unresolved conflicts. Now that you can see them clearly as principles rather than issues, you can often see quite simple things that can be done to tackle some of these conflicts and address the problems they present. They can then be removed as components of the overall problem. All that then remains are the unresolved conflicts between these decisive normative principles, which represent the nub of the problem.

> *Example: Suzanne and the social worker.* It's clear now from the normative principles that remain that there are four unresolved conflicts and problems: Suzanne's right to safety; equal opportunity justice and the virtues of independence and self-esteem that will come from this; the procedural justice she is due to right a wrong; and the virtue of her parents providing support without being overbearing and threatening her independence.
>
> It may be possible to satisfy some of these and remove them as components of the problem. For example, it may be possible to get from the community service an assurance, which satisfies Suzanne, that they have addressed the problem of Suzanne's safety and she now has nothing to fear.

Stage 4: Prioritising the remaining normative principles

All that remains now is to trace the underlying structure found in the interrelations between the normative principles that remain.

Hierarchy

As we said earlier, you will see that each principle has a certain value, a certain relative importance compared with other principles. As we prioritise them, we reveal the hierarchy among them, which gives us the structure to the particular problem, which we take to the next stage to design the best solution to the problem.

1 Within each type of principle

Indeed, you will see there is a hierarchy of value *within* each type of principle and *between* those of different types.

1.1 Rights

Within the category of rights, as we have already suggested, in some cases we would probably have no difficulty recognising that the right to life takes precedence over our rights to privacy, freedom of expression and assembly. Similarly, in some cases, where there is clear evidence of an imminent threat to public security, our right to safety and security might take precedence over our right to know, privacy and freedom of expression.

1.2 Justice

In some cases, where a social or ethnic minority has found it difficult to get the same opportunities as other groups, we might argue that this should be dealt with by introducing policies of affirmative action and positive discrimination, which give greater incentives to members of these groups than to others to enrol in training initiatives. Such a solution would underscore our belief that in this case equal opportunity justice is more important than achieving distributive justice, in which members of all groups would benefit equally from such programmes.

1.3 Virtues

In some cases we would probably agree that promoting someone's self-reliance takes precedence over other virtues, like generosity and helping others. This is likely to be true in the case of an elderly person, living alone in their own home, who wants to maintain his or her independence and refuses the offer of help from neighbours or the social services.

1.4 Values

The same is true of values: in some cases you might want to place greater importance on the democratic value of public accountability than you do on maintaining a market system that is free from such accountability and public regulation. The credit crisis that developed out of loosely regulated financial markets has brought many to this conclusion, insisting on greater transparency and accountability to the public.

1.5 Consequences

As for consequences, when they affect an individual or a small group you will have to decide how deep and wide they run through society, and which set of consequences for those involved has greater value.

> *Example: Dialysis patient.*   In the case of the dialysis patient, who was denied treatment because his behaviour made it difficult for the medical staff treating him and because it was thought his quality of life was not good enough, withdrawing treatment adversely affects the individual patient deeply. Set against that are the benefits for the medical staff treating him. These are felt more widely, but, of course, less deeply. For them it may be a few hours

a week struggling with a very difficult patient; for him it is a matter of life and death. So we would have to decide which weighs more heavily: the deep effects on one individual compared with the wide, though less deep, effects on the many.

2 Between types of principle

Of course, most of the moral problems we have to solve will reveal not just hierarchical relations *within* types of normative principles, but *between* them.

The importance we place on promoting the virtue of self-reliance among the elderly may not outweigh the freedom from harm if an elderly person is not capable of looking after him- or herself well enough. The beneficial consequences that come from catching criminals as a result of collecting private information on a new generation of supercomputers or through the use of public CCTV cameras may not justify the invasion of individual liberty.

Alternatively, in some cases the importance of correcting an injustice might take precedence over someone's right to confidentiality, or over someone's right to freedom of expression. And the importance we place on values, like the freedom of individual choice, might take precedence over the virtue of supporting someone by taking decisions for him, when we believe he is likely to make unwise decisions about his health.

Checklist

Structuring – the stages:
1. Identify the relevant normative principles.
2. Identify the decisive normative principles/Isolate and deal with those that are peripheral.
3. Where it is possible, resolve problems and conflicts between the remaining decisive principles.
4. Prioritise the remaining principles, revealing the underlying hierarchical structure.

Conclusion

It's likely that much of this is familiar to you. Most of us go through similar stages to solve the moral problems we confront, although on a more intuitive level. However, good moral thinkers probably work in the more deliberate and thoughtful way that we have seen in this chapter. Although it may seem time consuming, in practice, like most new skills and techniques, it isn't after we have used it a few times.

Whatever the problem, we have to reveal the underlying principles to solve it. Among these, there is an order of priority, which gives us the hierarchical structure to the problem. And with this, as we will see in the next chapter, we can set about designing the most effective solution.

19
Moral Thinking 3: Designing Solutions

With almost every serious moral issue there is good on both sides. Most are not fought over simple questions of good and evil, and right and wrong. Some are, it's true, but far fewer than we normally think. In most cases we are confronted by different ways of looking at the problem, all having good on their side. Usually there are more moral principles at stake than we acknowledge. So, it is not so much a matter of which side is right, but what is right about each side. All sides are right to some extent; it is not simply a case of the winner takes all.

Consequently, our decisions should seek to integrate as many as possible of the most important moral principles at stake in any situation. Our aim is to harmonise these different principles, rather than insist that only a few are right. The best solutions are those that maximise value in any situation: that meet as many of the preferences, interests and needs of those involved as possible.

One dominant normative principle

Nevertheless, we cannot avoid the possibility that, out of the hierarchy of normative principles we revealed in the last chapter, there may be one dominant normative principle that is more important than all the others. So the first thing we must clarify is whether this is, indeed, the case.

If it is, we must see whether it is outweighed by the combined effect of less important principles. If there isn't one dominant principle, or if it is outweighed by the combined weight of all the rest, then we must integrate and harmonise as many of the principles as we can in each of the possible solutions we devise.

In these we are attempting to resolve the conflicts between the decisive normative principles involved. You may find that one or two of your solutions resolve them all, but most will resolve only some. So we will be comparing and choosing between solutions on the basis of how well they maximise value by meeting as many as possible of the preferences, interests and needs of those involved.

Questions:

1. Is there one dominant normative principle?
2. If there is, is it outweighed by the combined weight of all the rest?
3. If there isn't or it is outweighed by the combined weight of all the rest, how can we integrate and harmonise as many as possible of the principles involved?

Example: Suzanne and the social worker.   In this case we set out the decisive normative principles involved in the following table.

Stakeholder	Decisive normative principles
Attendant	Justice – procedural
	Respect for the dignity of the individual
Parents	Virtues – support w/out being overbearing
	Virtues – self-reliance
	Autonomy
Suzanne	Right to safety
	Virtues – independence and self-esteem
	Justice – equal opportunity
Community service	Right to safety
	Justice – procedural

Possible solutions

To maximise value in this situation by integrating as many as possible of the normative principles involved you might design the following solutions to choose from.

Solution 1

As the social worker, to whom Suzanne has spoken about her problem, you could talk unofficially to the community service on Suzanne's behalf and then to her parents. This could be the best way of safeguarding Suzanne's right to safety, while avoiding a situation that might leave the attendant's career damaged by an official approach. Of course, it is possible that the community service might still react by removing Suzanne's home care. Just in case, it is worth talking to her parents who may be able to provide a safety net. The danger with this, of course, is that it may be at the cost of her independence.

Solution 2

Alternatively, you might consider talking directly and unofficially to the attendant. This again avoids the dangers of arbitrary procedural judgements made by the community service, which might rob the attendant of her chances of promotion and leave Suzanne without care. If the attendant responds well, the problem is solved. If she doesn't, she might take it out on Suzanne or simply refuse to help her again, which would not only be unfair, a breach of procedural justice, but would rob Suzanne of her independence.

Solution 3

Finally you could talk to Suzanne to see if you can allay her fears. If this is unsuccessful, you could then talk to her parents, asking them to support her in her quest for independence in the event that she does lose her attendant care by agreeing to you reporting the matter officially. Still, there would be the danger that they may not be able to help her without robbing her of her independence. If they can avoid this, although she will not have the justice and the official accountability she deserves, these are probably less important than the other normative principles: equal opportunity and the self-esteem from being independent. If the community service doesn't withdraw her help, but the attendant says she cannot work with her again, then either Suzanne gets a new attendant or her parents step in. Alternatively, the attendant may agree to accept responsibility and make changes.

Action	Decisive normative principles
Solution 1:	
Talk unofficially to the community service	Right to safety
	Justice – procedural
Talk to parents about	Virtues – independence
providing a safety net	and self self-esteem
Solution 2:	
Talk unofficially to the attendant	Justice – procedural
	Virtues – independence and self-esteem

Solution 3:

Talk to Suzanne	Right to safety
	Virtues – independence and self-esteem
	Justice – equal opportunity
Talk to parents	Virtues – self-reliance
	Autonomy

Choosing the best solution

Once you have designed possible solutions, you must choose between them. To do this there are three simple tests. If none of them pass these tests, you must work with them to find a better solution, adapting their structures as we did in Chapter 9.

Tests:

1. Non-overridable principles.
2. Proportionality.
3. Probability.

---

1 Non-overridable principles

First we must check that each solution meets the formal demands of moral thinking in the form of the three non-overridable principles we discussed in the last chapter. If any solution treats an individual involved as a mere means, or ignores his or her autonomy, or comes to a judgement that we could not will universally for all similar situations, then we must reject it.

Otherwise, we will have made a mistake as clearly as we do when we miscalculate in mathematics or wrongly deduce a conclusion in logic. When this happens we often feel uncomfortable about the solution, although we might struggle to find good reasons to explain exactly why, as you can see in the following example.

> *Example: Cleaners in a male environment.* In the early 1990s, two women cleaners, employed at the Goodwyn A gas platform being constructed near Fremantle in Australia,[1] complained that the 600 men employed subjected them to verbal abuse, graffiti and displays of hard- and soft-core pornography. While they accepted the soft-core porn – the semi-naked pin-ups – they drew the line at the offensive and degrading hard-core porn.

Their complaints to the union organiser and management were met with abuse and threats. The men insisted that on democratic principles, as the majority of the employees, they shouldn't be dictated to by a minority of two. This was a male environment, they insisted, and the women just had to accept it. They threatened to strike and the union took their side. Eventually the employer accepted the union's assurance that the problem had been resolved and dropped the case.

The women worked on, but after a year the stress became too great and they resigned. The case was then examined by the Western Australian Equal Opportunity Tribunal, which ruled that the women should receive A$92,000 in compensation for sexual harassment, which was to be paid by the union and the employer. They concluded that the employer had simply failed to deal with the problem, preferring instead to walk away from it once the union had given its assurance that the problem had been resolved.

But what should the employer have done, given such a difficult problem? Is this just an example of political correctness? After all, we simply have to tolerate some forms of behaviour even though we disapprove of them. Tolerance is an important moral value in democracy; we have an obligation to tolerate many things, even though we deeply deplore them. So at what point does tolerance give way to some other moral value? And then there is the democratic argument the men presented: that they are the majority of 600 to two, so why should they have to accede to the wishes of a small minority?

Questions:
1. Is this just political correctness?
2. At what point does tolerance, an important moral value in democracies, give way to some other moral value?
3. In a democracy, why should a majority be forced to accede to the wishes of a minority?

In its report the Equal Opportunity Commission accepted that it was far from easy to find a solution to this difficult problem, but it had to be confronted. Anything less amounted to simple capitulation and this is what the employer had done by walking away from the problem once the union had given its assurance that it had been resolved. Then it says tellingly, 'The short answer to the question posed is quite simply that we must do what we know to be right, to stop what we know to be wrong.'[2] In other words, we may not know the reasons why we are convinced that this is wrong, but still we must act on this simple conviction. But how do we simply know this to be wrong? There must be good reasons for our conviction.

The answer can be found in the formal nature of moral thinking and these non-overridable principles that define it. When we make a mistake in mathematical or logical reasoning we may know that we have made a mistake, although we might not be able to say exactly what it is. The same is true here.

> The reasons for the conviction that this was simply wrong can be found in these three non-overridable principles.

Two principles in particular were ignored by the men's actions and the justification they gave for them. First, respect for the dignity of the individual as an end in herself was ignored. The women were not respected as ends in themselves with their own intrinsic value and their own preferences, interests and needs. These were just ignored as having no significance in finding a solution. They were treated as having just extrinsic value: they were used as mere means to satisfy the men's preferences.

Second, the men ignored the requirement that we must be able to universalise our moral judgements: we must be able to put ourselves in the position of the women and will that we should be bullied in just the same way. The men needed to ask themselves, can they will that this should become a universal law? They bullied the women because they were different, but there are many types of differences: race, religion, age and so on. Would it have been right to have targeted a Muslim worker in the same way? Indeed, would it have been right to have targeted in the same way the differences that they or members of their own families exhibit?

Failure to comply with any of these three principles trumps any defence that might be given for such harassment. The reason why we and the Commission in this case often have a deep conviction that an action or judgement is just simply wrong without being able to find reasons for this belief is that it has failed to comply with one or more of these three non-overridable principles.

2 Proportionality

The second test is, perhaps, a little more complex. Once we are convinced that no one is being used as a mere means, we must make every effort to try to avoid one group or individual suffering disproportionately as a result of the possible solutions we have designed.

Of course, this doesn't exclude the possibility that there might be one dominant normative principle, like justice, which might dictate the solution we come to and disadvantage just one person. Indeed, this may be the result in Suzanne's case, if the only way of solving the problem is to go through official channels, which might damage the attendant's chances of promotion. Still, if this does appear to be the case, we must make every effort to minimise the effect and try to maximise as far as we can the individual's or the group's preferences, interests and needs.

To be clear about the effects of our possible solutions we need to ask questions about the nature of those affected. What follows are a number of questions we need to ask to get a clearer picture of the effects of doing what we propose. None of them require complex calculations, but asked routinely they will help you come to your decision.

2.1 The size of the group affected

First, what is the size of the group, the number of those who will be badly affected by the solution? In other words, what is the maximum negative impact?

> *Example: The 1989 Exxon Valdez disaster.* Since the pipeline and the terminal at Valdez, Alaska, had been operating for 18 years without a serious incident, it was obviously the calculation of those involved that, as oil prices had been falling and they needed to find cost savings, this could be done best by diverting investment away from emergency equipment and into other areas.
>
> But the maximum negative impact was, of course, immense. This was the largest oil spill in the history of the North American petroleum industry, causing immense harm estimated in billions of dollars to the local economy and to people's livelihood, let alone the incalculable damage to the Alaskan environment.

2.2 How deep and wide are the effects?

Then consider how deep and wide the consequences run throughout society. The effects of a heart surgeon's work are felt deeply by individual patients and their families, but not widely throughout society, whereas the effects of a disease control unit are felt widely, but not necessarily deeply. An accident underground in a coal mine is felt deeply by the families and the local community, but not widely, whereas a nuclear accident, like Chernobyl in 1986, has both wide and deep effects.

2.3 Cost/benefit analysis

If some people benefit at the cost of others, how large is the ratio?

2.3.1 Minority at the cost of the majority

If it is a minority that benefits at the cost of the majority, ask yourself the following questions:

1. **Significance of the benefits**
   Do the benefits to them make such a significant difference to their lives to justify the sacrifice of the majority?
2. **Significance of the sacrifice**
   How significant is this sacrifice? If it is fairly superficial, it may be justified in view of the significant benefits it brings to the minority.
3. **Nature of the minority**
   But then think about the nature of this minority. Are they transient, so that the benefits will be short-lived? Are they sufficiently wealthy to afford an alternative solution that they could fund themselves?

2.3.2 Majority at the cost of the minority

Then turn your attention to the other possibility, that it is the majority that benefits:

1. **Significance of the sacrifice**
   Is the sacrifice of the minority too great to justify the benefits to the majority?
2. **Alternative means**
   If the benefits do justify it, are there alternative means of achieving this without the minority suffering?

2.3.3 Long- or short-term sacrifices

And, finally, consider whether these sacrifices are long term or short term:

1. **Short term**
   If they are short term, is it possible for those involved to get over them so that they can then enjoy the benefits? Or do they represent too great a sacrifice for the benefits that will eventually accrue?

2. Long term
If these are long term, are the short-term benefits worth it?

Proportionality – questions:
1. What is the size of the number affected?
2. Are the effects deep, wide, or both?
3. Do some people benefit at the cost of others?
   3.1. How large is the ratio?
   3.2. Does a minority benefit at the expense of the majority or the majority at the expense of the minority?
   3.3. Are these short- or long-term effects?

---

3 Probability
The third and final test is to calculate as accurately as we can the probability that the outcome that we think will maximise value will actually be achieved. We have to know the probability that the action we propose will in fact have the good consequences we envisage. If it seems that the projected solution could only work in exceptional circumstances, then we will have to judge whether we should abandon this solution in favour of another that is more likely to come to fruition.

Of course, this may just be a rough and ready calculation, but it's one we are all accustomed to make whenever we take a decision. All professionals take decisions they think will have the best outcomes, but they will also have to assess how likely it is that these will come about. If the probability is low, it makes no sense to go down that route. Both calculations – of value and probability – are inextricably linked each time we make up our minds and take a decision.

Calculations of value and probability are inextricably linked each time we make up our minds and take a decision.

Example: Suzanne and the social worker.

Solution 1
With this solution there may be a high probability of failure, but it's difficult to calculate how great this is. Suzanne's parents may provide a safety net, but at the cost of her independence. Without knowing more about them we have no way of knowing whether they will respond in this way.

To make a judgement we would have to get more information from Suzanne about their likely reactions to such an approach. The same could be said for the community service: they may treat her unfairly and take her help away. However, we probably do have some assurance that they will respond in a professional manner and treat her fairly, if only because of the internal professional standards that they probably impose on themselves and by which they will expect their performance to be judged.

> **Solution 2**
> This is simpler, but everything hangs on our judgement of how the attendant will respond. It would certainly avoid the dangers of arbitrary procedural judgements that might be unfair on the attendant and may leave Suzanne without help.

As with the first solution, we would need more information to make a judgement, this time about the attendant and her state of mind.

> **Solution 3**
> This might seem the best solution; after all it safeguards Suzanne's safety and her independence, the two most important principles at stake in this case. But, again, we have to be sure about how her parents will react if called upon to help: whether they will respect her independence. And, like the first solution, we cannot be certain that the community service will treat both Suzanne and the attendant fairly, although the probability is weighted in favour of this in view of the internal safeguards that probably exist in the system to ensure good professional standards.

If we can feel confident about this probability, Suzanne won't have to rely on her parents and, therefore, will not only be assured of her independence and the self-esteem that comes from it, but also her safety and the continued help she needs.

Working with our structures

However, if none of our solutions satisfactorily deal with the problem or the probability that we can achieve this is low, we will have to go back to our four problem-solving strategies that we examined in Chapter 9: we will have to change the structure of the problem situation, approach it from a different direction, start from a different point, or create a new structure.

> *Example: Workplace random testing.* In 1995 a dispute broke out in a factory in northern France when a local official insisted that all employees should be randomly tested for drugs and alcohol to ensure the safety of workers using machinery. The workers objected that this was an invasion of their privacy and a restriction on their freedom to lead whatever lifestyle they chose.
>
> They feared that information could be gathered and records kept on all sorts of details relating to their private lives. Irrelevant details could be used as the basis for discrimination at work: whether they smoked, were overweight or whether they were being treated for a medical condition, all under the guise of enforcing health and safety regulations. Indeed, it could then lead to the testing of all employees on any pretext.

This is a problem that affects many occupations which involve activities that could threaten the safety of workers and the public. Airlines restrict their cabin crews' consumption of intoxicating substances and it is argued that the same regulations should be extended to train and bus drivers, ferry masters and so on. This is a compelling argument, but then so is the workers', so how do we go about solving it?

Probably the most obvious way is to change the structure. In Chapter 9 we found that this can be done in one of three ways:

1. Split it up.
2. Rearrange it.
3. Reinterpret it.

1 Split it up

With this problem the simplest method is to split the structure up. This will reduce a bewilderingly difficult problem into three simpler problems, whose solution is easier to find:

1. invasion of the workers' privacy – gathering information on their activities in their **non-working hours**;
2. testing involving **all sorts of things**;
3. testing **every type of employee** – the slippery slope argument.

1.1 Non-working hours

The solution to this problem is to restrict the invasion to just those activities that could affect their performance in such a way as to endanger themselves and others. So, the fact that they take too little exercise and are overweight would be of no interest to the employer, unless it could be shown that this has a tangible influence in the short term on the safety of their work.

1.2 Testing all sorts of things

As for the second problem, this can be solved best, perhaps, by restricting the employer's interest to just those activities the influence of which can be detected days after consumption **and only if** substantive evidence can be shown that it affects the safety of their work by putting themselves and others at risk. The fact that an employee smoked cigarettes over the weekend should be of no interest, whereas, if he were still under the influence of drink or drugs, would be.

The fear with this, as it is with the third problem, is that such invasion of privacy might be extended to all manner of things and to every type of employee – the slippery slope argument.

1.3 Extending it to every type of employee

But this, too, can be solved in the same way through a binding agreement that restricts testing to only those employees whose activities in their non-working hours can be shown to have an influence on their work and can pose a high risk to their own lives or those of others.

Of course, much of this now seems obvious, but it wasn't at the time to those involved in the complex issues of a difficult and emotional problem. These simple strategies can give organisation and clarity to an otherwise confusing problem, as you can see in the following example.

> *Example: Exploitation of women by advertisers.* Over the years women's organisations in many countries have protested that the use of female images to sell all manner of things is offensive in that it is dehumanising, degrading and sexist. On the other hand, advertisers argue they have a right to free expression.

This is a difficult, complex problem. On the one hand there is the right of advertisers to free expression and to act in accordance with the values of the free market, a system of values that dominates thinking in most western societies, while on the other hand there is a large number of people who believe they are being exploited for the profits of large corporations to the benefit of much smaller groups of shareholders.

2 Start from a different point

One way of tackling this is to adopt the third strategy in Chapter 9: to start from a different point. In other words, focus your attention on different parts of the structure and start from there. The easiest way of doing this with most problems is to start by analysing the key concepts around which the problem is organised.

As we've seen, at the heart of concepts are structures made up of organising principles that organise our ideas. One or two of these are likely to dictate the way we generally use the concept. Therefore, by concentrating on those we usually ignore we are able to locate different points to start from. They throw different light on the problem and present interesting angles from which to approach the problem.

At the heart of concepts are structures made up of organising principles. Choose a different one to throw new light on the problem.

A key concept that is frequently used in this problem is 'offence': feminist organisations often complain that advertisements using the female form are unnecessarily offensive and on these grounds should be withdrawn. The problem, of course, is that what is offensive to one group is not to another. Thus, advertisers are free to defend their work by arguing that the majority of the public see their commercials as inoffensive and quite harmless. It is only feminists and the most strident champions of political correctness that have a problem with it.

Moreover, not only is 'offence' the subject of widely different interpretations, but, when we analyse the concept, we find a key difference in ideas that seems to support the advertisers' argument. While we all have the right to freedom of expression, we don't have a right not to be offended. I might be deeply offended and annoyed by what a politician says on the television, but this is the price I pay for living in a democracy and upholding the right to freedom of expression. So it would seem that those who object to offensive advertising, whether they are women, ethnic minorities, religious groups, or even those of a certain age group, have no case.

Offence:

1. Subjective interpretations.
2. We have no right not to be offended.

But analysing the concept also sets clear limits to this interpretation and goes some way towards freeing us from the subjectivist argument that it's all a matter of interpretation.

Some forms of offensive advertising cause harm. They may cause anxiety and stress, which result in serious health risks, or they may cause economic harm by reducing the employment chances of a social or ethnic group because of the way they are portrayed. In these and similar cases there is an important normative principle – the right to be free from harm – which in these circumstances may trump freedom of expression. As John Stuart Mill famously argued in *On Liberty*, '... the only purpose for which power can be rightfully exercised over any member of a civilised community, against his will, is to prevent harm to others.'[3]

So now we have the basis of a solution. Advertisers should be free to create and use these advertisements as long as there is no harm to others. If evidence can be shown that it does result in substantive harm, then this should set the limits to such advertising.

Checklist

Checklist – Designing a solution:

1. Is there a dominant normative principle?
2. Is it outweighed by the combined effects of less important principles?
3. Do the solutions break any non-overridable principles?
4. Does any individual or group suffer disproportionately?
5. What is the probability that the outcome will be achieved?
6. Which solution maximises value?
7. Working with our structures:
   7.1 Change the structure.
   7.2 Approach it from a different direction.
   7.3 Start from a different point.
   7.4 Create a new structure.

Conclusion

Most of us are not taught moral thinking in the same way that we are taught mathematical, scientific and even logical thinking. Instead, we're given convenient moral prescriptions to learn; simple moral templates to apply whenever the appropriate situation appears. But, as we've seen in this chapter, these are very complex issues in which all sides are right to some extent. So to reach the best decision we have to design a solution, rather than take the standard model down from the shelf.

To do this we have to integrate as many as possible of the most important moral principles at stake in any situation. That way we will meet the important preferences, interests and needs of those involved. Now, we can turn to critical thinking and evaluate our solution to make sure our thinking is consistent and we have not overlooked anything.

20
Moral Thinking 4: Evaluating Solutions

When writers complete their first draft, they make the mental shift from the writer within them to the editor. The change in perspective can be insightful and transforming. The same transition occurs when we move from creative to critical thinking. Freed from the tangled undergrowth of our own initial thoughts and feelings, we see things in a way we haven't seen them before.

Nevertheless, this can be a confusing process, so it will help you to organise it and make it more straightforward if you work steadily through each of the checklists at the end of Chapters 10 to 16. As you do this, you will see that moral problems inevitably give rise to some things more than others. In this chapter we will focus on these, so that you develop a clearer idea of what to look for and the things you can do to prevent them reoccurring.

Arguments

Evaluating our arguments involves checking their consistency, which we found in Chapters 10 and 11 involves checking their components and the connections between them.

1 Components
With any familiar system of ideas and beliefs, we are always likely to take some things for granted. This is particularly true of our moral thinking. There cannot be many systems of beliefs that we hold closer to us than our moral beliefs. They seem to define who we are. The routine patterns of our thinking are stronger and more difficult to displace. As a result we are vulnerable to two common errors: suppressing premises that we simply take for granted and confusing facts with values.

1.1 Are any missing? – suppressed premises

Holding our moral beliefs so closely, it can seem incomprehensible that anybody should or could think differently. It's all too easy, therefore, to include in our arguments unstated premises that we have suppressed, often without knowing or because we think they are too obvious to need mention.

> *Example: Energy supply.*   Imagine you are a government minister responsible for energy supply. A company submits plans to build large wind turbines off the coast of a remote island. The population of the island is only 10,000, whereas the alternative sites are near urban areas on the mainland with populations of at least 50,000. The turbines will produce large amounts of clean, inexpensive electricity at a time when demand is growing. What's more, the islanders themselves will be able to have electricity in their own homes for the first time.

Given this, it's not unreasonable to assume that the islanders will welcome the project with some enthusiasm. Besides all the benefits they will enjoy from having electricity in their homes, there will be the increased business from the contractors and the local employment that will be generated. But, to your surprise, you find that there is overwhelming opposition to it. While they recognise the benefits of electricity, they have a unique culture, which they fear will disappear under the impact of television and the pervasive influence of commercial advertising.

> *Example: News editor.*   You are a news editor working on a local paper for a large national newspaper group. You receive a notification from head office that they will shortly be introducing new training programmes designed to help all those in the newsroom become 'multi-skilled'. In particular, this means training all reporters to be photographers and all photographers to be reporters.

You think this is an excellent idea and you take for granted that all those to be trained will think likewise. After all, it will improve their skills and increase the range of work they can do, making them much more valuable to employers. But, when you tell them about it, you are surprised by the lack of enthusiasm and the scepticism with which the news is greeted. It never occurred to you that some members of staff would suspect this is a way of reducing costs through redundancies and 'natural wastage', while others insist that they joined the profession as reporters or photographers, not some amalgam of the two.

As you can see, in each of these examples it seems natural to take certain assumptions about what we value for granted without ever realising that it is possible that people will think differently.

1.2 Confusing facts with values

Indeed, we can become so convinced that it is right to do a certain thing that we don't even recognise it as a value judgement at all and, instead, treat it as a fact. Consequently, we deduce a conclusion containing a value judgement from premises that appear to be purely factual. As we learnt in Chapter 10, this is invalid: no value judgement can be deduced from any set of premises which do not themselves contain a value judgement. Without knowing it, we have smuggled our own opinions in as if they were facts.

Moral thinking is, perhaps, more prone to this than any other form of thinking. Many of the words we use, like 'honesty', 'goodwill' and 'generosity' are mixed, both fact and value. Using them in what appears to be a factual argument, we can smuggle in a value judgement without realising it.

> *Examples: Islanders, photographers and reporters.* In both of the examples above it would not be strange to explain to the islanders, the photographers and the reporters that they were all being offered an 'opportunity'. But this is a mixed concept: not only does it carry its descriptive content, but it is also prescriptive in that opportunities are generally considered to be good things and should be taken when they are offered.

2 Connections

The same closely held conviction that our moral beliefs are right can influence the way we draw conclusions from our premises, particularly in our use of qualifiers and in the way we process terms.

2.1 Qualifiers

When our arguments involve our moral beliefs, we are more easily persuaded into categorical claims when, in fact, there might be good reason to have doubts. Slowing ourselves down to weigh up accurately the strength of the evidence and the weight of the supporting arguments, and then select just the right qualifier that reflects this, seems much more difficult when we are discussing issues about which we already have clear and strong moral convictions.

But we need to check not only that our qualifiers reflect accurately the strength of assurance that we can reasonably hold; we also have to be sure that the strength of our claims remains the same from premises to conclusion. As we connect our premises to our conclusion, it's easy to allow the conclusion to assume the categorical form ('all', 'every', 'always', etc.), when our premises may be in a more qualified form ('almost all', 'almost half', 'few', etc.).

Qualifiers:
1. Do my qualifiers reflect accurately the strength of the evidence and the weight of the supporting arguments?
2. Does the strength of my claims remain the same from premises to conclusion.

2.2 Processing terms

The same applies to the way we process our terms. Our moral discussions often go round in circles or hit a non-negotiable dead end. They break down for no obvious reason and there seems nothing we can do to resolve it. In many cases this is the result of assuming our terms mean more or less than they actually do. Consequently, in the conclusion we assert more or less than the premises allow us to. Although other people might disagree with your conclusion, they cannot explain why, because they can't find a fault in your argument.

> *Example: 'Obligation' and 'obliged'.*   If you were discussing a person's moral obligations to someone or something, having described these obligations in the premises of your argument, you might think it not unreasonable to argue from there to the conclusion that they are 'obliged' to do what those obligations entail. But in fact, there seems to be no necessary connection between what someone accepts as an obligation – what they think they ought to do – and what they are obliged to do and will therefore influence their actions.

As the philosopher G. E. M. Anscombe explains,[1] we might know what a plant needs, what it ought to have, but it will only affect our actions if we want the plant to flourish: there is no necessary connection between what in your judgement the plant *ought* to have and what you *want* it to have.

Evidence

All of this illustrates just how resolute the routine patterns of our thinking can be when we tackle moral problems. Perhaps more than any other aspect of our thinking, their influence is felt most in our use of evidence. As we describe and draw inferences from it our thinking falls into familiar patterns that we have used many times.

Indeed, the problems begin even earlier. As we generate our ideas in the first place, we find it difficult to put ourselves in someone else's moral shoes. In Chapter 3 we found that generating our ideas involves thinking outside our own limited perspective in order to experience vicariously the thoughts and feelings of others by empathising with them on different levels. As our moral ideas seem to define who we are, this can present a tough, unyielding challenge.

1 Empathy – the thought experiment

To know whether our solution is the right one we must imaginatively place ourselves in the position and circumstances of those who are affected by our decision. We must experience the impact of doing what we propose to do. We can then test whether there is any further objection to this solution: whether we would really want this for ourselves if we were in this position. In this way we convert our *beliefs* about what we value into *values*: we convert what we *believe* is the best solution into what we *know* is the best solution.

> *Example: World peace.* I might argue that I value world peace, although I am not prepared to give up my job to join the Peace Corps or the United Nations to work to bring it about. In this case it seems I am merely *talking about values*, about what I *believe* to be valuable, rather than *valuing*.

To know that I do in fact value this I must learn to give myself the experience of being in these circumstances, working in a difficult situation with all the personal sacrifices this would entail. Only then will I know if I really want to do this, that I *value* it, and not just *believe* that I value it. In the same way, it's not until we have used our empathetic imagination to experience vicariously the effects on others of implementing our solution, that we can know whether this is the right one. Up until then we are merely *talking about values*, rather than *valuing*.

When we employ this type of thought experiment, we confront the experience as accurately as we can without actually being in that situation: we test our beliefs about values against our pre-existing values to see if we can integrate them within them. Only if we *desire* what we *believe* ought to be the case can we be said to have assented to a moral judgement with real understanding and sincerity. Without this we cannot be said to have really 'bought into the idea'.

> *Example: Teachers and trainers.*   As all teachers and trainers will know, this mirrors exactly the way we learn. Teaching and learning involve not just a simple process of passively transmitting statements for students to understand and remember, but in their actively processing ideas. Otherwise they will remain just discrete statements recalled by students without any relevance. They will not be statements of 'facts', since they have not been processed, but only remembered without any meaning or significance.

Learning, like valuing, comes about through a process which analyses, criticises and evaluates new ideas, setting them in the context of our already existing structure of interrelated ideas. In this way, we test and implement them. We compare them with structures of ideas we already possess, making them our own by integrating them within our own network of beliefs and understanding.

> *Example: The nervous candidate.*   Colin Radford gives us an interesting example that illustrates the distinction involved here.[2] He cites a nervous candidate in an exam, who, in the panic of the moment, produces all the facts she has been taught without believing the arguments she produces. To an observer she is producing exactly what she has been taught as the right answers, but can she be said to know them when she doesn't actually believe them?

The example certainly suggests that we can know without believing; that by simply remembering things and spilling them out on paper we do in fact know them. But most students from an early age know that you can remember the most complex arguments accurately without understanding anything about them or having any reasons to believe them. To know something calls for more than passively remembering discrete items of information. We have to process them actively by evaluating the justifications given for them and by coming to our own judgements as to their relevance and significance to the wider network of our beliefs. Without this, we might remember without being able to say genuinely that we know.

The parallel process in moral thinking is to place ourselves imaginatively in the position of those who will be affected by the decision we make and vicariously experience their thoughts and feeling so we can integrate them within our own network of beliefs and values in the same way.

> *Example: Suzanne and the social worker.*   Once we conduct this sort of thought experiment on the third solution we chose, we may discover doubts about whether Suzanne will, indeed, value the normative principles of equal opportunity and self-esteem over her desire for justice and official accountability. Although *we* might prefer this, placing ourselves imaginatively in her position might reveal doubts we had not previously entertained: that she might have an over-whelming sense of personal injury that must be addressed first.

2 Describing the evidence

Once we have checked how well we've generated these ideas, we can turn our attention to the influence our moral convictions have on the accuracy of our descriptions of the evidence. In Chapter 12 we examined the various ways our established patterns of ideas can influence the way we describe our evidence. So we have to ask ourselves some of the same questions:

Do I use a sufficient number of examples to reach my generalisation? Are they a fair representation?
Do I exaggerate or underestimate the evidence, claiming more or less than it will allow?

When I use words, like 'typical', 'normal', and 'average', have I revealed all their implications and then checked that they represent a fair and accurate description?

Many of these problems are the result of having strong emotions and clear convictions that shape our thinking regardless of the evidence. Consider the following example:

> *Example: The official and the superstore.* You are an official in the Ministry for Local Government with responsibility for preparing reports and recommendations to the minister on local commercial planning. A large chain of superstores submits an application to build a new superstore in a small town. This will serve an area untapped by the company or any other chain of superstores. But the nearest two towns with superstores report the closure of local shops and businesses, and the decay of the central commercial areas, where once there were thriving communities. You receive a petition signed by 16,000 local people demanding that the application be rejected. This represents about 68 per cent of the town's population. What will you recommend?

Our evaluation of the evidence presented here is likely to be shaped by prior political and ethical convictions. Patterns of ideas and values that routinely shape our thinking about such matters would kick in. In the introduction we found that, prior to 2007 and the recession brought about by the banking crisis, the thinking of many of the most prominent and influential bankers and political leaders was shaped by their belief in the importance of lightly regulated markets and in the Neo-Darwinian notion that these sorts of problems are best left to the market to sort out in the best way possible for all. This blinded them to many of the dangers that were already evident.

So, it is not inconceivable that the same assumptions could influence our judgement in this example. We might assess the evidence of the petition and the report on the experience of the two local towns in the light of our commitment to what we believe to be the cardinal values of competition and consumer sovereignty, which, we believe, should be sacrosanct. We might be convinced that, given their freedom to operate unimpeded, they will meet the preferences of all and not just those of a few thousand local residents. With these values and ideas, it might be difficult for us to appreciate the argument for the less well defined importance of communities and communal life to people.

3 Drawing inferences from the evidence

Having arrived at our description of the evidence, we must then draw relevant and reliable inferences from it. If we have used an analogy to draw inferences, as many moral arguments do, we must ask ourselves:

> Are there significant differences between the analogy and the actual situation?
> Are these differences reflected in the conclusions we draw from them?
> Is our conclusion of the right strength, reflecting all the similarities and differences between the two?

Example: The official and the superstore.   In this example you might be tempted to use the analogy of Darwin's theory of evolution by natural selection to support your argument for free, unregulated competition. You might justify your decision by arguing that cut-throat competition was the natural state of affairs, which will bring to the top the strongest and most efficient. This is part of the natural law and the inevitable outcome of history, so to resist it is not only inefficient, but in the long-term futile.

But then you must take into account significant differences between what you are advocating and the analogy you are using. Darwin's theory of evolution not only recognised that for many species co-operation was the key to survival, but his theory was blind: it could not foretell that the strongest and most efficient would survive, just that the outcome would be determined by functional improvement and the nature of this depended on the nature of the environment. This might mean that those who survive have quite different advantages to those you might cite in your description of the strongest and most efficient. Indeed, their survival might be the product of the advantage that living and co-operating in a community gives them.

Such caution over the way we use our analogies will help to ensure our inferences are both relevant and reliable. In addition, as we discovered in Chapters 13 and 14, we must also check that we haven't oversimplified the case by using stereotypes, straw men or by special pleading, and that we've avoided creating invalid causal connections.

Language

Finally, we must evaluate how we have used language to describe the problem. All too often we discover that the language we have used has so shaped and manipulated our thinking that we just haven't seen things that should have been obvious from the start.

Unless we're careful, we can find that the language controls us, rather than us controlling it. In the process we struggle to get to the heart of the problem. The best way of protecting our thinking against this, as we found in Chapters 15 and 16, is to check the clarity and consistency of the language we use.

1 Clarity

Unfortunately, the way we use some moral language can beg important questions or exert emotional influence. Concepts like 'responsibility', 'equality', 'guilt' and, in the abortion debate, a 'person', all submit to different interpretations, each one carrying with it implications for the discussion in which they are used. So we have to be clear about the ideas that lie within the words we use. In particular we have to ask ourselves:

Have I obscured my ideas by using jargon?
Am I sure that the abstractions I use mean the same to other people?
Have I allowed my own thinking to be manipulated by the emotional influence that loaded language exerts?
Have I manipulated my own thinking by begging the question?

In particular, it is very easy to describe the problem in such a way, using moral words vaguely, to give our arguments everything we need.

Example: Responsibility. We might argue about a particular criminal case that the person was responsible for his actions and, therefore, should be punished. But the argument hangs on when we believe somebody can be held to be responsible for their actions and, in turn, this depends on when we believe their actions have been free and not compelled. One definition that might attract general support is the Aristotelian view that an act is compelled when its origin is external, when it is brought about by influences beyond the individual's control, so that the person contributes nothing to it. In such circumstances the individual cannot be held to be responsible.

But, then, what do we include in this? An individual may think or behave in a certain way that is not of her own choosing, but the result of the society in which she lives and the need to conform, to feel normal. The American behavioural psychologist B. F. Skinner argues that certain forces, like education, moral discourse and persuasion, are as much a form of control as any form of physical coercion or threat of force.

> *Example: Responsibility.*   Perhaps, then, we should argue that a person is responsible as long as he is free to decide what to do, which follows directly from his character alone and not from any external force however defined. His decision is caused by the person he is, by his character. In this case responsibility rests on our freedom to act on the basis of self-chosen ends, influenced by our own experiences, thoughts, motives, desires and needs.

But even here I can argue that my decisions are dictated by influences over which I have little or no control. There are various forms of internal compulsions we know little about and, even when we do learn about them, we have limited or no means of resisting them. And anyway, how can anyone be responsible for his actions, since they grow out of his character, which has been shaped, moulded and made what it is today by influences, some hereditary, but most stemming from his early parental environment, that were not of his own choosing?

Even if we have the ability to change, to overcome the influence of our early environment, the will to overcome these early disadvantages is of no credit to us. We are just lucky, because the strength of will to overcome our early environment is itself a product of that early environment. We can no more blame others for their inability to change than we can congratulate ourselves for our ability to do so.

As this illustrates, it is all too easy to accept unknowingly a set of assumptions that lie behind a particular concept and allow our thinking to be manipulated by it. Revealing these assumptions and giving sharper clarity to the meaning of the concepts we use helps us bring to light for ourselves, as well as for others, the underlying implications of our arguments that we may have missed.

2 Consistency

Then, once we're clear about these implications, we have to make sure that they remain the same in the course of our argument; that we don't change the way we use concepts. We need to ask ourselves:

> Do I maintain the same meaning for the words I use, or do I allow them to change in the course of my argument?
> Does the persuasiveness of my argument depend on equivocation in my use of words?

This is the fallacy of equivocation that we examined in Chapter 16: the meaning of a concept changes in the middle of the argument from one premise to another, making the argument and its conclusion invalid. In one part of the argument the concept is used to identify one referent, but then in another part it is used to identify a different one.

Unfortunately, much of the equivocation that infects our thinking occurs with deceptive subtlety. One of its most common manifestations is in references to races, nationalities and countries. You might read any of the following:

> 'America invaded X.'
> 'American greatness depends on freedom.'
> 'The interests of America depend upon free trade with Australia.'
> 'The average American stands for gun ownership'.

But what do we mean in each case when 'America/n' is used? Each case involves different referents. The first statement refers to the American military; the second, perhaps, to American business, commerce or industry; the third could refer to American farmers or consumers; and the fourth to that percentage of American citizens who own guns. And, of course, you can substitute any nationality in similar sentences to get the same effect.

Checklist

Checklist – Evaluating solutions:

1. Arguments:

  1.1 Components

      Are any missing – suppressed premises

      Confusing facts with values

1.2 Connections
        Qualifiers
        Processing terms
2. **Evidence:**
    2.1 Empathy – the thought experiment
            Converting beliefs about values into values
    2.2 Describing the evidence
            Sufficient examples
            Fair representation
            Exaggerating and underestimating
            'Typical', 'Normal', 'Average'
    2.3 Drawing inferences from the evidence
            Using analogies
            Stereotypes, straw men, special pleading
            Creating invalid causal connections
3. **Language:**
    3.1 Clarity
            Jargon and abstractions
            Loaded language
            Begging the question
    3.2 Consistency
            Equivocation

Conclusion

Although the process of moral decision-making, as we have described it, from generating our ideas, through conceptual and creative thinking to critical thinking, might have seemed at times to be complex, involving more detailed deliberation that you would normally entertain, developing our skills in each stage is the key to becoming more effective moral thinkers. Improving any skill first involves analysing it into its parts. To improve your golf swing, your first task is to analyse it so you can identify the problem and work on it.

However, as we have found, with our moral thinking this can be difficult. The routine patterns of our thinking are stronger and more difficult to displace. But if Mark Pastin is right that high-ethics organisations are simply better at what they do, learning to become good moral thinkers promises to reward our efforts with handsome dividends.

Conclusion

We began this book by describing humankind as inveterately conservative, pledged to routine patterns of behaviour and timid of innovation. On a geological scale we are still close to our primitive origins with all their fears, sentiments and programmed responses. Of the four to five million years of our existence, barely 10,000 have been spent in learning and 'civilisation'. And for much of this time things have changed very slowly, if at all. Just 250 years ago we were living in societies that resembled in almost every detail the societies in which our forefathers had lived two or three centuries earlier.

We have only very recently become progressive and even then only partially and artificially so. Our primitive past has left us with all the marks and weaknesses of a mind resistant to new ideas. In *Totem and Taboo*, Sigmund Freud describes how easily we fall into habits and inhibitions for reasons not discovered, or easily forgotten. Fixed and sacred, any departure from them is filled with fear and dread. As recently as 1633 Galileo was being forced, under the threat of excommunication, to renounce publicly his view that the Earth went round the Sun.

We tend to congratulate ourselves that we have come a long way since then, but not so far. We display the same reluctance to embrace new ideas and anxiously protect inherited patterns of beliefs and expectations. Entry into some professions is still determined more by whom you know than by how well you think. Undergraduates receive high marks for showing how well they can recycle the opinions of authorities, rather than for the originality of their own thinking. In the business world, large corporations follow conventional wisdom and award their CEOs massive performance bonuses, even when their decisions have resulted in unprecedented losses that threaten the survival of the corporation.

Compounding this problem still further, in the modern era our intellectual perspectives have become narrower. The difference between the medieval and modern worlds is marked by the rise of the specialist: someone who knows more and more about less and less. As our intellectual world has contracted, not only have we been more inclined to give way to specialist opinion where we no longer feel qualified to comment, but we have been more willing to accept the narrower vision defined by the values and routines of our own area of expertise.

Both problems have left us ill-equipped to manage change. The challenges we face call for a different kind of thinking. Rather than allow ourselves to ride comfortably within the well-worn grooves of our handed-down beliefs, to think as we have always thought, we must think about our thinking while we think. In this book we have described this as second-order thinking. It means learning to generate more of our own ideas, to structure them using our causal and conceptual thinking skills, and then to use our creative skills to adapt them to meet the demands of changing times.

The methods and techniques you have learnt to become good thinkers may at times have seemed more deliberate and detailed than your normal thinking. But learning any new method is always front-loaded. In time it will bed itself in to become part of your normal thinking processes. Nevertheless, there will always be that sense of awkwardness that comes from being asked to work in a different way and at a different pace and depth.

But then, in return, the rewards for your determination to think deeper, to question what seems unquestionable, are greater than most of us can imagine. You will learn to generate a richer mixture of more subtle ideas knit together in complex patterns of interrelations. Out of these you will learn to design your own solutions that will always have the power to surprise you with their insights and originality.

Notes

Introduction

1. Ernest Dimnet, *The Art of Thinking* (London: Cape, 1929), p. 48.

Part 1 Original Ideas

1. Christopher Caldwell, *Select All*, 1 March 2004.

Chapter 1 Reprogramming our Thinking

1. R. M. Hare, *Moral Thinking* (Oxford: Oxford University Press, 1981), p. 49.
2. Herbert A. Simon and W. G. Chase, 'Skill in Chess', *American Scientist* 61 (1973), pp. 394–403; quoted in James Surowiecki, *The Wisdom of Crowds* (London: Abacus, 2006), p. 32.
3. Sydney Finkelstein, Jo Whitehead, and Andrew Campbell, *Think Again* (Boston, MA: Harvard Business Press, 2008), pp. ix–x.
4. Finkelstein, Whitehead and Campbell, *Think Again*, pp. 15–17.
5. Bertrand Russell, *History of Western Philosophy* (London: Allen & Unwin, 1967), p. 14.
6. Paul Tillich, *The Shaking of the Foundations*, 1949 (Harmondsworth: Penguin, 1964), pp. 118–21.
7. Aldous Huxley, 'Green Tunnels', in *Mortal Coils*, 1922 (Harmondsworth: Penguin, 1955), p. 114.
8. Charles Handy, *Beyond Certainty: The Changing Worlds of Organisations* (London: Hutchinson, 1995), p. 104.
9. *New York Times*, April 1, 1934.
10. Ernest Dimnet, *The Art of Thinking* (London: Cape, 1929), p. 187.
11. Peter Ackroyd, *Newton* (London: Chatto & Windus, 2006), p. 26.
12. Ackroyd, *Newton*, p. 27.
13. The study appeared in *The Proceedings of the National Academy of Sciences*, which you can find at http://www.pnas.org/content/104/18/7723. abstract.

Chapter 2 Asking the Right Questions

1. Mike Martin and Roland Schinzinger, *Ethics in Engineering* (New York: McGraw-Hill, 1989), pp. 43–4; quoted in Damian Grace and Stephen Cohen. *Business Ethics: Australian Problems and Cases* (Melbourne: Oxford University Press, 1998), p. 148.

Chapter 3 Generating Ideas

1. P. B. Medawar, *Induction and Intuition in Scientific Thought* (London: Methuen, 1969), p. 53.

2. Medawar, *Induction and Intuition*, p. 26.
3. Boris Starling, *Visibility* (London: Harper, 2007), p. 14.
4. I am grateful to Marcus Groombridge LLB (Hons) Cert. PFS of Joseph Oliver Ltd for this example.
5. Rudolf Flesch, *The Art of Clear Thinking* (New York: Harper & Row, 1951), p. 121.

Part 2 Structuring Our Ideas

Chapter 4   Causal Thinking

1. These examples are from the *Guardian* Unlimited crossword page, which you can find at www.guardian.co.uk/crossword.
2. P. B. Medawar, *Induction and Intuition in Scientific Thought* (London: Methuen, 1969), p. 48.
3. Lisa Tsoi Hoshmand and Donald E. Polkinghorne. 'Redefining the Science-Practice Relationship and Professional Training', *American Psychologist*, Vol. 47, No. 1 (1992), pp. 55–66.
4. A fuller account of this example can be found in Richard D. Altick, *Preface to Critical Reading*, 5th edn (New York: Holt, Rinehart & Winston, 1969), pp. 283–5.

Chapter 5   Conceptual Thinking – Analysis 1:
Second-Order Thinking

1. Bertrand Russell, *The Problems of Philosophy*, 1912 (Oxford: Oxford University Press, 1986), p. 28.
2. Charles Handy, *Beyond Certainty: The Changing Worlds of Organisations* (London: Hutchinson, 1995), pp. 161–3.
3. James D. Watson, *The Double Helix* (New York: Mentor, 1969), p. 78.
4. Watson, *The Double Helix*, p. 55.
5. Ludwig Wittgenstein, *Philosophical Investigations*, 1953 (Oxford: Blackwell, 1992), p. 32.

Chapter 7   Conceptual Thinking: Synthesis

1. P. B. Medawar, *Induction and Intuition in Scientific Thought* (London: Methuen, 1969), p. 26.
2. Medawar, *Induction and Intuition*, p. 53.
3. David Hume, *A Treatise of Human Nature*, 1739–40 (London: Dent, Everyman's Library, 1968), Vol. 1, p. 239.
4. Dorothea Brande, *Becoming a Writer*, 1934 (London: Macmillan, 1984), p. 151.
5. Brande, *Becoming a Writer*, p. 160.
6. Brande, *Becoming a Writer*, p. 149.
7. Brande, *Becoming a Writer*, p. 151.
8. *New York Times*, 1 April 1934.
9. P. D. Smith, 'The genius of space and time', *The Guardian*, 17 September 2005.
10. James D. Watson, *The Double Helix* (London: Mentor, 1969), p. 55.

Part 3   Creative Thinking

1. Lisa Tsoi Hoshmand and Donald E. Polkinghorne, 'Redefining the Science-Practice Relationship and Professional Training', *American Psychologist*, January 1992, p. 61.
2. D. Schön, *The Reflective Practitioner: How Professionals Think in Action* (New York: Basic Books, 1983).

Chapter 8   Problem Solving 1: Analogies
1. Richard Dawkin, *The Selfish Gene* (Oxford: Oxford University Press, 1982).
2. Adrian Desmond and James Moore, *Darwin* (London: Michael Joseph, 1991), p. 420.
3. Quoted in Bill Lucas, *Boost Your Mind Power* (London: Duncan Baird, 2006), p. 89.

Chapter 9   Problem Solving 2: Adapting Structures
1. For a more complete account of Quaker's acquisition of Snapple, read Sydney Finkelstein, Jo Whitehead and Andrew Campbell, *Think Again* (Boston, MA: Harvard Business Press, 2008), p. 16.
2. Sir Arthur Conan Doyle, 'The Problem of Thor Bridge', in *The Case-Book of Sherlock Holmes*, 1927 (London: Penguin, 1951), p. 153.

Part 4   Critical Thinking

Chapter 11   Thinking with Arguments 2: The Connections
1. Oscar Wilde, 'Lady Windermere's Fan', in *The Importance of Being Ernest and Other Plays* (London: Penguin, 1987), p. 15.
2. Wilde, 'Lady Windermere's Fan', p. 17.
3. Oscar Wilde, *The Picture of Dorian Gray* (Oxford: Oxford University Press, 1974), ch. 3, p. 35.
4. Arthur Conan Doyle, 'The Greek Interpreter', in *The Memoirs of Sherlock Holmes*, in *The Complete Sherlock Holmes' Short Stories* (London: John Murray & Jonathan Cape, 1980), pp. 481–2.
5. L. Susan Stebbing, *Thinking to Some Purpose*, 1939 (Harmondsworth: Penguin, 1961), pp. 29–30.
6. Arthur Conan Doyle, 'The Boscombe Valley Mystery', in *The Adventures of Sherlock Holmes* (Harmondsworth: Penguin, 1988), p. 92.

Chapter 12   Thinking with Evidence 1: Describing It
1. André Malraux quoted in L. Susan Stebbing, *Thinking to Some Purpose* (Harmondsworth: Penguin, 1961), p. 45.

Chapter 15   Thinking with Language 1: Clarity
1. Helena Echlin, 'Critical Mass', in *The Sydney Morning Herald*, 10 February 2001; the complete article appeared in *Areté*, www.aretemagazine.com.
2. *The Sunday Times*, 18 January 1998.

3. Quoted in Rudolf Flesch. *The Art of Clear Thinking* (New York: Harper & Row, 1951), p. 57.
4. *The Guardian*, 9 June 1980.

Chapter 16 Thinking with Language 2: Consistency

1. L. Susan Stebbing, *Thinking to Some Purpose* (Harmondsworth: Penguin, 1961), pp. 183–4.

Part 5 Moral Thinking: A Case Study

1. Code of Ethics, 1988, The Institution of Engineers, National Office, 11 National Circuit, Barton, ACT 2600, Australia, p. 3.
2. Mark Pastin, *The Hard Problems of Management: Gaining the Ethics Edge* (San Francisco: Jossey-Bass, 1986), p. 129.
3. Pastin, *The Hard Problems of Management*, p. 132.
4. Pastin, *The Hard Problems of Management*, p. 132.
5. Charles Handy, *Beyond Certainty: The Changing Worlds of Organisations* (London: Hutchinson, 1995), pp. 183–4.
6. '"Employability" and Trust', *Conference Board meeting*, Chicago, 12 Sept 1996; you can find this at www.greatplacetowork.com.

Chapter 17 Moral Thinking 1: Generating Ideas

1. L. T. Hosmer, *The Ethics of Management*, 3rd edn (Chicago: Irwin, 1996), p. 26.
2. I am grateful to the Department of Social Work at the University of Newcastle in New South Wales, Australia, and particularly to its head, Professor Mel Gray, who very kindly allowed me to use this case study.
3. H. J. Paton (trans.), *The Moral Law: Kant's Groundwork of the Metaphysic of Morals* (London: Hutchinson, 1948), p. 84.
4. Holy Bible, *Leviticus*, chs 9 and 11.
5. Gitta Sereny, *Into that Darkness: From Mercy Killing to Mass Murder* (London: André Deutsch, 1974), pp. 200–2.

Chapter 19 Moral Thinking 3: Designing Solutions

1. For a more detailed account of this case, read Damian Grace and Stephen Cohen, *Business Ethics: Australian Problems and Cases* (Oxford: Oxford University Press, 1998), pp. 35–6.
2. Duncan Graham, '$92,000 damages for porn in workplace harassment', *Sydney Morning Herald*, 22 April 1994, p. 3; quoted in Grace and Cohen, *Business Ethics*, p. 35.
3. John Stuart Mill, *On Liberty*, 1859 (Harmondsworth: Penguin, 1984), p. 68.

Chapter 20 Moral Thinking 4: Evaluating Solutions

1. G. E. M. Anscombe, 'Modern Moral Philosophy', in *The Collected Philosophical Papers of G. E. M. Anscombe*, Vol. 3, *Ethics, Religion and Politics* (Oxford: Blackwell, 1981), pp. 26–42; first published in *Philosophy*, 33, 1958.
2. Colin Radford, 'Knowledge by Examples', *Analysis*, 27, 1966; see also, 'Does Unwitting Knowledge Entail Unconscious Belief?', *Analysis*, 29, 1969, pp. 103–7.

Bibliography

Ackroyd, Peter, *Newton* (London: Chatto & Windus, 2006).

Anscombe, G. E. M., 'Modern Moral Philosophy', in *The Collected Philosophical Papers of G. E. M. Anscombe*, Vol. 3, *Ethics, Religion and Politics* (Oxford: Blackwell, 1981), pp. 26–42; first published in *Philosophy*, 33, 1958.

Campbell, D. R., 'Evolutionary epistemology', in P. A. Schilpp (ed.), *The Philosophy of Karl Popper* (La Salle. IL: Open Court, 1974), pp. 413–63.

Conway, D. and R. Munson, *Elements of Reasoning* (Belmont, CA: Wadsworth, 2003).

Copi, I., and Carl Cohen, *Introduction to Logic* (New York: Macmillan, 1997).

Dawkin, Richard, *The Selfish Gene* (Oxford: Oxford University Press, 1982).

de Bono, Edward, *Practical Thinking* (Harmondsworth: Penguin, 1971).

de Bono, Edward, *Lateral Thinking for Management* (London: Penguin, 1990).

de Bono, Edward, *Serious Creativity* (London: Harper-Collins, 1995).

Desmond, Adrian, and James Moore, *Darwin* (London: Michael Joseph, 1991).

Dimnet, Ernest, *The Art of Thinking* (London: Cape, 1929).

Echlin, Helena, 'Critical Mass', in *The Sydney Morning Herald*, 10 February 2001; for the complete article, see Areté, www.aretemagazine.com.

Finkelstein, Sydney, Jo Whitehead and Andrew Campbell, *Think Again* (Boston, MA: Harvard Business Press, 2008).

Flesch, Rudolf, *The Art of Clear Thinking* (New York: Harper & Row, 1951).

Forrest-Pressley, D., G. McKinnon and T. Waller, *Metacognition, Cognition, and Human Performance* (San Diego, CA: Academic Press, 1985).

Gladwell, Malcolm, *Blink: The Power of Thinking Without Thinking* (London: Penguin, 2006).

Grace, Damian, and Stephen Cohen, *Business Ethics: Australian Problems and Cases* (Melbourne: Oxford University Press, 1998).

Handy, Charles, *The Empty Raincoat* (London: Arrow Books, 1995).

Handy, Charles, *Beyond Certainty: The Changing Worlds of Organisations* (London: Hutchinson, 1995a).

Handy, Charles, *Gods of Management* (London: Arrow Books, 1995b).

Handy, Charles, *Understanding Organisations* (London: Penguin, 1999).

Hare, R. M., *Moral Thinking* (Oxford: Oxford University Press, 1981).

Hoshmand, Lisa Tsoi and Donald E. Polkinghorne. 'Redefining the Science-Practice Relationship and Professional Training', *American Psychologist*, 47:1 (1992), pp. 55–66.

Hosmer, L. T., *The Ethics of Management*, 3rd edn (Chicago: Irwin, 1996).

Hume, David, *A Treatise of Human Nature*, 1739–40 (London: Dent, Everyman's Library, 1968).

Huxley, Aldous, 'Green Tunnels', in *Mortal Coils*, 1922 (Harmondsworth: Penguin, 1955).

Kanfer, F. H., 'The scientist-practitioner connection: A bridge in need of constant attention', in *Professional Psychology: Research and Practice*, 21 (1990), pp. 264–70.

Kuhn, T. S., *The Structure of Scientific Revolutions* (Chicago: Chicago University Press, 1971).

Margolis, H., *Patterns, Thinking, and Cognition* (Chicago: Chicago University Press, 1987).

Martin, Mike, and Roland Schinzinger, *Ethics in Engineering* (New York: McGraw-Hill, 1989).

Medawar, P. B., *Induction and Intuition in Scientific Thought* (London: Methuen, 1969).

Mill, John Stuart, *On Liberty*, 1859 (Harmondsworth: Penguin, 1984).

Pastin, Mark, *The Hard Problems of Management: Gaining the Ethics Edge* (San Francisco: Jossey-Bass, 1986).

Paton, H. J. (trans.), *The Moral Law: Kant's Groundwork of the Metaphysic of Morals* (London: Hutchinson, 1948).

Polkinghorne, D. E., *Narrative Knowing and the Human Sciences* (Albany, NY: State University of New York Press, 1988).

Ramachandran, V. S., and Sandra Blakeslee, *Phantoms in the Brain: Human Nature and the Architecture of the Mind* (London: Fourth Estate, 1998).

Russell, Bertrand, *History of Western Philosophy* (London: Allen & Unwin, 1967)

Russell, Bertrand, *The Problems of Philosophy*, 1912 (Oxford: Oxford University Press, 1986).

Schön, D., *The Reflective Practitioner: How Professionals Think in Action* (New York: Basic Books, 1983).

Schön, D., *Educating the Reflective Practitioner* (San Francisco, CA: Jossey-Bass, 1987).

Simon, Herbert, A., and W. G. Chase, 'Skill in Chess', *American Scientist*, 61 (1973), pp. 394–403.

Smith, P. D., 'The genius of space and time', *The Guardian*, 17 September 2005.

Starling, Boris, *Visibility* (London: Harper, 2007).

Stebbing, L. Susan, *Thinking to Some Purpose*, 1939 (Harmondsworth: Penguin, 1961).

Sternberg, Robert J., *Why Smart People Can Be So Stupid* (New Haven and London: Yale University Press, 2002).

Stricker, G., and R. H. Keisner, 'The relationship between research and practice', in G. Stricker and R. H. Keisner (eds), *From Research to Clinical Practice* (New York: Plenum Press, 1985), pp. 3–14.

Surowiecki, James, *The Wisdom of Crowds* (London: Abacus, 2006).

Tillich, Paul, *The Shaking of the Foundations*, 1949 (Harmondsworth: Penguin, 1964).

Toulmin, S., *Human Understanding: The Collective Use and Evolution of Concepts* (Princeton, NJ: Princeton University Press, 1972).

Watson, James D., *The Double Helix* (New York: Mentor, 1969).

Wilson, John, *Thinking with Concepts* (Cambridge: Cambridge University Press, 1976).

Wittgenstein, Ludwig, *Philosophical Investigations*, 1953 (Oxford: Blackwell, 1992).

Glossary

The following glossary is designed to give you quick and convenient access to definitions of the more technical terms used in the text.

Accidental generalisations Some generalisations, although they are universal in form, cannot support counterfactual or subjunctive conditionals, because there is nothing analogous about the relationships they describe. Even though I can claim that 'All the coins in my pocket are dated 1990', this does not allow me to support a subjunctive conditional to the effect that if I were to put another coin in my pocket this too would be dated 1990. It is merely an accidental generalisation.

See also Counterfactual and subjunctive conditionals.

Affirming the antecedent and denying the consequent A hypothetical or conditional proposition is marked by the distinctive 'if/then' structure as in the proposition, 'If an athlete is found to have taken performance enhancing drugs, then he will be disqualified.'

There are two valid forms of arguments that use a hypothetical proposition: to 'affirm the antecedent' and 'deny the consequent'. The two invalid forms are to 'deny the antecedent' and to 'affirm the consequent'.

See Chapter 11.

Analytic proposition If a proposition is true analytically it is true by virtue of itself alone: it is not necessary to refer to anything beyond its own terms. For example, 'All bachelors are unmarried men', 'All cats are animals', and 'All bicycles have two wheels', are all true analytically: they are true by virtue of what we agree to put into them in the first place. The fact that we agree the word 'bachelor' shall mean 'male' and 'unmarried', makes the statement true. In the same way, when we analyse the meaning of 'cat' and 'bicycle', we find their meaning, too, links two or more characteristics in 'all' cases.

See also Empirical proposition.

Argument by analogy When we argue by analogy we assert that things, which resemble each other in some respects, will resemble each other in some further respect. We might conclude from the fact that A, B and C all have characteristics x and y, and A and B in addition have characteristic z, that C too will probably have characteristic z. However, the fallacy of false analogy is often committed when we ignore differences and push similarities beyond what is reasonable.

Autonomy All individuals consider themselves to be ends-in-themselves and not mere means to achieve someone else's ends. In other words, we believe we have intrinsic, not just extrinsic, value. We attach paramount importance to our autonomous status as the fashioners of our own ends with freedom to make our own choices.

A significant implication of this is that our moral decisions are not driven by our desires – what we *want* to do – but by what we think we *ought* to do: not by prudential reasons about what will most effectively satisfy our desires, but by moral reasons. If they were driven by our desires, we would no longer be ends-in-ourselves and we would no longer have a choice: it would not be us that determine what we should do, but our desires and appetites. The actions and lives of individuals must be determined by the dictates of their own reason, by their own self-imposed judgements.

Begging the question   Begging the question occurs when you accept as an assumption what you are supposedly arguing for as a conclusion. Strictly speaking, this is what we know as arguing in a circle or, more familiarly, the fallacy of the vicious circle. We use a premise to prove a conclusion and then use the conclusion to prove the premise. It is revealed in four common forms: common notions, moral words, verbal propositions and vague definitions.
See Chapter 15.

Composition   The fallacy of composition is committed when we assume that what is true of the part is also true of the whole.
See also Division.

Conditional proposition   *See* Hypothetical proposition

Contraries   Contraries refer to those things that do not exclude their opposite, but include it as their most extreme form. Both represent the two extremes of a continuous series of changes. So, where the statement, 'This is white', has only one opposite – 'This is black' – it has many contraries including 'This is not white', 'This is coloured', 'This is grey', 'This is dirty', as well as 'This is black.'
See also Opposites.

Conversion   Conversion is the process of interchanging the subject and the complement of a sentence. It follows from the proposition 'No Xs are Ys' that 'No Ys are Xs'. The subject (X) and the predicate (Y) can be interchanged, that is, the converse is also true. But while total exclusion is a reversible relation, total inclusion is not. We cannot similarly argue that given 'All Xs are Ys', then 'All Ys are Xs'. While we can argue that 'All dogs are animals', we cannot reverse this and argue that 'All animals are dogs'. This would be an example of illicit conversion. Nevertheless, partial inclusion is reversible. We can argue not only that 'Some accountants are businessmen', but also that 'Some businessmen are accountants.'

Counterfactual and subjunctive conditionals   We generally talk about two types of conditionals: counterfactual and subjunctive. The first is perhaps more usually associated with historians who ask what would have happened if something else had occurred rather than that which did in fact occur. So, counterfactual conditionals have the form: 'If A had been the case, then B would have occurred.' With subjunctive conditionals it is forward looking, in that we ask what will happen if we do something: 'If A should occur, then so would B.'

Deductive thinking   Deduction is a form of argument in which the conclusion is already contained within the premises. It can therefore be described as 'conclusive reasoning', because the conclusion never states more than is contained in the assumptions that make up the argument, whereas an inductive argument always does. In an inductive argument we start with singular observation statements that certain events, all similar in some important respect, have occurred, and then we derive a universal generalisation that applies to all events of this type, observed and unobserved, past, present and future.

See Chapter 10.

Denying the consequent *See* Affirming the antecedent and denying the consequent.

Distributing our terms To distribute a term is to refer to every member of the class of things it represents. If we distribute the term 'businessmen', we might say, 'All businessmen treat their workers badly', whereas if we were only to use the partial qualifier, 'Some', we would not distribute it.

Division The fallacy of division is committed when we argue that something, which is true for the whole, is also true of its parts taken separately.

See also Composition.

Empirical proposition An empirical proposition is one that is based wholly or in part on the evidence of our senses.

See also Analytic proposition.

Equivocation When we use words in two or more different ways in the same argument, we commit the fallacy of equivocation if that argument depends on them maintaining constant meaning throughout.

Fallacy of false dilemma We assume that the problem we're dealing with has an either/or solution; that there are just two alternatives, when in fact there may be several.

See Chapter 14.

Hypothetical proposition The hypothetical or conditional proposition has two parts: the 'if' clause, known as the antecedent, and the 'then' clause, known as the consequent, as in the proposition: 'If an athlete is found to have taken performance enhancing drugs, then he will be disqualified.'

See also Affirming the antecedent and Denying the consequent.

Illicit conversion *See* Conversion.

Illicit obversion *See* Obversion.

Inductive thinking See Deductive thinking.

Invalid causal connections

The *post hoc* fallacy (*post hoc ergo propter hoc* fallacy – 'After this, therefore because of this'): the mistake of assuming that just because an event follows another, it must be caused by it:

Cause/correlation: the mistake of confusing a cause with a correlation.

Multiple causes: the mistake of assuming that there is only one cause when there may be several interrelated causes and not just one.

Underlying causes: in some circumstances, where there appear to be multiple factors operating, there may either be an underlying cause explaining them all or they may not be causally related.

Fallacy of false cause (*non-sequitur* – 'does not follow'): we commit this fallacy when we draw a conclusion that doesn't follow logically from the premises. More loosely, it is basing a conclusion on insufficient, incorrect or irrelevant reasons.

Irrelevant inference *signoratio elenchi* (ignoring the issue): we appear to strengthen our argument by proving another that is irrelevant to the issue. Instead of keeping to the point, we shift attention to a different question on which we feel a lot more confident:

The Person: *ad hominem* (to the man) the argument is sidestepped by discrediting the person who proposed it.

Popularity: *ad populum* (to the people) deals with a difficult argument by appealing to the sentiments of popular opinion. It sidesteps or supports the argument by appealing to mass emotion, assuming that whatever the crowd thinks must be right.

Authority: *ad verecundiam* (to awe or reverence) diverts attention from a difficult argument by making an appeal to a prestigious or authoritative name or figure, a revered authority, even conventional propriety.

Fear: *ad baculum* (to fear) deals with an opponent's argument by evoking the fear that their arguments cannot be trusted.

The greater evil: discourages action against some admitted evil by citing an even greater evil, about which the original argument is not proposing to do anything.

The counter accusation: *tu quoque* (you're another) – someone replies to a charge made against them by making the same or similar charge against that person.

The Compromise: the argument that is presented as a compromise between two undesirable extremes, so that anyone who refuses to accept it appears unreasonable.

The Law of Contradiction   *See* Opposites

The Law of the Excluded Middle   *See* Opposites

Loaded language   This is language that carries with it more than what it means descriptively, usually emotional content, which manipulates our responses without us being aware of it.

Necessary and sufficient conditions   A condition is sufficient if its truth is all that is required for a belief to be true, or a certain event to occur. When an assumption is a sufficient condition for a belief to be true, it is said to entail that belief. In other words, given the assumption, the belief necessarily follows, so that if the assumption is true, then so, too, is the belief.

An assumption is a necessary condition if it *must* be true in order for another belief to be true or an event to occur. When a proposition X necessarily cannot be true, unless another proposition Y is true, then the truth of Y is by definition a logically necessary true condition for X.

Non-overridable principles There are formal rules to moral thinking as there are to logical, mathematical and scientific thinking. When we break these, we make mistakes as we would in these other forms of thinking if we were to break their rules. When a scientist presents a scientific explanation, she knows it must be empirical, testable and universal in its claims. Likewise in moral thinking: our judgements must be universal; they must respect the dignity of each individual, treating them as ends and not as mere means; and they must preserve each individual's autonomy, so that they are free to make their own choices and not coerced into behaving the way we want them to.

Obversion This is the process of changing a proposition into its logical equivalent: from the affirmative to the negative form. The four basic forms are:

1. All As are Bs into No As are non-Bs.
2. No As are Bs into All As are non-Bs.
3. Some As are Bs into Some As are not non-Bs.
4. Some As are not Bs into Some As are non-Bs.

Illicit obversion occurs when it does not necessarily follow that those who are excluded from one class are also excluded from the other. To say that 'All golfers are competitive' is not the same as saying, 'All non-golfers are non-competitive.' The fact that someone is not a golfer doesn't mean they are non-competitive.

Opposites Between opposites, like 'mortal' and 'immortal', there is no common ground. But for things to be opposites, they must comply with two logical laws: the Law of Contradiction and the Law of the Excluded Middle.

The Law of Contradiction simply says that A is not not-A; that something cannot be in the same sense A and not-A. The Law of the Excluded Middle says either A or not-A; that there is no middle ground – the two terms are mutually exclusive. The combined effect of these is that something has to be A or not-A and both of these are mutually exclusive.

See also Contraries.

Overridable principles While there are three non-overridable principles in moral thinking (universalism, respect for the dignity of the individual and autonomy), the remaining principles are not. In any situation, we have to choose which are the most important in order to reach the best moral solution to the problem. None can trump any other, although in any situation some will be more important than others.

Some reflect our concerns about justice – a sense of fairness; others are about what we believe we have a right to; others are about values we think ought to be respected; then there are the virtues we think it is important to promote; and, finally, there are the harmful consequences we believe we should avoid or the good consequences that we should bring about.

1. Justice
2. Rights
3. Values
4. Virtues
5. Consequences

Premises   An argument is a set of sentences, one of which is the conclusion and the others, called premises, are offered as the grounds for the conclusion. The premises are said to imply or entail the conclusion.

Processing terms   When we process terms accurately, we use them in the conclusion to mean exactly what they mean in the premises. When we badly process terms, we assume they mean more or less than they actually do and, therefore, in our conclusion we assert more or less than the premises will allow.

Proposition   A proposition is an indicative sentence, which can be true or false, as opposed to a question or a command. It can also be distinguished from the sentence itself in that a proposition is the meaning of the sentence. So, two sentences can be quite different linguistically, yet contain the same proposition.

Qualifiers   These indicate the strength of the claim you are making, words like 'some', 'most', 'all', and 'few'.

Respect for the dignity of the individual   In moral thinking, universalism dictates that we must treat others as we would expect to be treated ourselves. As we place the highest intrinsic value on ourselves, this means we must place the same intrinsic value on others. In other words, in the same way that we would resist being treating as a mere means for someone to achieve some end of their own choosing, we must likewise avoid treating others as a mere means to achieve our own ends. We must respect the dignity of the individual as an end in him- or herself and not as a mere means of promoting our own ends.

Sound arguments   An argument is sound if and only if it is a valid argument and has true premises. Therefore, we can challenge the soundness of an argument either by criticising it for being invalid, or by arguing that one or more of its premises are untrue.

Special pleading   The fallacy of special pleading occurs when we are so convinced of our side of the argument that we present just the evidence that supports our view, ignoring all that contradicts it. Alternatively, we do this when we use an argument in one context, but refuse to use it in another where it would lead to an opposite conclusion.
   See Chapter 14.

Straw man fallacy   This is committed when we oversimplify our description of a situation or a proposition, either deliberately or accidentally, so that we can dismiss it as false.
   See Chapter 14.

Suppressed premises   Often in our arguments there are unstated premises, which we have just suppressed, because we assume the other person knows or agrees with them so they can be taken for granted. Our arguments may be valid, but we won't know this until we have revealed the suppressed premise.

Syllogism One of the most common forms of deductive reasoning, a syllogism is an argument that moves from the most general premise, known as the major premise, to the particular premise, known as the minor premise, and finally to the conclusion, which follows logically from the first two premises and forms a valid argument.

Tautology When propositions say nothing about how things are in the real world and are true independently of the way things are, they are said to be tautologies. Literally, it means saying the same thing. We see this most clearly in the form of analytic truths, like 'All bachelors are unmarried men', which are true by virtue of the meaning of their constituent terms. Tautologies are not refutable because they are, in fact, trivially true. Whatever the content, and they may have no content at all, it is irrelevant to their truth.

Universalism In moral thinking we must be prepared to prescribe our moral judgements independently of the role we occupy and whether we gain or lose by their application. We are not just saying that this is what *I* should do in this situation, but that *all people* similar to me and in a similar situation should act in accordance with the same rule. This is the Golden Rule: 'Do unto others as you would have them do unto you.'

Every action should be judged in the light of how it would appear if it were to be a universal code of behaviour. It should not be based on subjective feelings or inclinations. To think morally is to think objectively, according to our reason, beyond our own interests and feelings. And, as the paramount feature of reason is consistency, this means, by definition, that our judgements must be universal: they must apply to all similar people in similar circumstances. The eighteenth-century German philosopher Immanuel Kant famously encapsulated this in his 'categorical imperative':

> Act only on that maxim through which you can at the same time will that it should become a universal law.
>
> (qtd in Paton, 1948, p. 84)

Validity When we examine the validity of a deductive argument we are concerned with its form, not with its truth, the substance of the argument. Validity is a way of ensuring that if we do have true premises, then we also guarantee that our conclusion is true. When an argument is valid, it is not possible for its premises to be true, while its conclusion is false. It can have false premises and a false conclusion, but never true premises and a false conclusion. An argument is valid if and only if it is not possible for all its premises to be true and its conclusion to be false.

See also Deductive thinking.

Index

References to illustrations are printed in bold.